# MANCHESTER HISTORIC ASSOCIATION COLLECTIONS

Volume I

1896–1899

HERITAGE BOOKS
2012

# HERITAGE BOOKS
### AN IMPRINT OF HERITAGE BOOKS, INC.

Books, CDs, and more—Worldwide

For our listing of thousands of titles see our website
at
www.HeritageBooks.com

A Facsimile Reprint
Published 2012 by
HERITAGE BOOKS, INC.
Publishing Division
100 Railroad Ave. #104
Westminster, Maryland 21157

Copyright © 1992 Heritage Books, Inc.

— Publisher's Notice —
In reprints such as this, it is often not possible to remove blemishes from the original. We feel the contents of this book warrant its reissue despite these blemishes and hope you will agree and read it with pleasure.

International Standard Book Numbers
Paperbound: 978-1-55613-574-3
Clothbound: 978-0-7884-9462-8

# ARTICLES OF ASSOCIATION.

THE undersigned hereby associate together to be a corporation under chapter 147 of the Public Statutes of the state of New Hampshire, to be known as the MANCHESTER HISTORIC ASSOCIATION, the purpose of which Association shall be to collect, preserve, and publish whatever may relate to the early and later history of the city of Manchester and the surrounding towns, that formed in its early history and settlement one and the same community, and to preserve such articles or relics of the aborigines and early settlers of the country, and records of colonial and later wars, as may be obtained by the Association.

The first meeting of the Association shall be holden, without further notice, on the 18th day of December, 1895, at eight o'clock in the afternoon, at the rooms of the Manchester Board of Trade, at which meeting, or some adjournment thereof, there shall be chosen by ballot, such officers of the Association as shall be provided for by the constitution adopted by the Association.

The annual meeting, qualification of, and condition of membership, raising of money, and all other matters necessary to be done and performed to fully carry out the objects of the Association shall be provided for by the constitution and by-laws to be by them adopted.

The place of business and chief office of the Association shall be located in the city of Manchester, county of Hillsborough, and state of New Hampshire.

Witness our hands and place of residence this the 18th day of December, A. D. 1895.

MOODY CURRIER,
GEORGE C. GILMORE,
JOSEPH KIDDER,
JOHN C. FRENCH,
DAVID CROSS,
JOSIAH CARPENTER,
GEORGE F. WILLEY,
HENRY W. HERRICK,
JOHN DOWST,
EDWIN P. RICHARDSON,
SYLVESTER C. GOULD,
JOHN G. CRAWFORD,
DAVID L. PERKINS,
JOHN G. HUTCHINSON,
GEORGE W. BROWNE,
CHAS. B. STURTEVANT,
HERBERT W. EASTMAN,
JOSIAH G. DEARBORN,
EDGAR J. KNOWLTON,
WILLIAM E. MOORE,
SAMUEL C. KENNARD,
FRANCIS B. EATON,
WILLIAM H. MORRISON,
DAVID PERKINS,

All of Manchester, N. H.

---

CITY CLERK'S OFFICE, Manchester, N. H.

Rec'd Jan'y 2, 1896, and recorded in City Book of Corporations, Vol. 4, Page 77.

By me, N. P. KIDDER,
*City Clerk.*

STATE OF NEW HAMPSHIRE.

OFFICE OF SECRETARY OF STATE,
CONCORD, JAN. 17, 1896.

Received and recorded in Record of Voluntary Corporations, Vol. 8, pp. 314–16.

EZRA S. STEARNS,
[L. S.] *Secretary of State.*

# CONSTITUTION.

ARTICLE 1. The object of the Manchester Historic Association shall be to collect, preserve, and publish whatever may relate to the early and later history of the city of Manchester and the surrounding towns, that formed in its early history and settlement the same community, and to preserve such articles or relics of the aborigines and early settlers of the country, and records of colonial and later wars, and other objects of interest, as may be obtained by the Association.

ARTICLE 2. The Association shall consist of such persons as shall be elected by major vote of members present at any annual or quarterly meeting of the Association, and who have paid the amount of the membership fee provided in this constitution. The election of members shall be by ballot, except by unanimous consent of the members present.

ARTICLE 3. The membership fee shall be the sum of two dollars, to be paid at the time of the application, and any person who shall be refused membership shall have the amount so paid refunded. The annual dues of the members shall be one dollar, to be paid on or before the annual meeting of each year. The Association may assess taxes at the annual meeting on its members, provided that such taxes shall not in any one year exceed the sum of two dollars. Any member neglecting to pay the annual dues, or any tax assessed, for the space of one year shall cease to be a member. Any person may become a life member of the Association on the payment of the sum of twenty-five dollars at one time, and any person becoming a life member shall be exempt from the payment of annual dues or any tax that may be levied by the Association. Such persons, not residents of New Hampshire, as the Association shall deem for its interest to make honorary members of the same, may become such on a vote of the Association at any meeting thereof, and no fees or dues shall be required of such honorary members.

ARTICLE 4. The annual meeting of the Association shall be held on the third Wednesday of December in each year, at such time and place in the city of Manchester as the President shall designate, notice thereof to be given through the daily press of Manchester. Quarterly meetings shall be held on the third Wednesdays of the months of March, June, and September, notice of the same to be given as is provided for annual meetings.

ARTICLE 5. Special meetings shall be called by the president, and in his absence by one of the vice-presidents, on application of six members, notice of such meetings to be published in the daily papers of Manchester and notice sent through the mail to each member at least two days before such meeting, which notice shall contain the purpose and object for which the meeting is called, and seven members shall constitute a quorum for the transaction of business, but a less number may adjourn.

ARTICLE 6. The officers of the Association shall be elected at the annual meeting and shall be a president, two vice-presidents, a treasurer, a recording secretary, a corresponding secretary, a librarian, a historiographer, an executive committee of seven members, of which the president and recording secretary shall be *ex-officio* members, a committee of five on publication, and such other officers as may be deemed necessary by the Association. The executive committee shall be the auditing committee and have general supervision and direction of the affairs of the Association.

The officers herein provided for shall perform the duties indicated by their respective titles, and shall hold their office for the term of one year and until others are elected in their place, provided the first election of officers under this constitution shall be made at such time and place as the Association may determine.

ARTICLE 7. This constitution may be amended at any annual or quarterly meeting, as the Association shall deem expedient, by a vote of two thirds of the members present, provided that written notice of the proposed amendment be given at the last preceding regular meeting.

# PREFACE.

THE following pages will attest their own value. With two exceptions the articles have been prepared expressly for the Association, and it was deemed fitting those should be included. The first year of the Manchester Historic Association has met with a success which seems to assure it a flattering future. It certainly is of the utmost importance that the historic data passing away with the decease of our older citizens should be obtained and placed on record before it is forever gone. One personal statement often makes valueless the hearsays of many. The first is history, the other tradition. If such facts as can be are gathered from time to time and presented to the Association, the printed volume from year to year will be of inestimable worth. The valley of the Merrimack is rich in its legendary lore as well as history that has been such an important factor in the making of the state and nation. If the Association awakens the interest of the inhabitants of what was once old Derryfield to the importance of preserving those facts, it will have performed a mission which following generations will have reason to appreciate. Said Hon. Edward Everett, "Know the history of your own town first, then that of your state and country."

Respectfully submitted.

GEORGE W. BROWNE,
SYLVESTER C. GOULD,
EDGAR J. KNOWLTON,
WILLIAM H. MORRISON,
FRANCIS B. EATON,

*Publication Committee.*

# CONTENTS.

## VOLUME I.—PART 1.

REMINISCENCES OF MANCHESTER, 1841 TO 1896,
        *David L. Perkins* . . . . 9

NEW HAMPSHIRE MEN AT LOUISBURG AND BUNKER HILL,
        *Rev. William H. Morrison* . . 27

DERRYFIELD MEN AT BUNKER HILL,
        *Hon. George C. Gilmore* . . 32

BOATING ON THE MERRIMACK,
        *George Waldo Browne* . . . 35

DERRYFIELD SOCIAL LIBRARY,
        *William H. Huse* . . . . 44

CASTLE WILLIAM AND MARY,
        *Hon. John G. Crawford* . . . 51

NEW HAMPSHIRE BRANCH OF THE SOCIETY OF CINCINNATI,
        *Hon. John C. French* . . . 66

GRACE FLETCHER,
        *Hon. John C. French* . . . 73

"THE SWEET BY-AND-BY,"
        *S. C. Gould* . . . . . 81

OLD DERRYFIELD AND YOUNG MANCHESTER,
        *David L. Perkins* . . . . 84

SEMI-CENTENNIAL OF MANCHESTER,
        *Fred W. Lamb* . . . . 112

ELECTION SERMONS IN NEW HAMPSHIRE,
        *S. C. Gould* . . . . . 117

# REMINISCENCES OF MANCHESTER.
## 1841 to 1896.

AN ADDRESS BY DAVID L. PERKINS BEFORE THE MANCHESTER HISTORIC ASSOCIATION, MARCH 18, 1896.

*Mr. President and Gentlemen:*

It has been said of us, almost by way of reproach, that we have no ancient castles in America; no stately ruins to remind us of mediæval times; but, on the whole, our transatlantic friends must admit that we have got along quite successfully without them, and let us hope that the time may never come when baronial castles shall dot the horizon of our fair land. As for ruins, our people are too busily employed in their various avocations in building up the new even to think of them, much less to lament their absence from our virgin landscape. Our perspective is altogether too bright and alluring for that. Some hundreds of years hence our successors may cultivate the scars and wrinkles that will serve a purpose in that line; but at present we are full of life, full of resources, full of hope and youth. But it is not the present purpose to dwell upon ruins, or castles, even in the air; but merely to suggest as best we may, a few milestones which in the experience of a single life have brought us to our present magnificent estate.

There are scores among us who can recall a time when the present site of Manchester was hardly more than a worthless sand bank; a prolific fishing resort; and with nothing more suggestive of thrift or of value in its character and surroundings than an obscure little spinning mill at Amoskeag. Later on a manufacturing village grew up on this side of the river; and as the cotton industry throve, the village blossomed into the beautiful and far-famed city of to-day. My father came hither in June, 1841, as the first male instructor in the public schools of the new Manchester, in the new high school building on Lowell street at the corner of Chestnut, then almost literally in the woods. There were no railroads here, no telegraph wires. Even gas as an illuminating agent was practically unknown. The telephone, electric lights, street motor cars, and the modern fire-alarm service are of comparatively recent date; and the steam fire-engine only preceded them a very little. There were no street pavements here, and the sidewalks were limited to the village needs,— a village of about three thousand five hundred souls. I doubt if there was a private bath-tub, a domestic heating furnace, a coal stove, or an elevator in the town.

There was little to attract attention south of Merrimack street or north of Lowell, and east of Union street there were no buildings at all until the suburbs were reached. The now elegant northeast section, then of uneven surface, covered with little patches of feed for cattle, rude granite boulders, scrub oaks and pines, not arable, and hardly fit for grazing, was yet used for a pasture, and was enclosed with a rough stone wall. The time came when the authorities placed a neat wooden rail fence around Concord common, then the only park of any pretensions, and it seemed almost like a case of metropolitan extravagance. The vicinity of Birch and Washington streets, now known as the "Barbary Coast," was wet and marshy, and abounded in alder bushes, where the rabbit and the partridge lingered as if regretful of the coming change. The territory south of Hanover street and east of Union was covered by a heavy pine forest as far out as Hallsville; and through the woods to the south a tract of cleared land, comprising some twenty acres or more, was familiarly known as "the Ryefield." As late as 1850 or 1851, Daniel Webster delivered an address from a raised platform at a fair of the New Hampshire Agricultural Society, held in this immediate vicinity. He was the "observed of all observers" in a procession that marched up Elm street, and from his open barouche, with bared head, he bowed, like the god that he was, to the ladies on either side of the street, who waved their handkerchiefs.

A deep glen or ravine extended northeasterly from the Valley cemetery, and a brook that rippled down between the heavily shaded banks, thence through the cemetery valley, is well remembered by thousands of our fellow-citizens. This shaded dell served us boys as a not too remote Arcadia, where we often repaired of a school holiday with wooden tomahawks, in imitation of the Indians. It was only at long intervals that we got as far out as the shores of Lake Massabesic, for we had no other means of transportation than those afforded by nature. At a point near West Brook street, where Judge David Cross now lives, the Old Falls road, so called, curved around, first westerly and then to the north, until the Amoskeag bridge and the north River road were reached. On a high bluff, at its intersection with Elm street, a small weather-stained house stood guard for many years; and halfway around the curve, at the foot of the hill, a small, ancient, black-wooded schoolhouse was a familiar object. The pasture, the outlying orchard, and the adjacent graveyard have now disappeared forever. Cows no longer feed placidly along the hillside; the school children of the olden days are gathered to their fathers, or scattered far and near; while the bones of the dead have been ruthlessly removed. This ancient burying-ground was in the immediate vicinity of, and perhaps included, the present site of the Manchester Locomotive Works. The father of General Stark was buried here.

The sand bluff where the Governor Smyth mansion now stands, and the one south of it across West Salmon street, then under the shade of willows and elms, were rich with the deposit of Indian arrowheads and other aboriginal curios, and many a valued collection has been exhumed therefrom. There was a deep ravine just north of Penacook street, crossing Elm from the old fair ground, with its riotous little trout brook now rapidly disappearing from human view. When Smyth's block was built at the corner of Elm and Water streets, as late as 1853, it was thought by some of the wise heads of that day to be a crazy enterprise, because it was so far removed from the business center of the town; and now even Rock Rimmon bids fair to become a huge setting like a gem of nature in the midst of a thriving, busy settlement. I have a distinct recollection of a deep ravine south of Granite street and west of Elm, where nature had formed a charming amphitheater. A platform was erected in this temple of nature, where temperance lecturers and Fourth of July orators held forth to audiences seated upon benches arranged one above another on the hillside, and all under the grateful shade of primitive trees. Along in the forties a man from over the river was found drowned in a shallow pool in this ravine, with a jug of rum by his side. In view of this tragic event some of the temperance people conceived the idea of giving the town an object lesson, and it took the form of "a drunkard's funeral," in which the corpse played a conspicuous part. A procession was formed, and marching through Elm street a halt was made before several places where liquors were dispensed, and the "mourners" groaned several times in unison.

Political feeling, then as now, was exciting and absorbing. July 4, 1844, a presidential year, the two parties held rival meetings in Manchester,— the Whigs in this same ravine, and the Democrats among the pines in the neighborhood of Tremont square. Some fifteen thousand strangers were in town, and no end of the militia. Charles Francis Adams, of Massachusetts, addressed the Whigs, and George Barstow, the historian, was the Democratic orator.

I caught many a fine brook trout on Hanover common in my boyhood, out of an artificial pond that existed there for fire purposes, supplied by the "Mile brook," so called. This brook had its rise on Oak hill, and thence from Hanover square by a culvert it supplied another artificial pond on Merrimack common, now known as Monument square, and still another small reservoir on Concord common, at a point where the fountain now stands. These small bodies of water afforded the school children of that day excellent facilities for skating, and, alas! at times, even for drowning; and for the latter purpose several adults availed themselves of the little pool on Concord common. In recent years these ponds have been filled in and completely grassed over, as they were no longer needed for fire purposes, and with an increasing density of population the impure waters were thought to be a menace to the health of those who lived in their vicinity. I recall with pleasure the sunken barrel on the south bank of Hanover common, from which the thrifty housewife, the ruddy maid, or perchance the man of the house, with pail in hand, drew a supply of sparkling spring water for family use. The children were wont to slake their thirst at this same perennial fountain, and occasionally one of them fell headlong into the barrel, a fate that once befell the writer of these notes. From this bounteous spring the public fountain at the corner of our city hall is supplied with the pure juice of the rock, and in the heat of a summer's day it is an untold blessing to our weary, toiling, care-worn masses. Yet Mayor Abbott was unmercifully ridiculed for introducing this boon, though if he had done nothing more, this alone would serve as a fit monument to his memory.

At the southeast corner of Merrimack common there was a low boggy place, where for many years an irregular clump of ungainly trees served as an eyesore and reproach; but, like the mile brook that meandered across Elm street and lost itself in the deep glen south of Granite street, they have long since disappeared from view.

In that day the neighbors around Concord common were accustomed to parcel out among themselves small garden spots on the upper or east section, where they raised such vegetables as suited their fancy, and he was thought to be a slothful farmer who could not supply his table therefrom with green peas and cucumbers as early as the Fourth of July. We chased rabbits among the scruboaks, pines, and granite boulders north of Concord street and east of Union, for in this whole section there were no houses west of Janesville, and one may know now that he is in Janesville or Towlesville when the streets run crossways like the great avenues in Washington.

The ground where the Governor Straw mansion stands, north of Harrison street and east of Elm, was occupied by a little black, weather beaten, single-storied farmhouse and barn, and it was then away out in the country to us boys. Here we spent many delightful hours hunting hens' nests on the haymow, and chasing butterflies over the sun-clad fields with a schoolfellow whose father occupied the premises. Sweet flag was found here along the margin of a little brook. There were picturesque relics of a decaying wooden mill of small pretensions on the river road, this side of the General John Stark place, and another near the present intersection of Lake avenue and Massabesic street, where leeches were found and where we sometimes went in bathing.

On the west side, from the eddy at Amoskeag to Granite street south, a long mile, there were hardly more than a half dozen houses, including the Agent Reed mansion, now standing, and the Butterfield farmhouse, a district that is now densely populated. And who can forget the ancient pound and the pesthouse on Bridge street just north of our Derryfield park? The colonial buildings on the poor farm over the hill on the Mammoth road presented a stately aspect of thrift and comfort to our minds, and Stevens pond, a little farther east in the low land, where hornpouts and pickerel were found in abundance, was to us a perpetual joy. Many an old inhabitant would think he had strayed beyond his bailiwick if found within the limits of "the new discovery." A few years ago this territory was a dense jungle under the shadows of Amoskeag hill; now it is a flourishing settlement in the northeast section. In the early times Thanksgiving shooting matches were held near a little tavern stand at the intersection of Bridge and Russell streets in Janesville. Very many interesting changes in the topography of our city might be noted here, but time and space forbid. In preparing a paper like this, where the material is so abundant, it is always difficult to know just what to include, and when done it is ever a source of regret that something more had not been added. Yet something is due to the cause of brevity. Prolixity is easy enough, and with the best endeavor a selection of the fittest is not always easy of attainment.

The character of the pupils who then attended our public schools, as I remember them, was vastly different from those of today, being largely composed in the higher grades of young men and young women, at least they seemed so to me. In those days both urban and country teachers were often compelled to fight for the right of way, and sooner or later the test was reasonably sure to come as to whether a new teacher could fight as well as teach, and frequently the fighting preceded the teaching. In the large audience room of the Lowell-street school, where nearly two hundred pupils were frequently assembled, an iron box stove four feet long was the only heater, and when well packed with chunks and well fired it was thought to be a pretty safe reliance, though in zero weather the occupants of the back seats near the windows may now be pardoned if they entertained a different opinion ; but they had the best that the market then afforded. In fact, it is only within recent years that modern heating appliances have been introduced into our public schools, and water was only to be had by going after it among the neighbors. When I attended the Spring-street grammar school, there were two large box-stoves, one on either side, east and west, the boys occupying the east half and the girls the west, divided by a broad aisle, and there were times when the privilege of standing around one of these stoves was esteemed an especial favor. It was the custom in the early days for the larger boys to take turns in the care of the schoolrooms, and it was no idle pastime to sweep out and build the fires on a cold winter's morning. The dainty pupils of today would think they had fallen upon hard lines if required to exchange their luxurious surroundings for the meagre school facilities of their parents. And yet, though education is now rendered comparatively easy and pleasant, it can hardly be said that Daniel Websters are more plentiful than in the frugal early days of the republic. Indeed, it is as true now as ever, that we fail to realize the real worth of a gift dollar until we have been compelled to work hard all day to earn one hundred pennies. Corner lots that were then sold for eight cents per foot cannot be had now for ten dollars a foot, so changed are the conditions under which we live.

If our boys were to deport themselves like the merry boys of the forties, they would soon find themselves in the reform school during their minority, but there was no reform school then. The adults, too, were often careless of their p's and q's, for the primitive little jail at Amherst was hardly capable of holding twenty guests. It is within my recollection when a lot of machine-shop boys held a policeman by main force while a confederate went through his pockets for a key to the local bastile, with which a comrade was liberated, and it was considered a fairly good joke on the policeman, for there were less than a half dozen of these noble guardians to preserve the peace in a turbulent community. The machine-shop boys, some four or five hundred of them, were a rough-and-ready crowd, and they came near to ruling the town. A trouble signal from one of "the gang" was sure to be answered with stalwart vigor, and our police heroes well knew the part of discretion.

The only place in the village, as late as 1841, for the accommodation of public gatherings, was a dingy little affair christened with the high-sounding name of "Washington Hall." The old building is still preserved, and is now located on Amherst street halfway west from Chestnut. It stands in from the street and is reached by an alleyway. A private school was kept here at one time, and it was my fortune or misfortune to be one of the attendants. On coming to this side from Amoskeag, the first Baptist church worshipped in this hall from 1838 to 1840, when their new brick church was completed, at the northwest corner of Manchester and Chestnut streets. This church, together with the Masonic Temple on Hanover street, and many other buildings, was destroyed in Manchester's great fire of July 8, 1870, of which I was a witness. Many hot election contests have taken place in this old building.

Concord common was then a crude reservation, and the stately trees of today have all attained their present grandeur within my time. The only tree of primitive growth now left is the old gnarly oak in the southwest corner of the park. The vicinity of Concord common was then the aristocratic section.

Judge Samuel D. Bell lived at the corner of Amherst and Chestnut streets, and his comfortable home of that day has been converted into a corner grocery. Dr. Thomas Brown, very prominent in his day, lived nearly opposite Vine street, on Amherst, and his fine residence, standing in from the street, has long since become a cheap tenement house. Hon. Mace Moulton, once a member of congress, and said to be the father of sheriffs in New Hampshire, lived on Amherst, south side, between Elm and Vine. Hon. George W. Morrison lived for a time in the brick house at the corner of Vine and Amherst streets, and it has since blossomed into a thriving groggery. Warren L. Lane, the third mayor of Manchester, lived and died on Pine street, at the head of the common; and for a time Hon. Moody Currier, ex-governor of the state, was his next door neighbor. Hiram Brown, our first mayor, lived only a short distance away, on the present site of the Hanover street Congregational church; and Phinehas Adams, agent of the Stark corporation, occupied the site of the Catholic orphanage. Ex-Mayor E. W. Harrington and Hon. Nathan Parker were close by on Hanover street. The latter lived where the government building now stands. Alonzo Smith, one of our early mayors, lived at the corner of Concord and Union, and his house was a frontier post. He was the proprietor, or one of the proprietors, of a lumber yard located on the present site of St. Paul's Methodist church; and the lot north of it, the present location of the First Baptist church, was vacant property, enclosed with a high board fence. I find by consulting the early directories that F. B. Eaton, Herman Foster, Walter French, ex-Gov. E. A. Straw, J. T. P. Hunt, A. C. Wallace, and the Rev. C. W. Wallace lived in this section of the town. Robert Ayer, a well-to-do merchant, lived in a comely vineclad cottage where the cathedral now stands, at the corner of Pine and Lowell streets, and he had the most attractive garden of shrubs and flowers in town. It was quite aristocratic. A double, single storied, and white-painted wooden schoolhouse stood in the place of the Unitarian church of to-day, corner of Concord and Beech. From this point southeasterly as far as Towlesville, the ground was low and marshy. The Mile brook took its tortuous course through this section, and frogs were musical there in the springtime, and the busy muskrat was found there in his season. But all is now changed. The low places are made even, and tidy streets and pleasant homes give no clue to the former low estate.

I have a vivid recollection of a Fast Day game of oldtime round ball, the parent of our national game, that was played on Concord common opposite the Central fire station, in 1848, between the Ransom Guards of Vermont and some Manchester recruits for the Mexican war. The late Col. Thomas P. Pierce, afterwards postmaster of Manchester, was one of the contestants. The levity of the players seemed strangely out of place to me, for my juvenile conception of a soldier's lot ended in his being shot to death for the glory of his country and the pride of his posterity; and indeed the gallant Col. Ransom met that fate on the plains of Mexico, and my conception of the fitness of things was thus justified.

In 1841 the Union building, so-called, now occupied and owned by the Manchester National Bank, was the first building erected on the west side of Elm street, and in this year there were few buildings on the street. Ex-Mayor Harrington told me on one occasion that he walked from Manchester to Hooksett to secure the refusal of this building from Hon. R. H. Ayer, the builder, in which to carry on his business, and he was entirely successful in his mission and in his business. The "Union Democrat" was published here at one time, and "The Mirror" was domiciled across the way in Riddle's block.

The Concord Railroad was opened to Manchester from the south July 4, 1842. As late as 1844 my father kept a bookstore and small circulating library in Towne's old block near Amherst street, next door south of Z. F. Campbell's drugstore, and its number was 48 on the old plan of streets. From this fact some idea may be had of the changes that have taken place in Manchester in the past fifty years. A stage coach started for Concord each week day at 8 A. M., via Bow and Hooksett, William G. Hoyt driver. There were also stage lines connecting Manchester with Lowell Portsmouth, Gilmanton, Exeter, and New Ipswich.

On the night of March 26, 1845, Jonas L. Parker, the town's collector of taxes, who had several thousand dollars on his person, was beguiled into the pine forest that extended south and east from the corner of Union and Hanover streets, and was brutally murdered. The exact spot is believed to be at the rear of Dr. Hiram Hill's lot on Manchester street, now known as No. 327. This was a murder of national celebrity, and strange to relate, the murderer has never been revealed, the old adage to the contrary notwithstanding. Well do I remember the spot where lay the mangled and ghastly remains of the murdered man. I was then but seven years old, and I went to the place of the murder on the following morning in company with my father and with many a horror-stricken citizen, entering the woods by a cart road that crossed diagonally through the forest to the little hamlet beyond. This whole territory is now densely populated. I recall something of the intense excitement that pervaded the community, and for several months the good housewife was sure to repeat the daily admonition to her menfolk, that there was danger in remaining away from home after dark.

There are many now living who recall a row of Elm trees up the middle of Elm street, above Lowell, of which there has been no trace for many years, except in memory. At the June session of the legislature in 1846, Manchester was incorporated as a city, and on the first day of August the charter was accepted by a popular vote of 485 to 134.

The pine grove north and west of the corner where the city hall now stands was a favorite resort of the machine-shop boys for wrestling bouts and for indulgence in other athletic sports, and if the truth were told, many of their pastimes were anything but gentle, and I dare say that many a dispute was settled there with fists when other arguments had failed. The famous Stark Guards, a star military company of that day, also held their annual field sports here, and I have heard the late Hon. George W. Morrison relate that as captain he was expected to accommodate the standing man in a wrestling match. He was a skilled wrestler of that day, and no doubt he was able to fill the bill to the satisfaction of his loyal and royal company.

And now for a few moments let us change our point of view, from which it will appear that had the progenitors of our city been gifted with a prevision, they could hardly have improved upon their undertakings. There are always men enough in every community who are experts at pulling down, but these men were gifted with a genius for building up, and they builded better than they knew. The Amoskeag Company was incorporated in 1831, and was capitalized at $1,600,000. Its plant included the old spinning mill of 1809, the Bell mill, and the Island mill at Amoskeag. The Island mill was destroyed in 1840, and I witnessed the burning of the Bell mill, March 28, 1848. In the old mill of 1809, yarns were spun from hand-picked cotton, for there were no machine pickers then, and these skeins of yarn to some extent took the place of currency in local business transactions, for our currency was in its infancy and it was a feeble infant at that. The enterprise, however, proved unsuccessful, and in 1825 it passed into more experienced hands. In 1826 the Bell mill was added to the original plant, and also the Island mill on the island south of the covered bridge. A picturesque foot-bridge connected the island with the mainland at a point near the Bell mill on the site of the present P. C. Cheney paper mill, and a commodious boarding-house on the island survived until after the beginning of the civil war. Our fellow townsman, Ephraim K. Rowell, lived there nearly seventy years ago. In early times the yarn that was spun from the hand-picked cotton was given out among the surrounding towns to be woven on hand looms, at from two to seven cents a yard, according to quality, and thus were the maids and matrons of that day enabled to turn a not over nimble penny for themselves. Subsequently tickings were woven by machinery at the Island mill, and perhaps to some extent in the Bell mill, and they soon acquired a wide reputation under the trade-mark of the " A. C. A. Tickings," of which we hear even now. Soon after being incorporated, the new Amoskeag Company caused a careful survey to be made with a view to future operations, from which it appeared that the east bank of the river afforded the better facilities for the engineering operations necessary for the laying out of canals, and in a general way for the upbuilding of a manufacturing center at this point. The next move was quietly to buy up all the available adjacent land on either side of the river so as to control the water power and flowage as far north as was needful to prevent competition, and in this they were measurably successful. It was a part of the plan to lease water privileges to other manufacturing companies, for whom the Amoskeag Company was to erect mills and boarding houses. As early as 1835 lots were placed on the market, but it was not until 1837 that active operations were begun. The first cotton mill on this side of the Merrimack river was erected for the Stark corporation in 1838, the year of my birth, and in this year the Amoskeag Company laid out the site of the future city, the main thoroughfare being given the name of Elm street, which it has ever since retained. Not only was the first cotton mill erected here in the year of my birth, but the name of Manchester was adopted in the year that my father was born, 1810, so that all these changes have occurred in the brief span of a single life. A cemetery, public parks, church and school lots, wide streets, and other reservations, were set apart for public uses, and a large lot covered with pitch pine trees at the corner of Elm and Merrimack streets was dedicated to the use of a tavern stand, which was availed of by the late venerable William Shepard, who erected a famous hostelry thereon, which has but recently given place to the Pembroke block of modern times. Merrimack common was then covered with pines, birches, and alders. The first public land sale was held October 24, 1838. The first house, a one-story cottage, erected on land thus purchased, was in 1839, at the corner of Chestnut and Concord streets, and it gave place only recently to the People's Tabernacle church.

I think it was in 1839 that the first fire engine was purchased for the use of the community, a famous hand-tub known as "Merrimack No. 1." In 1840 the Amoskeag Company erected their machine shop on the lower canal, where a vast amount of machinery was built for new mills here and elsewhere, and subsequently the Amoskeag steam fire engines were manufactured here that have found their way into every part of the civilized world, originally invented by our fellow citizen, Nehemiah S. Bean. In 1841 the Amoskeag Company also built two large mills known as Nos. 1 and 2.

The east side, therefore, now assumed an air of importance that was very distasteful to the old inhabitants at the center of the town. They were apprehensive that the pretentions of the upstart newcomers in the " new village " would result in swelling the tax rate. This feeling was at high tide when we came to Manchester, but henceforth, so rapid was the growth of the " new village " that the old inhabitants were soon swallowed up in the onward march, though for several years they sturdily resisted every effort looking to a development of the future city. In this same year the old settlers in the rural districts and at the center were exasperated at the action of the selectmen in calling a town meeting at Washington hall, thus ignoring the ancient place of meeting. They were also bitterly opposed to an article in the warrant with reference to a new town house to be located in the " new village " at public expense. But the new villagers prevailed, and it was voted to build the new town house with a loan not to exceed $20,000, and it was accordingly built in the summer of that year at an expense of about $17,000. It was surmounted by a pretentious cupola, an elaborate spread eagle, a town clock, and a fine toned bell of twenty-eight hundred pounds. They had a healthy habit of keeping within their appropriations. But the ill feeling between the old and the new still lingered, and finally culminated in an incipient riot at one of the early town meetings held in the new town hall. I think this must have been as early as 1843. The factions were threshing over the old straw when one Copp, an athlete, undertook to enforce his arguments with his fists, when the fight became general. Judge S. D. Bell, the factotum of that day and afterwards our chief justice, read the riot act. A deputy sheriff undertook to suppress the belligerent Copp, whereupon the boys set upon the sheriff and chased him as far as the railroad station, where he crawled under a platform to save himself from threatened castigation. But in time the old settlers became reconciled to the new order of things, and peace again reigned in the Warsaw of the Merrimack. This town house stood on the site of the present city hall, and on the 12th day of August, 1844, I was a witness to its destruction by fire. At that time it was thought to be a marvel of architectural beauty.

The hamlets outlying the then " new village " were Janesville, in the immediate vicinity of the McCrillis carriage shop; Towlesville, southerly from Janesville, where a slaughter-house was the attraction for us boys. Hallsville was on the way out to Manchester Center, where the old meeting-house was located, and where the annual town meetings had been held " from a time whereof the memory of man runneth not to the contrary." And here at the Center was the ancient postoffice. Youngsville, then as now, was out Hanover street and near to Lake Massabesic. Goffe's Falls, at the outlet of Cohas brook, was a place of some renown in its early history as a fishing resort, and I believe there was a sawmill and gristmill there in the old colonial times. It is now a thriving manufacturing village four miles to the south of our city hall. Bakersville is at the south end of Elm street. On the west side of the Merrimack, Amoskeag was a prosperous village until her industries were diverted to the east side, and Piscataquog to the south was a pretentious place, where lumbering and flatboat building for the navigation of the Merrimack was carried on, and where West India goods and groceries, wet and dry, had long been dispensed to the profit of dealers, and to the delectation of bibulous rivermen and other sturdy yeomen. These two ancient boroughs were annexed to Manchester in 1853, one from Goffstown and the other from Bedford. Amoskeag had long been a celebrated fishing place, first for the Indians and then for the white men who succeeded them. Many a thrilling tale of this neighborhood has come down to us through Indian legendry, and many an amusing story is related of the prowess of our immediate predecessors in their " hustle " for the juicy salmon and the elusive lamprey eel. For centuries Amoskeag Falls was a favorite resort for Indians. Here they cele brated their tribal rites, practiced their wild orgies, and negotiated treaties with their savage neighbors. A bridle path was blazed through the primeval forest to this point prior to 1649 for the renowned Eliot, that the gospel of peace might be preached to a new world of heathen. But it is by no means certain that Eliot preached here, though it is so stated with considerable positiveness in Potter's History. Alas, the poor Indian!

The island south of the bridge, reached by a little foot-bridge, was a sort of fairy land for the boys of my time, and the old boarding house, inhabited by bats and swept by every blast, was indeed our island castle. Frequently at low water we crossed over to our deserted castle upon the rocks in the river bed, jumping from one to another. At one time Capt. James M. Varnum had an extensive bleachery here. The great ledge on the northeast border, extending out towards the high bridge, has long excited the curiosity of visitors on account of its deep and curious potholes. They have the appearance of having been chiseled out by the aborigines with infinite care and patience centuries ago, in which to secrete their booty captured in fierce warfare with other sanguinary tribes. That, at least, was our conjecture. Cotton Mather described them as follows in a letter published in the "Philosophical Transactions" in London: "There is a huge rock in the midst of the stream, on the top of which are a great number of pits, made exactly round, like barrels or hogsheads of different capacities, some so large as to hold several tons. The natives know nothing of the time they were made, but the neighboring Indians have been wont to hide their provisions there in the war with the Maquas. God had cut them out for that purpose for them. They seem plainly to be artificial." It is more probable, however, that these deep and curious places in the solid rock were formed by revolving pebbles kept in motion by a constantly recurring flood of waters. The savants, I believe, have agreed upon this as the better opinion. I recall one place in particular where a pothole had been worn through a shelving rock so that the rush of waters might have been seen below, only that a huge boulder had become suspended therein by some convulsion of nature. Some of these basins have the capacity of a hundred gallons or more, and their sides are as smooth and regular as though they had been wrought by the cunning hands of a skilled artificer. Youths and maidens of a summer's eve were wont to dance upon the island green. Ah! how pleasant are these memories. The little foot-bridge went out more than thirty years ago.

And now in looking back, I linger with pleasurable emotions as I recall at springtime the sound of many waters beating upon the rocks at Amoskeag, even afar off. It is a curious fact that when listening to the familiar sound of the school bell, especially if I happen to be in a suburb, or remote from my school district, I feel the old longing to bestir myself, lest I be reckoned with as a truant. And the evening curfew, sounded from our city hall, transports me with a feeling of restfulness to the days of my boyhood.

There have been few disturbances in Manchester that by any stretch of imagination can be termed riotous, and I recall but two that have cast a blur on the fair fame of our beautiful "Queen City." One was the anti-Catholic riot of many years ago, and the other was the firemen's riot of 1859. Labor disturbances have been exceedingly rare, and I recall but two in the whole history of our municipality. Indeed, Manchester has been wonderfully blessed in this particular, for the policy of our great manufacturing establishments has generally been conservative, humane, and just. Here the lamented Horace Greeley opened his campaign for the presidency almost in sight of his birthplace, and many a time have I crossed the old McGregor bridge of which he spoke so feeling on that ever memorable occasion. It was carried away by a flood in 1851.

With hundreds of others I have thus witnessed the astonishing growth of a sand bank, which at first hardly any one could afford to own, into a flourishing city. First it was Tyngstown, an ungranted tract, and Harrytown, the latter, perhaps, in memory of the mythical "old Harry." Then after September 3, 1751, by grant of the royal governor, Benning Wentworth, with added territory from Chester and Londonderry, the whole was known as Derryfield, because, it was humorously said, the Derry farmers pastured their cattle here. Then it was a fishing resort, near which a few hundred pounds of cotton yarn were spun per week or month. Now it is a beautiful city of nearly sixty thousand people, the wealthiest community in the state, with a valuation in 1895 of $28,861,122, and one of the leading manufacturing cities in this great country, where cloth enough is woven every week to make a belt around the world. The little hamlets scattered here and there in the early forties have been united in one compact, harmonious, and prosperous whole, with a diversity of industries that bids fair at no distant day to yield a population of a hundred thousand souls. Years ago the Amoskeag was the largest manufacturing company in the world that put its products on the market in a finished state, and to-day it has no rival. There are in Manchester, at the present time, about 14,000 operatives, male and female. There are about 20,000 looms and 600,000 spindles in our thirty-one mammoth mills, capitalized at $8,600,000, with an average weekly pay-roll of about $92,000. Our broad paved streets are lighted, and our commodious street cars are propelled by chained lightning, which we call electricity. We have seven beautiful public parks. Thousands of stately blocks and elegant private residences adorn our fair city. Our people are supplied with an abundance of pure water in every house. Our public schools rank among the best in the country. Our fire service is without a rival. Our militia is organized upon lines of patriotic duty; and for miles along the river banks there is heard the hum of industry, to testify that thousands of toilers earn honest bread in the sweat of their brows and by the skill of their hands. There are churches and hospitals for all. There are homes founded in charity for the indigent and infirm. There are Christian institutions that reflect the love of God in the duty of man to man, and no one may go astray through want of kindly, Christian admonition, and of helpful, loving hands. Such is the Manchester of to-day. What will it be even fifty years hence if our successors keep pace with the progress that has led us to this, our first semi-centennial conclave?

# NEW HAMPSHIRE MEN AT LOUISBURG AND BUNKER HILL.

AN ADDRESS BY REV. WILLIAM H. MORRISON BEFORE THE MANCHESTER HISTORIC ASSOCIATION, JUNE 17, 1896.

*Mr. President and Gentlemen:*

I have been asked by our president to talk to you tonight about New Hampshire at Bunker Hill because this 17th of June is the anniversary of that battle in which New Hampshire took a prominent part. It is a curious fact, however, that June 17 was famous in New Hampshire annals long before the men from the Granite hills stood on the heights of Charlestown and taught Englishmen how Yankees could fight for their rights. And so before I speak of what is in all your minds let me tell you something of another event which happened on this same June 17, thirty years before the battle of Bunker Hill. Fifteen leagues from Cape Roy, the southwestern extremity of Newfoundland, lies the cold and rocky island of Cape Breton. Its northern and western sides are steep and inaccessible. On the southeastern side it is level and indented with fine bays and noble harbors.

England, by treaty, gave this island to France, and got in exchange Nova Scotia and Newfoundland. On a neck of land south of one of the finest harbors on the island France built the city and fortress of Louisburg. A wall of stone thirty-six feet high and a ditch twenty feet wide surrounded the city. The only land entrance to the town was at the west gate over a drawbridge, defended by a circular battery mounting sixteen guns. On the west side rose the citadel which, with other batteries, contained for the defense of this place 148 cannon.

It had taken France twenty-five years to build these magnificent works of defense, and cost her in money $6,000,000. In all North America there was nothing to compare with this northern fortress. When, in 1744, war between France and England began, Duquesnel, the French commander at Louisburg, heard of it first and surprised and captured the little English garrison at Cousean. This called the attention of the colonists to the importance of Louisburg and inspired a strong wish for its reduction. The man who first suggested the taking of this fortress was William Vaughan of Portsmouth. He had learned from fishermen the strength and situation of this place and conceived the design of taking the city by surprise. He was in Boston when Massachusetts decided upon the expedition, and on fire with enthusiasm, came post haste to Portsmouth to enlist the men of New Hampshire in the scheme.

The assembly was in session when his errand was announced, and voted to raise men and money for the work.

As it turned out, New Hampshire was ready first, and impatient of delay, its men, under the head of Pepperell and Vaughan, sailed in advance of the rest of the expedition. At Cousean they were stopped by the ice, and thus they were joined by the men from Massachusetts and Connecticut. On the last day of April they made their first landing at Louisburg.

Vaughan, ever ready for any daring adventure, now led forward the New Hampshire men, first captured and burned the naval stores of the place, and the next morning entered the royal battery with only thirteen men, which he held until reinforcements from the main body reached him. It was the taking of this battery that gave the colonists their first advantage and finally resulted in the surrender of the fortress on the 17th of June, 1745. And when the keys of the place were given up, Massachusetts, New Hampshire and Connecticut stood side by side to receive them. For this splendid victory Warren, who commanded the British fleet, and Pepperell, who commanded the land forces, were rewarded by England, but the real hero, the man who did most to bring about this success, William Vaughan, was never rewarded, but died in London, a disappointed man at the way the mother country had treated him. Now we are ready for the other part of my story, and one that reflects just as much credit on New Hampshire as this.

Thirty years have passed since the tri-color was humbled by the cross of St. George on the heights of Louisburg. In spite of valiant service done by the colonists, England has become an unbearable tyrant, and the men of these colonies rebel. Down in Portsmouth harbor there is a fort which brave spirits captured, carrying away the guns and powder which is so much needed. Boston is garrisoned by 10,000 British veterans. Out at Concord there are some stores which General Gage, who commands this force, decides to destroy.

Paul Revere is watching him, and when the lanterns from the steeple of the old North church give the signal he is off like the wind "to give the alarm through every Middlesex village and farm, for the country folk to be up and to arm."

The British march out to Lexington, and thus, under the shadow of the Church of God, the embattled farmers stand and fire the shots heard round the world.

Massachusetts fought that battle alone, and sent the trained cohorts of Britain back into Boston a fleeing rabble. But to the north of her, like hound in leash, listening for the signal, stood her sister, New Hampshire. As the shadows of night settled over the earth on that ever memorable 19th of April, east, west, north, and south, sped the messengers, and like the gathering of the clans at the call of Roderick Dhu, the hardy sons of New England grasped their rifles and hastened to Boston.

O that the pen of Walter Scott, winged as it was when he wrote that immortal poem, might do justice to the scenes that took place all through this valley and around our Granite hills, when the news of Lexington reached New Hampshire !

Scarcely had the clocks in the farmhouses sounded the hour of one in the morning of April 20, when sixty men, all armed and equipped, started from Nottingham common for Boston. In his sawmill at Amoskeag falls was John Stark at work that day, when up the river came a boy on horseback with the news of that battle. Leaving his saw in the cut, and in his shirt-sleeves, he mounted his horse, and leaving a hasty message for his family, galloped down the valley, calling upon his old comrades of the French war to follow him. And here again is a sight for a poet. The spectacle of that horseman sniffing the battle from afar, riding as fast as his noble steed can carry him, while at his back come the hardy frontiersmen, at first in ones and two, then in scores, then in hundreds, until, when he rides into Concord the next morning, he is leading a thousand New Hampshire men, every one of them ready to follow John Stark to the death, if need be. The next morning at least 3000 men from New Hampshire were at the service of Massachusetts, to help her in the struggle. John Stark and Enoch Poor were made colonels by that colony, and at once proceeded to form these men into regiments.

Stark's regiment was the first formed, as it was also the largest in the whole Continental army. Here, as at Louisburg, thirty years before, the men of New Hampshire shrink from no duty, but do their full portion of driving the British out of Boston. June 15 arrives, and with it the news that Gage has decided to seize the heights of Charlestown on the 18th. General Ward, commanding the colonists, determined to forestall him.

On the night of the 16th, 1000 men from Massachusetts and Connecticut silently occupied Breed's hill, the higher of the two eminences, and before morning had thrown up a redoubt which sheltered them from the guns of the British ships of war floating in the harbor. When the bombardment opened, as it did as soon as light, General Putnam, seeing that more men were needed, ordered a portion of Stark's regiment to the hill. By 11 o'clock the whole of Stark's and Reed's New Hampshire regiments were on their march. At Charlestown Neck they found a large body of troops halted by the storm of cannon balls which swept their pathway. Stark called upon these men to open and let his men through. They did so, and the New Hampshire men passed over the Neck and upon the hill.

When they reached the redoubt they found the Massachusetts

men, under Prescott, stationed there, while the Connecticut men, under Knowlton, held the breastworks on the right. On the left from the redoubt to the river was a wide gap, and here Stark and Reed, with the New Hampshire men, took their places, behind a breastwork made up in part of a stone wall and in part of a rail fence stuffed with hay. In the meantime the British are not idle. Boat after boat is landing soldiers upon the Charlestown shore. In the steeple in the North church is a group of officers. One of them is General Gage. On being asked if he thinks the Yankees will fight, he answered: "If a certain John Stark of New Hampshire is there I know they will, for I have seen that man fight." At 3 o'clock the British advance. The plan is to carry the breastwork on the left and flank the redoubt. To do this the best troops in the British army are stationed on the right. As they sweep up the slope the patriots hold their fire till within point blank range, and then a storm of bullets hurls back the whole British line.

It is certain death to face those deadly rifles, for every man behind them can bring down a squirrel as far as he can see it.

Once more the red line advances and once more it is sent reeling back to the shore. Twice have they tried to break through the breastwork on the left. Now the British decide to change their plan and a third time they move forward, this time concentrating their forces upon the redoubt. The Americans have made a gallant fight, but now their ammunition is gone, and after one volley they have nothing but clubbed muskets with which to fight and are soon overpowered and driven out of the redoubt. Not so with the New Hampshire men. They still held the rail fence and the stone wall in spite of all attacks, but when Prescott's and Knowlton's men retreated from the hill they must leave, too, or be flanked, and so, falling in behind Massachusetts and Connecticut, New Hampshire was the rear guard that saved the Americans from capture, as well as defeat.

# CAPTAIN JOHN MOORE'S COMPANY.

By George C. Gilmore, before the Manchester Historic Association, June 17, 1896.

*Gentlemen of the Manchester Historic Association:*

The subject assigned me for the evening exercises is Capt. John Moore's company, Col. John Stark's regiment of Derryfield (now Manchester), at the battle of Bunker Hill, fought one hundred and twenty-one years ago today. This battle, one of the most famous in its results in history, is of especial interest to Manchester, for eighteen of the men of that band of heroes were from here, and we only wish it was possible to know when and where they died and are buried. Captain Moore's company at the battle occupied the extreme left of the American forces, next to the Mystic river, where the British troops made two desperate charges to dislodge them, without success. The third charge was made on the redoubt, and the result is well known in history. One of the singular outcomes of this battle was, there is no record that a single man of this company of sixty-four men was killed or wounded, for they were certainly in the thickest of the fight. General Devens, in his address at the centennial anniversary of the battle of Bunker Hill said: "The second repulse was terrific." "In front of our works," says Prescott, "the ground was covered with the killed and wounded, many of them within a few yards; while before the rail fence the dead, in the homely phrase of Stark, 'lay thick as sheep in a fold.'" Ten men of this company went with Benedict Arnold on his perilous expedition to Quebec, and one of them was taken prisoner by the French.

## CAPTAIN JOHN MOORE'S COMPANY.

Baker, Benjamin, private, Manchester.
Boyd, Nathaniel, sergeant, Manchester.   Promoted to lieutenant, June 18, 1775.
Emerson, Charles, private, Manchester.
Emerson, George, private, Manchester.
George, Benjamin, private, Manchester.
Goff, John, private, Manchester.
Hart, Arthur, private, Manchester.
Harvey, Lemuel, private, Manchester.
Martin, Nathaniel, private, Manchester.   With Arnold in the Quebec expedition, and was taken prisoner.
Martin, Timothy, private, Manchester.
McKnight, David, private, Manchester.
McNeil, John C., private, Manchester.
Moore, John, captain, Manchester.   Promoted to Major, June 18, 1775.
Moore, Goffe, private, Manchester.
Stark, Archibald, private, Manchester.
Stark, Caleb, private, Manchester.
Campbell, Hugh, private, Bedford.   Discharged July 7, 1775.
Callahan, John, private, Bedford.   Said to have been killed during the war.
Cutting, Jonas, private, Bedford.
Dobbin, John, private, Bedford.   With Arnold in the Quebec expedition.
Eagan, Luke, private, Bedford.
Fling, Patrick, private, Bedford.   With Arnold in the Quebec expedition.
Hogg, George, private, Bedford.
Houston, James, private, Bedford.
Johnson, Calvin, private, Bedford.   Died in the service during the war.
Kerr, John, private, Bedford.   With Arnold in the Quebec expedition.
Matthews, Joseph, private, Bedford.
Matthews, Hugh, private, Bedford.
McClary, Thomas, private, Bedford.
McLaughlin, Thomas, lieutenant, Bedford.   Promoted to captain June 18, 1775.
Murphy, Patrick, private, Bedford.   With Arnold in the Quebec expedition.
Moore, David, private, Bedford.
Newman, William, private, Bedford.
O'Neil, John, private, Bedford.
Patten, Samuel, private, Bedford.   Promoted to corporal June 17, 1775.
Orr, James, private, Bedford.
Allds, John, private, Litchfield.
Bixby, Edward, private, Litchfield.
Butterfield, James, fifer, Litchfield.

Lawler, David, private, Litchfield. With Arnold in the Quebec expedition.
McQuig, David, sergeant, Litchfield.
Patterson, William, corporal, Litchfield.
Turner, John, private, Litchfield.
Hutchinson, Solomon, private, Merrimack.
McClure, Thomas, private, Merrimack. With Arnold in the Quebec expedition.
Wier, John, private, Merrimack. With Arnold in the Quebec expedition.
Caldwell, Samuel, private, Dunbarton.
Gage, Joshua, private, Dunbarton.
Glidden, James, private, Dunbarton.
Huse, Thomas, private, Dunbarton.
Johnson, Abraham, private, Dunbarton.
Mills, John, private, Dunbarton.
Smith, Jonathan, private, Dunbarton. With Arnold in the Quebec expedition.
Glover, Henry, drummer, New Boston.
Gregg, John, private, New Boston.
Hogg, James, private, New Boston.
Hunter, John, private, New Boston.
Jordan, John, sergeant, New Boston.
Martin, Samuel, private, New Boston.
McPherson, James, private, New Boston.
McPherson, John, private, New Boston.
Hutchins, Nathaniel, lieutenant, Hopkinton. With Arnold in the Quebec expedition. Transferred from Baldwin's company; no date given, probably to take the place of Thomas McLaughlin, promoted to captain.
Follinsby, Moses, private, Weare. With Arnold in the Quebec expedition,
Cyphers, John, private. Residence unknown.
Gibson, James, private, Bradford. Transferred from Baldwin's company to Capt. John Moore's, July 7, 1775.

## FOOT NOTES.

Moore, Samuel, private, Bedford. Discharged June 7, 1775.
McMurphy, John, private, Bedford. Enlisted July 16, 1775.
Clay, John, private, Candia. On roll August 7, 1775.
Capt. John Moore removed in 1778 to Norridgewalk, Maine; he died in 1809.
David Farmer, of Derryfield, in Goffstown company.

# BOATING ON THE MERRIMACK.

A PAPER BY GEORGE WALDO BROWNE, READ BEFORE THE MANCHESTER HISTORIC ASSOCIATION, SEPT. 16, 1896.

No period in the history of the busy Merrimack from the morning of July 17, 1605, when it was discovered by de Champlain, to the present date is fraught with more exciting interest than the boating days of the first half of this century and immediately preceding the appearance on its banks of the iron horse, which was to bring such a revolution in the methods of traffic. Boston had already become a promising metropolis of 20,000 inhabitants, while all along the northward course as far as Concord, N. H., thriving villages had come into existence, demanding increased business facilities and better and cheaper means of transportation than were afforded by the slow moving ox trains or the desultory rafting on the river practiced to uncertain extents at occasional intervals. But before the stream could be successfully utilized as an inland maritime highway the passage of its falls must be rendered feasible by locks and the rocky shallows and devious windings be escaped by artificial waterways.

The first step in this direction was the building of the Middlesex canal, which was projected by Hon. James Sullivan and begun in 1794, to be completed in 1803. This waterway stopped at what is now known as Middlesex village, about two miles above Lowell, and was twenty-seven miles in length. Immediately upon its completion other companies and individuals, aided more or less by the Middlesex corporation, undertook to continue the work of making the river navigable by building locks, dams, and canals where needed until a point two miles north of Concord was reached — fifty-two miles in length — Judge Samuel Blodget fitly completing the great scheme of engineering by his canal of Amoskeag, which was formally opened on May Day, 1807. That part of the system below Amoskeag, comprising the dams and locks at Merrill's falls, near Granite bridge, and Griffin's falls below, was done by the Union Lock and Canal Company, superintended by Isaac Riddle of Bedford.

To Superintendent Riddle belongs the credit of conceiving the possible benefits likely to accrue from river boating, and in association with Major Caleb Stark of Dunbarton he constructed the first canal boat that ever plied on the Merrimack. The work was done at Bedford Center and the boat was so different from anything the people had seen as to call forth numerous expressions of surprise and often of ridicule. The nearest approach to its style of construction that we have now is the flat-bottomed scow used to bring brick down the river from Hooksett. This odd craft, when completed, was drawn to Basswood Landing on the Piscataquog, near the bridge, by forty yokes of oxen, and launched amid the tremendous cheering of a large crowd of curious spectators. This boat, appropriately named the Experiment, was promptly loaded with lumber and started on its pioneer trip to Boston, where it was hailed with greater demonstrations than at its starting point, the firing of cannon mingling with the shouts of the spectators. The newspaper of the day, the Boston Centinel and Federalist, had the following notice concerning the arrival of Captain Riddle's boat:

"Arrived from Bedford, N. H., Canal Boat Experiment, Isaac Riddle, Captain, via Merrimack River and Middlesex Canal."

This was in the fall of 1812, and Captain Riddle immediately found himself beset with orders for the shipment of large contracts of lumber and merchandise. His business increased so rapidly that in 1816 a store and boat house was built at Piscataquog bridge, and two years later locks were built just above the island at the mouth of the river.

It is not apparent that other individuals at that time sought to imitate the example of Captain Riddle, but even before his boat had made its initial trip the Merrimack Boating Company had been organized in Boston to transport freight from that place to Concord and way stations through Middlesex canal and Merrimack river. The first boat belonging to this corporation was taken up the river in October, 1814, and commenced on regular trips the following June. In 1817 steam power was unsuccessfully applied and the project abandoned after one trial. From the beginning of operations by this company thirty years of uninterrupted and successful boating followed on the Merrimack. It is true passengers had to depend, as before, on the stage coaches, but all the products of the country were taken to market, and such merchandise as was needed brought up on the return trip to the places along the route. The granite in Quincy market was transported from Concord by these boats.

The season opened as soon as the river was clear of ice in the spring and continued until cold weather. Five days were consumed in the upward trip and four days in going down the river. Twenty tons was considered an average load as far as Lowell and fifteen tons above that point, except during low water, when not more than half that burden could be carried. At the beginning, $13.50 was the charge for up freight to the extreme landing in Concord, and $8.50 for down transportation; but these prices were gradually reduced, until in 1838 only $5 and $4 were the respective charges. The total amount of business done during the years 1816–1842 was $468,756, going upward, and $220,940 downward. Before the boating began $20 a ton was charged by the teams for the entire route.

The Merrimack Boating Company was succeeded by the Concord Boating Company in 1823, and that in turn gave up business in 1844. The largest number of boats believed to be on the river at any one time was twenty. These boats, built to meet the peculiar requirements of river navigation, were not less than forty-five feet or over seventy-five feet in length, and from nine to nine and one half feet in width at the middle. Those on the Merrimack were generally of the greatest length, nine feet wide at midway but a little narrower toward the ends, flat-bottomed across the center but rounded up at bow and stern, so that while they were three feet deep at mid-length the sides were barely a foot high at the extremities. Two-inch pine planks were used in their construction, these being fastened to three-by-four-inch cross joints and side knees of oak, with cross timbers of the same wood at the ends. The seams were calked with oakum and pitched. No cross thwarts were needed, but a stout plank nailed across from side to side about a foot forward of midway served the double purpose of strengthening the boat and affording support to a mast raised to carry a square sail attached to a cross yard, and which under favorable circumstances could be made to assist in the propulsion of the heavily loaded boat. These spars varied somewhat in length, being from twenty to twenty-four feet long and six inches in diameter at the foot. A rope running through a single block at the top enabled the boatman to hoist or lower the sail at will.

The main means of propulsion against the current were the setting poles in the hands of two strong bowmen, who were assisted, at such times as his attention was not occupied in steering the unwieldy craft, by the skipper in the stern. These poles, commonly called pike poles, were fifteen feet long, two inches in diameter and made round and smooth out of the best ash wood, with the lower end armed with an iron point. At intervals between the canals, when a favoring breeze made it practical, the sail was run up and gave material aid; but after all it was the muscle of the brawny pike men that carried the heavily laden barge onward and upward toward its destination.

The peculiar method of propulsion is thus described by one who was familiar with the work: "To propel the boat by poling, a bowman stood on either side of the bow, with his face toward the stern, and thrusting the pike end of his pole down beside the boat in a slanting direction toward the stern until it struck the bottom of the river, he placed his shoulder against the top of the pole, and, with his feet braced against the cross timbers in the bottom of the boat, he exerted the strength of his body and legs to push the boat forward. As it moved, he stepped along the bottom of the boat, still bracing his shoulder firmly against the pole, until he had walked in this manner to the mast board—or, rather, until the movement of the boat had brought the mast board to him. He then turned around and walked to the bow, trailing the pole in the water, thrust it again to the bottom of the river and repeated the pushing movement.'' It must be understood that the cargo was piled along the middle of the boat so as to allow of a narrow passageway on each side.

The passage down the stream was of course easier and more rapid, the men relying principally on scull oars for means of propulsion, these oars being about the same length as the poles, with six inch blades on the lower portion. The oarsmen stood close to either side of the boat and about six feet from the bow, each working his oar against a thole pin fastened on the opposite gunwale, and, the oar handles crossing, it was necessary that they be worked together, which moved the craft evenly on its way.

The steering oar was nearly twenty feet long, and secured at the middle to a pivot on the stern cross timber. The blade was about twenty inches in width, and this like the others was made of the toughest and strongest ash. The steersman at his post in the stern had his pike pole and sculling oar at hand to lend such assistance as he could to the bowmen whenever he was not occupied in guiding the boat along the laborious course.

The agent at Concord lower landing hired the men making up the crews of the company, from $16 to $26 a month being paid. A large proportion of these boatmen were from Manchester and Litchfield. Brought up in the knowledge and experience of fishing at the Falls and rafting lumber down the river, they were superior boatmen. Among them was Joseph M. Rowell, who had been a raftsman, and of whom it is related as a specimen of what might be required of a man in that capacity, that he rafted in one day two lots of lumber from Curtis eddy, nearly opposite No. 5 Amoskeag mill, to Litchfield, nine miles, and walked back each time with a forty-pound scull oar on his shoulder. For this day's double work he got three dollars. Despite the hardships of his earlier life, Mr. Rowell lived to a good old age.

Among the best known of the rivermen was Capt. Israel Merrill, who had the distinction of being pilot of the steamer that made its "experimental" trip up the river in 1817. He was a tall, powerful man, of whom many reminiscences of bravery and hardihood are still related. He received a gold medal for saving two men from drowning in the river, at the imminent risk of losing his own life. John McCutchens, afloat on a raft of lumber above Eel falls, and finding it getting beyond his control, leaped into the water to attempt to swim to the bank. Unable to do this he was carried over the dam built just above the falls, but managed to catch upon a wooden pin on the top of the planking. Captain Merrill, seeing his perilous situation, swam down to the place and pulled him to a rock, from which they were rescued soon after by some men in a boat. Matthew McCurdy fell into Pulpit stream and was swept down against a jam of logs, where he clung until Captain Merrill swam to his assistance. It was this same redoubtable captain that made the long-talked-of race with another boatman from Concord to Boston, coming in at the end of this eighty-one-mile stubbornly contested trial a boat's length ahead of his rival, who paid for his folly by the loss of his life from over-exertion.

The quickest trip of which there is record was made in 1833 by Samuel Hall, John Ray, and Joseph M. Rowell, who started with a boatload of men from the mouth of Piscataquog river at eight o'clock on the morning of June 30, went to Medford, into Medford river, back into Middlesex canal and into Boston, got a load of goods and reached home on the evening of July 3, having been only four days on the trip and return. The last boat on the Middlesex canal made its final trip in 1851.

As a rule travel was suspended at sunset, the men planning so as to be near one of the convenient stopping-places along the route at nightfall. The passage of the Middlesex canal consumed one day; another enabled them to reach Cromwell's falls, fifteen miles this side; the third took them through Amoskeag locks; and the fourth, everything proving exceptionally favorable, found them at their destination. The rendezvous at Amoskeag was the old Blodget house, kept respectively by Samuel P. Kidder, "Jim" Griffin, and Frederick G. Stark.

Samuel P. Kidder was the first agent appointed by the boating company to superintend the Union canals and collect tolls, continuing until his death in 1822, when he was succeeded by Frederick G. Stark, who held the position to 1837. The books kept by both these agents are now in the possession of Frederick G. Stark, of Manchester, a nephew of the first-named. Through his courtesy the writer has examined the several volumes and gives the following extracts to illustrate the methods and amount of business.

```
" No. 97              Daniel Jones                         18 Shotts.
    " July 8, 1829
" Bow Canal    103M Pine Lumber and Timber @ 34    35.02
               " 62M Shingles                @ 03    1.86
                                                   ——— $36.88

" Hooksett Canal  103M Pine Lumber and Timber
                                             @ 18   18.54
                  " 62M Shingles             @  2    1.24
                                                   ———  19.78

" Amoskeag Canal  103M Pine Lumber and Timber
                                             @ 50   51.50
                  " 62M Shingles             @  6    3.72
                                                   ———  55.22
                                                      ———
                                                      $111.88
            " Paid July 28th."
```

The amount of business for the month of October, 1821, was $759.80; while for the same month in 1831 it was $1,598.65, having more than doubled in the decade.

"Amoskeag Canal Work Roll for September, 1825.

"Israel Colson, James Ray, George Clark, David Young, William P. Harwood, Abiel Saunders, Ziba Saunders, Charles Dale, Jacob Richardson, Jacob Currier, William Palmer, Adam Gilmore, Viranus Webster, Joseph Rowell, Alpheus Stevens, Reuben Kimball, Parker Whidden, Nathan Stearns, Joseph Butterfield, Hezekiah Kitrege, Isaac Nichols, —— Blodget, Ebenezer G. Preston, Jonathan Young, Jr., Samuel Jackson."

Accidents were less common than might have been expected. One boat capsized at Goffe's Falls, and Edward Killicut was killed. Another was carried over Amoskeag falls, a yoke of oxen attached to it being saved from the same fate by the presence of mind of Joseph M. Rowell, who rushed into the water and cut the rope that held them.

In the midst of the bustle and hard-earned success of these stalwart sons of old-time progress came the announcement of that new power which was to rob them of their means of livelihood. Naturally this aroused bitter opposition on their part, and as an illustration of the reluctance of the spirit of the times to accept the new way for the old, the Boston Transcript of Sept. 1, 1830, said: "It is not astonishing that so much reluctance exists against plunging into doubtful speculation. The public is itself divided as to the practicability of the railroad." A member of the Massachusetts legislature was on record as saying: "Railroads, Mr. Speaker, may do well enough in the old countries, but will never be the thing for so young a country as this. When you can make the rivers run back it will be time enough to make railways." The waters of the Merrimack continued to run according to the laws of gravitation, but the railroad, in spite of all human opposition, came, and, like an avenging Nemesis, followed almost identically in the tracks of the skeleton of departed greatness,— the canals, which had made its coming possible.

There is no doubt that the adventurous lives led by the boatmen tended to bring out the rougher element of their natures, and a considerable number drank, gambled, and entered zealously into the more boisterous sports; but they were always faithful to duty, kind-hearted to a fellow-being in distress, and many of them carried beneath their coarse jackets more than an average allowance of real manhood. They belonged to a very necessary class of citizens in their day, but which in the evolution of the swiftly following years has been supplanted by another, and only a memory of their usefulness remains. The shriek of the car-whistle ended the boatman's song, while his inspiring watchword as he toiled laboriously toward the upper waters of old Amoskeag, " One more stroke for old Derryfield," found its death knell in the heartless snort of the iron horse, which threw at once those hardy men out of the only employment they knew. Here and there some shattered landmark dimly remains to remind us of them and their gigantic work, but the wooden dams and locks have long since crumbled away, the canals have been filled and their banks leveled, while the icy floods of spring have played such sad havoc with the granite abutments that even they fail to stand as their monument.

# THE DERRYFIELD SOCIAL LIBRARY.

A Paper by William H. Huse, read before the Manchester Historic Association, Decemebr 23, 1896.

What treasures are found in parental garrets! With what delight do children ransack the accumulations of past years and live fictitious lives amid the belongings of their ancestors. Ofttimes are these treasures appreciated more as the boy becomes a man and sees their real value. Such has been my experience. My delight when a boy, as in my father's attic I played with a few old leather-bound books that lay in an ancient bookcase, has been replaced by a better appreciation, as I learned that they were the remains of the Derryfield Social Library, an institution that was the forerunner of our present public library, and which was a powerful factor in molding the lives of our fathers.

The only printed mention of the library I can find is in Mr. Potter's "History of Manchester," where he tells us that "in the latter part of 1795 the project of a social library was started by the inhabitants of Derryfield and vicinity. Those interested in the project associated under the name of the Proprietors of Derryfield Library. January 4, 1796, they bought their first books of E. Larken, of Boston, at a cost of $32.94. On the 12th of December of the same year they voted to form a society by the name of The Proprietors of the Social Library in Derryfield. The number of the first proprietors or their names is unknown. The proprietors were incorporated in December, 1799, at which time they numbered forty-six, and had seventy-eight volumes of valuable books in the library. Additions were made from time to time, but the interest in it began to abate, and at length in 1833 no annual meeting was held, and the library was at an end, each proprietor appropriating such books as he chose." The office of the secretary of state contains a copy of the act of incorporation.

## STATE OF NEW HAMPSHIRE.

[L. S.] IN THE YEAR OF OUR LORD ONE THOUSAND SEVEN HUNDRED AND NINETY-NINE.

### AN ACT

For incorporating Certain Persons by the Name of the Proprietors of the Social Library in Derryfield.

*Be it enacted by the Senate and House of Representatives in General Court convened :*

That Daniel Davis and Samuel P. Kidder and their associates, proprietors of said library, and all such as may hereafter become proprietors of the same, be, and they hereby are, incorporated into a body politic by the name of The Proprietors of the Social Library in Derryfield, with continuation and succession forever; and in that name may sue and be sued, may plead and be impleaded in all personal actions, and may prosecute and defend the same to final judgment and execution, and they are hereby vested with all the powers and privileges incident to corporations of a similar nature, and may enjoin penalties of disfranchisement or fine not exceeding four dollars for each offense, to be recovered by said society in an action of debt to their use in any court proper to try the same, and they may purchase and receive subscriptions, grants, and donations of personal estate not exceeding one thousand dollars, for the purpose and use of their association. *Passed, December 26, 1799. Proprietors' names. May sue, etc. May enjoin penalties, etc. Hold personal Estate.*

*And be it further enacted,* That said society be, and they hereby are, authorized to assemble at Derryfield aforesaid on the first Monday in November annually, to choose all such officers as may be found necessary for the orderly conducting the affairs of said corporation, who shall continue in office until others are chosen in their room, and that said corporation may assemble as often as may be found necessary for filling up any vacancies which may happen in said offices, and for transacting all other business, excepting the raising of monies, which shall be always done at their annual meeting, and at no other time, at which time they shall vote all necessary sums for defreaying the annual expense of preserving said library, and for enlarging the same; and said corporation shall have power to make such rules, regulations, and by-laws for the government of said society as may from time to time by them be found necessary; *provided* the same be not repugnant to the constitution and laws of this state.

*Annual meeting.*
*Raise money.*
*Make By-laws.*

*And be it further enacted*, That Daniel Davis and Samuel P. Kidder, or either of them, are hereby authorized and empowered to call the first meeting of said proprietors at such time and place as they may appoint, by posting a notification for that purpose at the meeting-house in said Derryfield, at least fifteen days prior to said day of meeting; and the said proprietors at said meeting shall have the same power to choose officers and make by-laws as they have by this act at their annual meeting.

*First meeting.*

## STATE OF NEW HAMPSHIRE.

IN HOUSE OF REPRESENTATIVES, December 24, 1799.

The foregoing bill having had three several readings, passed to be enacted. Sent up for concurrence.

JOHN PRENTICE,
*Speaker.*

IN SENATE, THE SAME DAY.

This bill having been read a third time, was enacted.

AMOS SHEPARD,
*President.*

Approved December 26, 1799.

J. T. GILMAN,
*Governor.*

A true copy. Attest:
PHILIP CARRIGIAN,
*Sect'y.*

Among the books that now remain is the record book that was kept by the several librarians, and although many liberties were taken with it by us youthful vandals (I say "us," for I am not alone responsible), as many a leaf stub can testify, it is possible to get at the names of nearly all the proprietors and patrons of the library. The fact that the right to take books was occasionally sold, would indicate that it was not a public library, only the members of the association having that privilege. Compared with modern libraries, a large number of the books were religious in their character, and the Calvinistic trend of many was plainly seen in the lives and creeds of the people.

It was in the earlier years of the century that my grandfather brought up a boy named Moody Davis. He was a queer, thoughtful lad, and much given to strange remarks. One day there called at the house a man known to all the section as Uncle Ebenezer. He spent most of his time calling on his neighbors, made it a point to call about noon, never refused an invitation to dinner, and usually ate enough to last till the next day. At this dinner, for he staid, there was brought on a boiled pudding that was not only boiled but boiling. Moody received his portion and sat waiting anxiously for it to cool, at the same time intently watching the visitor bolt down his without any difficulty whatever. At last the boy's pent-up feelings found expression. "If I could eat hot pud'n like Uncle Ebenezer, I'd never be afraid of going to hell."

But all were not Calvinists. Hosea Ballou's Notes on the Parables were in the library and were read by many. Whether it was a result of this or not I cannot say, but even then a liberal interpretation of the Bible was occasionally to be found. One night a good man was reading to his family the story of Samson. As he came to the account of the foxes his wife interrupted him with "Hut tut, John, d'ye read right?" And John read again, "And Samson went and caught three hundred foxes and took firebrands and turned tail to tail and put a firebrand in the midst between two tails." Again he was interrupted. "Hut tut, John, d'ye think they were all foxes?" "Well," said John, deliberately, "I don't know but there might have been some skunks and woodchucks among them."

The earliest date found in the record book is May 14, 1802, and although Mr. Potter states that the library ceased to exist in 1833, the last date given on which a book was withdrawn is May 19, 1838. The number of books taken out for several years previous to this, however, was small, so that it is probable that the association died a slow death.

The list of members, as complete as can be obtained in the record book, is as follows:

David Adams.
Robert Adams.
Jesse Baker.
Phineas Baley.
Lieut. Hugh Boys.
Jacob Chase.
Nathaniel Connant.
Ann E. Couch.
Daniel Davis.
Moses Davis.
Samuel Davis.
David Dickey.
John Dickey.
Capt. John Dwinell.
Peter Emerson.
Joseph Farmer.
William Farmer.
David Flint.
John Frye.
John Gambel.
James Griffin.
Lieut. Daniel Hall.
John Hall.
Robert Hall.
Philip Haseltine.
Asa Heseltine.
Capt. Moses Heseltine.
Peter Hills.
Isaac Huse.
Samuel Jackson.
Nathan Johnson.
Samuel P. Kidder.
Benjamin Leslie.

George McAlester.
Samuel McAllester.
John G. Moor.
Capt. Joseph Moor.
Nathaniel Moor.
Samuel Moore.
The Widow Moor.
Eliza A. Nutt.
James Nutt.
James Parker.
John Perham.
William Perham.
Phineas Pettingill.
Stephen Pingry.
John Proctor.
John Ray.
Lieut. Job Rowell.
Reuben Sawyer.
Aaron Seavey.
Benj. F. Stark.
John Stark.
Widow Eliza (Elizabeth) Stark.
Ephraim Stevens.
Ephraim Stevens, Jr.
Thomas Stickney.
William Walker.
Lieut. Amos Weston.
David Webster.
Israel Webster.
Ephraim White.
Ruben White.
Stephen Worthley.
Jonathan Young.

A few of the librarians are known. Robert Perham held the office in 1814 and John Dwinell from 1815 to 1818. Mr. Perham's name does not appear on the pages as having taken out books, but it is presumable that he was a member. On one page we read that John Gambell went out of office December 7, 1826, and on the same page is found the statement that "Daniel Hall is libaren and Clark of the Librey for the time to come."

A few rights were transferred. John Frye sold his right to Aaron Seavey. The following item is found on one page: "January 19 this Day Capt. Moses heselton Sold his Right to leftenant hugh Boys of manchester."

The bookcase in which the remnant of the library reposed for so many years in my father's attic and in which the entire collection of books was probably kept is a plain case of pine painted a dull red, sixty-two inches high by thirty-nine wide, and eleven inches deep. Two doors fastened by handmade hinges hide from view five shelves that show the effects of wear and age. Under the shelves is a long double drawer with no handles, which looks so much like a panel that its existence had been forgotten and it was only quite recently that it was rediscovered and found to contain a few packages of dry herbs and tax books of the town of Manchester for seven years beginning with 1826. The library was doubtless kept in the house where the bookcase remained so long, for there was the village store with a hall overhead and there was the first postoffice at the Center.

The highest number of any book recorded was No. 110. As there were several books without numbers the library probably contained one hundred twenty volumes or more.

There were two columns on each page of the record book for fines for detention beyond a prescribed or reasonable time and on account of damage. The time fines ranged from two to fifty cents. This latter fine was for keeping a book from August 8 to November 7, but whether in the same or different years is not stated. These are representative fines for damage,— "tearing maps, 15 cents," and "tearing 2 leaves 10 cents."

At first the books seem to have had no numbers for the names were given in almost every record. From these names and the few books that remain the following list has been obtained:

Animated Nature, American Gazetteer, American Revolution, Arabian Nights, A Fool of Quality, A Bold Stoop for a Wife, A

Christian's Life, A View of Religions, Burton's Lectures, Burroughs' Memoirs, Burn's Justice of the Peace, Cook's Voyages, Carver's Travels, Columbian Orator, Davis' Sermons, Doddridge's Sermons, Don Quixote, Dyer's Titles, Exercises on Piety, Explicatory Catechism, Erskine's Sermons, Female American, Five Points of Christian Doctrine, Flowers of Modern Travels, Franklin's Works, Farmer's Letters, Gordon's History, Henry Tufts, Hickeringill's Works, Hunter's Sacred Biography, Howard's Life, Hervey's Meditations, Infantry Regulations, Josephus, Lady's Miscellany, Laws of New Hampshire, Letters from England, Life of Washington, Life of Joseph, Looking Glass, Morse's Geography, Maria Cecilia, Morse's Journal, Notes on the Parables, Newton's Prophecies, Pilgrim's Progress, Priest Craft, Paine's Writings, Pomfret's Poems, Riley's Narrative, Robison's Proofs, Religious Courtship, Rollin's History, Repository, Rasselas, Saints' Everlasting Rest, Scottish Chiefs, Sanders' Travels, Spectator (several volumes), The Deist, The Rising Progress of Religion in the Soul, The Mariner's Compass Rectified, Thoughts on Divine Goodness, Universal Dialogues, Valuable Secrets, Watts on the Mind, Winchester's Lectures.

Some of the books have interesting features. The author of The Mariner's Compass Rectified asserts that the tables " will last with Exactness as long as God upholdeth the Order and Course of Nature." The full title of Robison's Proofs is " Proofs of a Conspiracy Against all the Religions and Governments of Europe, Carried on in the Secret Meetings of Free Masons, Illuminati and Reading Societies, Collected from Good Authorities by John Robison, A. M." The author, who was English, evidently connected every effort of the Stuart pretenders and every attempt at revolution on the continent with all societies whose meetings were not open to the public.

It was in the volumes of The Spectator that I found in the old red bookcase in the attic that I first read that classic, " The Vision of Mirza," and made the acquaintance of Sir Roger De Coverley. A very few of the books in the old library are now read, but most of them have been replaced by others, for " of making many books there is no end."

# CASTLE WILLIAM AND MARY.

A Paper by John G. Crawford, read before the Manchester Historic Association, December 23, 1896.

The movement that was inaugurated a few years ago to erect a monument to the memory of General Sullivan, and my admiration for the grand military and civic record of that noble patriot, was what led me to investigate the subject in relation to the dismantling of Castle William and Mary. To make sure that the histories already published giving an account of the explorations were correct, I devoted much time to the accounts given by those who were familiar with these transactions and who gave the facts and circumstances in numerous letters and official reports, all of which were published in the "American Archives." The paper I am requested to present to you tonight is the result of these investigations, and if I should differ, as I shall, from those who have published these accounts, I trust that some other historian will show wherein I am in error, that in the end the true account may be given.

Historians are allowed to take great liberty with facts, but when they record important transactions and state matters which are not facts, then that which purports to be history not only ceases to be of value but becomes detrimental and misleading.

The errors which have occurred in all the histories of New Hampshire in relation to the expeditions which were planned and carried out to dismantle Fort or Castle William and Mary are so apparent that they certainly require some correction.

If the histories in their entire are to be judged from the standpoint, as to correctness, of their account of Fort William and Mary, then it may well be said "There has been no history of New Hampshire yet published."

Fort, or Castle, William and Mary was one of the line of forts established by England along the coast to defend the several harbors and ports of entry. Portsmouth at the time of the trouble between the colonies and the mother country was, next to Boston, the most important port along the New England coast. This fort was situated in Newcastle, some two miles down the harbor from Portsmouth. After the close of the French and Indian war there had been but little use to maintain a large force in it; only sufficient to care for the guns and munitions stored therein, and for revenue service. The expense of maintaining the fort, in supplying it with men and provisions, was borne by the colony of New Hampshire. The troubles which had been brewing between the colonies and England ever since the passage of the stamp act, which culminated in the War of Independence, made the occupation of the fortifications on the coast of great importance in the struggle soon to follow.

The house of representatives of the province of New Hampshire which convened at Portsmouth, the capitol, on Thursday, May 26, 1774, voted: "That there be allowed and paid unto the captain general of this province for payment of officers, soldiers, billiting, fire-wood, and candles for support of his majesty's Fort William and Mary for one year, viz,: from the 25th of March, 1774, to the 25th of March, 1775, the sum of two thousand pounds, lawful money, to be paid in four quarterly payments out of the money that is, or shall be in the treasury, with advice of council." This vote was sent up to the council by Mr. Jennes. The next day, May 27, the secretary brought from the board the vote for an allowance for the fort, with a verbal message from his excellency, Governor Wentworth, that he thought the allowance insufficient and desired some alterations might be made, by allowing a larger sum, or appointing a number of soldiers sufficient, with proper allowance.

The house took immediate consideration of the message from

the governor, and to show their loyalty to England, voted that the captain general be desired to give orders for the enlisting three men to be posted at his Majesty's Fort William and Mary for one year, commencing the 25th day of March, 1774, under such officer as he shall appoint.

This vote was sent up by Colonel Folsom and Captain Waldron. It was returned on the same day to the assembly, with a message from the governor, in which he said: "The vote of assembly for the support of his majesty's Castle William and Mary, dated this day, appears to me to be so inadequate that it is my duty to inform the assembly that I do not think it safe to entrust so important a fortress to the care and defense of three men and one officer." The members of the assembly were not disposed to vote a large sum or raise much of an army to occupy the fort. Already there was a movement to form another government and from this assembly were to come those men who were to lead the colony in its struggle for independence.

Committees of correspondence had been appointed in several of the colonies to consider the situation of the country, and on the next day, after voting three men to defend the fort, the assembly chose Hon. John Wentworth of the house, Samuel Cutts, John Gedding, Clement March, Joseph Bartlett, Henry Prescott, and John Pickering a committee to correspond with the committees appointed by the several houses of the sister colonies.

They took into consideration the "great difficulties that have arisen and still subsist between our parent country and the colonies on this continent," and declared they were ready to join in all salutary measures that may be adopted by them at this important crisis for saving the rights and privileges of the Americans." After choosing this committee and passing the resolution they took up the governor's message in reference to the support of the castle and authorized the enlistment of five men under an officer to be posted at the fort.

Governor Wentworth saw the tendency of the members of general assembly to join with the representatives of the sister colonies in appointing a congress of the colonies, and to prevent further action he adjourned the assembly from time to time until the 8th day of June, 1774, when he dissolved it.

The provisions made for the fort were carried out, and five men under the command of Captain John Corcoran were stationed there to defend it. This was the condition of affairs when, on the 13th of December, 1774, the movement was first put on foot to dismantle the fort, and it is this account given by the several historians of New Hampshire that we desire to call attention to, and to give, as far as the records will permit, a correct version of the affair.

In order to better understand the true history it is necessary to copy extracts from pages 298 and 299 of McClintock's History of New Hampshire. I am fully aware that McClintock's history is not considered reliable in its details, having been hastily gathered, and published without that verification which should accompany all histories, yet it stands before the public as the history of New Hampshire, and though this generation may be aware of its many deficiencies, it may be regarded as correct by the generations to come after us. Yet McClintock is not alone responsible for the many historical inaccuracies on these two pages, for the earlier writers upon this subject, including Mr. Amory, in his Life of General John Sullivan, and Headley in his work, Washington and His Generals, made the same mistakes.

" An order had been passed by the king in council, prohibiting the exportation of gunpowder and military stores to America. The committee of safety received a copy of it by express from Boston the 13th of December. They collected a company with great secrecy and dispatch, who went to Fort William and Mary at New Castle, under the direction of Major John Sullivan and Capt. John Langdon, confined the captain of the fort and his five men and brought off one hundred barrels of gunpowder. The next day another company brought off fifteen of the lightest cannon, all the small arms and some warlike stores.

" On the 13th of December, 1774, Paul Revere took his *first* public ride. While it may not have been so far reaching in importance as his later one, it richly deserves a place in history. It happened in this manner : The Boston committee of safety had just heard of the British order that no military stores should be exported to America. They accordingly sent Paul Revere on a fleet horse to Portsmouth to apprize the similar committee there of the news, and probably to urge them to secure the powder which was in Fort William and Mary in the harbor, as reinforcements were expected shortly from England. . . . . John Sullivan was a member of the *Provincial* congress that year, and had just arrived in Portsmouth from Philadelphia. . . . . Sullivan proposed the immediate capture of the place, and offered to lead the men to the attack. A military force was accordingly summoned as secretly as possible from the neighborhood, Sullivan and John Langdon took the command and the march was commenced towards the English fort. It was a hazardous undertaking. There was danger from the fort. If the captain became aware of their designs he was sure to turn the guns on them and destroy them. But no alarm was given; with a rush they gained the gate, captured the sentry, and before a challenge could be given had the captain and every man in the fort prisoners. The British flag was hauled down, the gunpowder, of which there were one hundred barrels in the fort, was immediately taken away and hid in the houses the patriots. *Sullivan concealed a portion of it under the pulpit of the Durham meeting-house.* A large part of this plunder afterwards did good service at *Bunker Hill.* Next day fifteen of the lighter cannon and all the small arms were carried away. The governor and his officers received no intelligence of the affair until it was too late to remedy it. . . . . It was the first act of armed hostility committed against the crown of Great Britain by an American."

The above quotation from one and one half pages of what is called history contains no less than sixteen errors, some of which I desire to call attention to, that the future historian of our state, — and no state stands in need of one more than New Hampshire,— may not repeat the same in giving an account of these expeditions.

The order in the British council, prohibiting the exportation of gunpowder, etc., may have been the primary cause for the dismantling of the fort but not the immediate cause. That order was not what the committee at Portsmouth received at the hands of Paul Revere from Boston. A gentleman in Boston, who evidently was informed upon the subject, said in a letter to Mr. Rivington in New York under date of December 20, 1774:

" On Monday, the 12th instant, our worthy citizen, Mr. Paul Revere, was sent express from only two or three of the committee of correspondence at Boston,— of whom no number under seven were empowered to act— to a like committee at Portsmouth, New Hampshire, informing them ' That orders had been sent to the governors of these provinces to deliver up the several fortifications or castles to Gen. Gage, and that a number of troops had the preceding day embarked on board the transports with a design to proceed and take possession of said castle.' This information was delivered by Paul Revere to Samuel Cutts, one of the committee at Portsmouth, who immediately called together the committee to consider the situation. Action was postponed until the following day. Some of the committee deeming a delay dangerous, determined to immediately seize the fort."

There was no secrecy about the matter. Notice of their intention was openly avowed on the streets of Portsmouth. In a letter written from Portsmouth, under date of December 17, 1774, the writer says:

" On Wednesday last a drum and a fife paraded the streets of Portsmouth, accompanied by several committee men and the Sons of Liberty, publickly avowing their intention of taking possession of Fort William and Mary."

Notice of this intention was sent by Gov. Wentworth to the commander of the fort. Captain Cochran, who was in command, in his report to Gov. Wentworth on December 14 said:

" I received your Excellency's favor of yesterday, and in obedience thereto kept a strict watch all night and added two men to my usual number, being all I could get. Nothing material occurred till this day, one o'clock, when I was informed there was a number of people coming to take possession of the fort, upon which, having only five effective men with me, I prepared to make the best defense I could, and pointed some guns to those places where I expected they would enter. About three o'clock the fort was besieged on all sides by upwards of four hundred men. I told them on their peril not to enter; they replied they would. I immediately ordered three four-pounders to be fired on them and then the small arms, and before we could be ready to fire again we were stormed on all quarters, and they immediately secured both me and my men and kept us prisoners about one hour and a half, during which time they broke open the powder house and took all the powder away except one barrel, and having put it into boats and sent it off, they released me from my confinement. To which I can only add, that I did all in my power to defend the fort, but all my efforts could not avail against so great a number."

This was not Paul Revere's first public ride. He had been sent express on important business on at least two occasions previous to his ride to Portsmouth. News of the passage of the Boston port bill was received in Boston on the 10th day of May, 1774. On Friday, the 13th, about noon, Gen. Gage arrived and landed at the castle. On the same day, the 13th, a meeting was held in Faneuil Hall to consider the edict for shutting up the harbor. Samuel Adams was moderator. They voted to invite the other colonies to come into a non-importation agreement till the act of blocking up their harbor was repealed. They voted to forthwith transmit the same to all the other colonies, and on Saturday, the 14th of May, just seven months before he rode to Portsmouth, Paul Revere was dispatched with important letters to the southern colonies. On the 20th of May he arrived at Philadelphia and delivered the letters and a meeting was called, which was attended by between two and three hundred people and the letters read. A committee was appointed to answer the same, and on the 21st Paul Revere started on his return, stopping on his way at New York and Hartford.

Revere was sent over the same route again the last of September, 1774, with dispatches to the general congress, and arrived October 5, 1774, at Philadelphia.

John Sullivan was a member of the continental congress which met September 5. This meeting could hardly be called a congress. It was a meeting of delegates from the several colonies to consider the situation and devise some measures to have the difficulties between the colonies and England adjusted. They drafted an address to the king, in which they made their final appeal for justice. Peyton Randolph was president. The first name signed to the address after the president's was John Sullivan. John Sullivan had returned from the sitting of congress and was at his home in Durham on the 14th of December, and did not go to Portsmouth until the 15th, as stated by Mr. Bennett, who is the authority for the statements made in Amory's Life of Sullivan.

The account given by Governor Bell in his History of Exeter, as taken from the lips of Gideon Lamson fifty years ago, is so far from the accounts given by all others, it ceases to be of any value, for any one can readily see the many errors contained therein.

The errors which have occurred in other histories have arisen from the mixing up of the two expeditions, the one on December 14, when the powder was removed, which occurred in the afternoon of that day, and the expedition on the night of the

15th, when the cannon and small arms were seized. The latter expedition was led by Major John Sullivan, and had the writers upon the capture of the fort applied the description to the work accomplished on the night of the 15th, they would not have been far from the truth.

On the 14th, when the forces started for the fort and removed the powder, expresses were sent to all the surrounding towns, and they came in to Portsmouth on the 15th. This is the statement of Captain Bennett, who relates his story many years after. He says he was at work for Mr. Sullivan, and on the 15th of December a messenger came to his house in Durham and informed Major Sullivan of the situation at Portsmouth, and Sullivan with others immediately started for the latter place.

In a letter written at Portsmouth under date of December 17, 1774, from which I have already quoted, the writer says:

" On Wednesday last a drum and fife paraded the streets of Portsmouth, accompanied by several committee men and Sons of Liberty, publickly avowing their intention of taking possession of Fort William and Mary, which was garrisoned by six invalids."

After describing the capture of the powder, which he says was carried up to Exeter, a town fifteen miles distant, he says:

" The next day after, while the Governor and Council were assembled in the Council Chamber, between two and three hundred persons came from Durham and the adjoining towns headed by Major Sullivan, one of the Delegates to the Congress. They drew up before the Council Chamber, and demanded an answer to the following questions: Whether there were any Ships or Troops expected here, or if the Governor had wrote for any? They were answered that his Excellency knew of no forces coming hither, and that none had been sent for; upon which they retired to the Taverns, and about ten or eleven o'clock at night a large party repaired to the Fort and it is said they carried away all the small arms. This morning about sixty horsemen accoutred, came into town, and gave out that seven hundred more were on their march to Portsmouth, from Exeter, Greenland, Newmarket, etc., and would be in that Town by eleven o'clock; their intention, it is suspected, is to dismantle the Fort, and throw the cannon, consisting of a fine train of 42-pounders, into the Sea."

Another writer, under date of December 20, 1774, after giving the account of the seizure of the Fort and removal of the powder, which agrees with the other accounts herein given, says:

" Previous to this, expresses had been sent out to alarm the country; accordingly a large body of men marched the next day from Durham headed by two generals,— Major Sullivan, one of the worthy delegates who represented that province in the continental congress, and the parson of the parish [Rev. Mr. Adams most likely], who having been long accustomed to apply himself more to the cure of the bodies than the souls of his parish, had forgotten that the weapons of his warfare ought to be spiritual and not carnal, and therefore marched down to supply himself with the latter from the king's fort, and assisted in robbing him of his warlike stores.

" After being drawn up on the parade, they chose a committee, consisting of those persons who had been most active in the riot of the preceding day, with Major Sullivan and some others, to wait on the governor and know of him whether any of the king's ships or troops were expected. The governor, after expressing to them his great concern for the consequences of taking the powder from the fort, of which they pretended to disapprove and to be ignorant of, assured them that he knew of neither troops or ships coming into the province, and ordered the major as a magistrate to go and disperse the people.

"When the committee returned to the body and reported what the governor had told them, they voted that it was satisfactory and that they would return home. But by the eloquent harangue of their *Demosthenes* they were first prevailed upon to vote that they took part with and approved of the measures of those who had taken the powder. Matters appeared then to subside, and it was thought every man had returned peaceably to his home. Instead of this, Major Sullivan, with about seventy of his clients, concealed themselves till the evening, and then went to the fort and brought off in gondolas all the small arms, with fifteen four-pounders and one nine-pounder, and a quantity of twelve and four-and-twenty pound shot, which they conveyed to Durham, etc. The day following being *Friday*, another body of men from Exeter, headed by Colonel Folsom, the other delegate to the continental congress, marched into *Portsmouth* and paraded about the town, and having passed several votes expressive of their approbation of the measures that had been pursued by the bodies the two preceding days in robbing the fort of the guns, powder, etc., retired home in the evening without further mischief."

The party led by Major Sullivan on the night of the 15th was conducted in great secrecy and no alarm was given. The capture of the powder on the 14th was in open daylight, there was nothing secret about it. They were fired upon from the fort but no one was injured. The entry was not made through the gate of the fort, but it was stormed on all sides. The four hundred patriots overcame the five soldiers and captured for the American army one hundred barrels of powder. This powder in the first instance was taken to Exeter and from there distributed among the neighboring towns for safety. Part of this powder was sent to the army on the frontier and sold to towns in the province. There is no evidence that any was sent to the army at Cambridge until after the battle of Bunker Hill.

On May 20, 1775, the provincial congress at Exeter " Voted the thanks of the convention to the persons who took and secured for the use of this government a quantity of gunpowder from Castle William and Mary in this province." After choosing a committee of safety, they voted that Nicholas Gilman and Mr. Poor be a committee to sell any quantity of gunpowder not exceeding four barrels to such frontier towns in this province as they shall think most need it. This was the first action taken in relation to this powder, and the sale was limited to the towns in this province.

On June 2, 1775, they voted "That the committee on supplies be desired to apply and obtain the quantity and quality of the powder brought from the Fort William and Mary; also take it into their possession and lay the state of it before the committee of safety."

The committee on supplies in making their report, found that the powder remaining at that date was stored in the following named places, viz.: Kingston, 12 barrels; Epping, 8 barrels; Poplin, 4 barrels; Nottingham, 8 barrels; Brentwood, 6 barrels; Londonderry, 1 barrel; Exeter, 29 barrels in eleven different houses. Four barrels were furnished to Portsmouth on the request made in April, 1775. They found stored in these different places 72 barrels, but none of it was reported as being at Durham.

The first powder sent to the army at Cambridge, at least in any quantity, was on June 18, the next day after the battle of Bunker Hill. On the day of the battle express was sent from the army to the committee at Exeter; he stopped on his way at Kingston, where Col. Josiah Bartlett resided, one of the committee. He immediately ordered a general meeting of the committee, and on the 18th Col. Bartlett wrote to Gen. Folsom saying, " Mr. Moreton left Cambridge on the evening of June 17 and rode all night, arriving at Kingston the 18th. He brought the news of the battle of Bunker Hill." The committee immediately ordered the selectmen of Kingston, where some of the captured powder was stored, to deliver to Samuel Philbrick six barrels of powder, to be by him conveyed to the army. They also ordered Major Cilley and the companies of Captains Elkins, Rowe, Clough, Adams, Titcomb, Gilman, Wentworth, Tilton, and Norris of Colonel Poor's regiment to march to Cambridge to join the army. All the companies except Captain Elkins's started for Cambridge.

June 21, there was sent to the army by Nathaniel Gordon one cask flints, quantity 3,200; five kegs bullets, weight 113, 110, 62, 123, 220 pounds each; 30 tents, poles, pins, etc., ten barrels of powder 100 pounds each.

June 23 "the selectmen of Newmarket were directed" to send by Nicholas Nichols four barrels of the provincial gunpowder, now in their custody, to be dealt out as the public service may require. On this order they received only one barrel, and on the 26th of June they received one more barrel.

On June 26 Lieutenant Bartlett was directed to pick out two of the largest, strongest, and best cannon taken from Fort William and Mary and convey them to Exeter to be sent to the army at Medford.

August 7, 1775, the committee of safety issued an order to Major Cilley as follows:

"SIR: You are desired as soon as possible to apply to the selectmen of the several towns in this colony with whom was lodged the powder taken last winter from Fort William and Mary, take an account of what is now in their custody, and request of them forthwith to convey the whole to Col. Nicholas Gilman at Exeter."

It may have found its way into the powder house at Exeter, and we find no further record of this particular powder until the report of the committee, made August 24, that they had on hand only eight or ten barrels.

The call of General Washington was made upon August 4 for powder, and General Sullivan reported to General Washington that he had of powder furnished by New Hampshire to his troops nineteen barrels of one hundred pounds each. Sixteen barrels of this was doubtless the six sent from Kingston and ten from Exeter.

Fort William and Mary was not again occupied by any English soldiers. On May 30, 1775, while the English man-of-war Scarborough was seizing vessels loaded with salt and provisions to be sent to General Gage's army, thirty or forty men from the vessel came ashore and tore down the greater part of the breastworks. The day before the Scarborough had seized a vessel loaded with provisions, and refused to deliver it up, and on this refusal between five and six hundred men in arms went down to the battery called Jerry's Point and brought off eight cannon, twenty-two and thirty-two pounders, all there were there, and brought them to Portsmouth.

Though foreign to the purpose of this address, I feel justified in saying in conclusion: The men who conducted the civil affairs of the province of New Hampshire had not their superiors in America. No colony contained a more patriotic and liberty-loving people, and none furnished to the army a grander man, an abler general, than that man who went from New Hampshire; the "Demosthenes" who inspired patriotism by his eloquence; the commander who stood by the side of the great Washington; the orator, the statesman, the jurist, the warrior,— Major-General John Sullivan; and not until one hundred years have passed away since he laid off his armor and went to sleep with his fathers, was the effort made to erect a monument to his memory.

Others who were less conspicuous in their country's service have been remembered by state and nation. The hero of Bennington stands in bronze to guard the entrance to our state capitol; his equestrian statue is, we trust, to adorn the spot where rest his hallowed remains, on the banks of our beautiful Merrimack; and the halls of our national capitol have received another statue of Gen. John Stark.

While we would not pluck one leaf from the laurel encircling the brow of our own hero, would it not have been quite as appropriate in the selection of the statue for the national capitol to have placed there one of him who sat in that first congress and by his eloquence called forth the patriotic sons of America? Himself

"Leaping from slumber, to the fight
For freedom and for chartered right."

The state and nation should unite in the erection of a monument that would by its grandeur symbolize the services rendered by Gen. John Sullivan.

When completed, what more appropriate inscription could be carved upon its tablet than the words uttered by himself in a letter from his camp on Winter Hill to the committee at Exeter, when political generals were using their utmost endeavors to injure his reputation and destroy his influence? He said:

"I call heaven and earth to witness, that thus far the good of my country has been my only aim.

"No private friendship or private quarrels shall take hold of my public conduct.

"I wish we could leave our private resentments in our closets when we are acting in public capacities, and consider only the means of promoting our country's good.

"I must observe that when they feel motives similar to those which actuated me at the time, malice will cease to reign in their bosoms, and envy learn to be silent."

EXTRACT FROM A LETTER FROM GENERAL SULLIVAN TO THE COMMITTEE AT EXETER.

WINTER HILL, March 24, 1776.

*Honorable Gentlemen:*

I have an account presented me by Captain Tilton, agreeable to the direction of General *Folsom*, for payment of seventeen pounds twelve shillings and sixpence.

It consists of six articles: One bill is nine pounds ten shillings, for boarding Artillerymen sent from the Army, to your assistance, and remained there three weeks without wages, and were carried there and brought back at my expense. The next is two pounds ten shillings and eleven pence, for Major *Cilley's* expenses; he was by the committee of safety appointed and detained as Mustermaster for your troops, and I supposed you would make no difficulty in paying his expenses. The next is one pound eleven shillings and one penny, for the expenses of Mr. *Nathaniel McClintock*, appointed my Aid-de-Camp, while present, and remained as a volunteer with your forces, at the request of your commanding officer, when I was absent, and was very useful to him; and his bill if paid, would not amount to the wages of a private soldier for the time he tarried. The next bill is for seventeen shillings and nine pence, expenses of the Captain of the Riflemen, sent there without my knowledge or consent, with a company to assist you if necessary. To crown the whole, is a bill of four shillings and sixpence, expended in securing the Tories in your capital when the enemy appeared off your harbor, when I was at headquarters and knew nothing of the matter.

This, gentlemen, is a state of the account handed me for payment, and which I am ready to pay, in case you think a single article ought to be paid by me.

Gentlemen, I am extremely sorry to find a person pretending so much patriotism as Mr. *Folsom* does, ever striving to give me pain and uneasiness, and this without the least provocation on my part. Every day do I hear of his insulting and abusive language, such as he well knows he dare not use if I were present. Every step he takes is pregnant with malice against me; and I am sorry to hear his malicious endeavors have but too great weight on some other minds; and by means of that I am daily censured in your cabinet; and for what, I know not.

I now appeal to you all, and call upon you to give one instance where I have made money at the expense of my country or where I have usurped a greater power than was at first delegated to me. What relations have I promoted or what part of my family have I enriched? which of my former friends have I promoted, or which of my former enemies have I persecuted with unrelenting fury? No, gentlemen, my motives are of a different kind; no private friendship or private quarrels shall take hold of my public conduct.

*I call Heaven and earth to witness that thus far, the good of my country has been my only aim.* This I have endeavored to evince by my conduct.

Consider, gentlemen, what sums of money I have already expended, and how many days I have hailed, clad with new and threatening dangers to my life; how I have refrained from the seat of domestick happiness, and confined by my country's cause at a distance, heard the fatal tidings of sickness and death in my own family, while I was contemplating my own dangers here.

Can all this be, gentlemen, and yet I not be in earnest? And shall he who basks in the sunshine of malice, and sleeps serenely in the bed of revenge, set my own friends, my fathers in political life, against me? Let gratitude, let pity forbid it; and let the heavenly justice take hold on the wretch whose sordid soul could never harbor a thought but that of gratifying his own malicious disposition, or bringing about his own promotion.

I most earnestly pray that Heaven may judge between us, and reward him that is insincere with infamy and disgrace.

I know, gentlemen, that some of you thought it a great stretch of power in me to select officers for a new regiment out of those you sent before. Let the enclosed paper witness the justice of the choice, and the confidence General *Washington* has placed in the field officers of that regiment, by trusting them with the most important posts, (never before entrusted to militia regiments), witness in favor of my judgment. Sure I am that those persons have not in private life been my intimate friends,— nay, some of them my most inveterate foes; but *I wish we could leave our private resentments in our closets when we are acting in publick capacities, and consider only the means of promoting our country's good.*

Surely, by my having the choice of thirty-one sets of officers, who had been under my immediate inspection, I could have a much better opportunity of selecting eight good ones, than you who were not here and could not know how they behaved. I made the choice, and the officers have done honour to themselves and the Province, and differ exceedingly from some of the Captains sent here before, who could neither sign a return nor give a receipt for the money they received at Head-Quarters, but by making their marks.

# NEW HAMPSHIRE BRANCH OF THE SOCIETY OF CINCINNATI.

CONTRIBUTED TO THE MANCHESTER HISTORIC ASSOCIATION BY JOHN C. FRENCH.

Some thirty years ago I heard an intelligent old lady describe an annual meeting of the Society of Cincinnati, held in Epsom in her girlhood days. Since that time I have persistently attempted to learn something of its organization, its members and records without success, until recently. In a memorial volume, published by the Massachusetts Society, I found mention of the branch in this state, and learned that its records were deposited with the New Hampshire Historical Society, and extracts published in the sixth volume of the society collection. On application to that repository of historical data, lo, and behold! the accommodating librarian produced to my astonished vision a large, well bound volume containing the records of the New Hampshire Branch of the Society of Cincinnati, covering a period of forty years, and I have a complete copy of the same duly transcribed.

It commences with a copy of a letter from Maj. Gen. Baron Steuben of West Point, N. Y., to Maj. General John Sullivan, dated July, 1783, urging a branch in this state. The first meeting was called at the house of Gen. Samuel Folsom, in Exeter, and the following heroic Revolutionary worthies were present and completed an organization. The records show in plain penmanship their signatures and term of service as follows:

| Name. | Rank. | Residence. | Term of Service. |
|---|---|---|---|
| John Sullivan, | Major-Gen., | Durham, | 4 years, 6 months. |
| Joseph Cilley, | Colonel, | Nottingham, | 5 years, 6 months. |
| Henry Dearborn, | Colonel, | Nottingham, | 7 years, 10 months. |
| Jonathan Cass, | Captain, | Exeter, | 6 years, 4 months. |
| Ebenezer Sullivan, | Captain, | Durham, | 7 years, 9 months. |
| Joseph Mills, | Lieutenant, | Nottingham, | 6 years. ........ |
| Daniel Gookin, | Lieutenant, | North Hampton, | 8 years, 1 month. |
| Samuel Adams, | Lieutenant. | .......... | ................ |
| Josiah Munro, | Captain. | .......... | ................ |
| Jonathan Cilley, | Lieutenant, | Nottingham. | ................ |
| Neal McGaffey, | Lieutenant, | Epsom. | ................ |
| Michael McClary, | Captain, | Epsom, | 6 years. ......... |
| William Parker, | Surgeon, | Exeter, | 3 years, 4 months. |
| Nicholas Gilman, | Captain, | Exeter, | 6 years, 3 months. |
| Joshua Merrow, | Lieutenant. | .......... | ................ |
| Amos Emerson, | Captain, | Chester, | 5 years. ......... |
| John Adams, | Lieutenant, | Stratham, | ................ |
| John Boynton, | Lieutenant, | Stratham, | 7 years. ........ |
| Samuel Cheney, | Captain, | Londonderry, | 8 years. ........ |
| Francis Frye, | Captain, | Wilton, | 9 years. ........ |
| Z. Rowell, | Captain, | Epping, | 8 years. ........ |
| Jonathan Perkins, | Lieutenant, | Epping, | 6 years. ........ |
| John Harvey, | Lieutenant, | Northwood, | 4 years. ........ |
| Jonathan Fogg, | Captain, | Kensington, | 3 years. 6 months. |
| Jeremiah Richards, | Lieutenant, | Hollis, | 3 years, 8 months. |
| James Reid, | Brig. Gen., | Keene, | 8 years. ........ |
| Jas. H. McClary. | ........ | Epsom. | ................ |
| John Sullivan. | ....... | Durham. | ................ |
| Joseph Mills. | ........ | Nottingham. | ................ |
| John W. Gookin, | Captain, | North Hampton. | ................ |

Of forty-two meetings, nine were held in Exeter, seven in Nottingham, four in Durham, three in Deerfield, fourteen in Portsmouth, one in Dover, three in Epsom, and one in Epping.

Maj. Gen. John Sullivan served as president eleven years; Gen. Joseph Cilley, five years; Major Joseph Mills, ten years; Col. Amos Cogswell, fourteen years, and Gen. Michael McClary served as treasurer thirty-nine years.

The long term of service of the officers will be noticed. The first New Hampshire Regiment, with numerous changes, served a longer time than any other volunteer regiment in the country. Comparatively few of the New Hampshire line officers joined the order, and those mostly resided in the limits of what was then Rockingham county.

Only four of the sons of the original members succeeded their fathers to perpetuate the order, and after forty annual reunions on " Independence Day," with convivial services commensurate with the times and occasions, the closing page sorrowfully reads as follows :

PORTSMOUTH, July 4, 1823.

Present, Michael McClary, Daniel Gookin.

Proceeded to the choice of officers :

Amos Cogswell, president; Bradbury Cilley, vice-president; Daniel Gookin, secretary ; Michael McClary, treasurer.

Examined the treasurer's accounts. There are in his hands one hundred forty-three dollars and seventy-eight cents ($143.78). Interest by him accounted for to July 1, 1823.

Voted, that the treasurer pay to Charlotte Page, daughter of the late Joseph Mills, fifteen dollars.

Voted that the treasurer pay to the children of John Sullivan, ten dollars.

Voted that the next annual meeting be held at Portsmouth.

DANIEL GOOKIN,
*Secretary.*

As the society failed to meet in 1824, the interesting question naturally arises, *Where is the fund and the accumulated interest ?*

It had been voted to change the fund from state to United States securities, and the receipts from interest had averaged about $150 annually for the forty years, but the treasurer's books were not rescued from oblivion.

The secretary's records are in admirable condition, and were presented to the New Hampshire Historical Society in 1843 by the son of Daniel Gookin, the last secretary.

At the close of the war, the officers of the American army who had shared the common danger and whose friendship had been cemented by eight years of conflict, desired to combine themselves into a society based on the principles of friendship and charity, " to endure as long as they shall endure," or " any of their posterity." General Washington was chosen president. Out of respect to the Roman citizen and soldier, Cincinnatus, it was called the " Society of Cincinnati," the general society to meet triennially, and branch societies in each of the thirteen states to meet annually on the Fourth of July.

An officer was eligible to membership who had held a commission in the army three years, and who assigned a month's pay to the fund, and his eldest male descendant could be his successor to membership.

For over a century this honored and revered society has demonstrated its pure patriotism and benevolence, and to become a member has been considered of the highest honor. The "hereditary succession" feature was early assailed and denounced by the politicians and press in the chaotic condition of affairs at that time as forming an "hereditary peerage" dangerous to the Republic.

The general society, Hon. Hamilton Fish president, holds regular meetings, but most of the state societies have failed to continue existence. Massachusetts and New York societies still exist, being prominent and wealthy.

In these booming days, the Sons of the Revolution and the Daughters of the Revolution are tracing and perpetuating the memory of their ancestry. Why do not the descendants of the New Hampshire line officers revive and reorganize the state branch of the Order of Cincinnati?

The Loyal Legion has the same "hereditary succession" feature, while it was the design of the Grand Army of the Republic to exist only during the lifetime of those engaged in the Civil War.

Gen. (Gov.) Benjamin Pierce, of Hillsborough, was vice-president of the Massachusetts society from 1836 to 1839, and was succeeded by his three sons, Col. Benjamin K. in 1841, General (President) Franklin in 1852, Henry D. in 1873, and his grandson, Kirk Dearborn Pierce, in 1889.

John B. Varick, of Manchester, as successor of Col. Richard Varick, who was mayor of New York city twelve years, is a member of the New York society, and he, with Mr. Pierce, are probably the only two members now residing in the state belonging to the honorable Order of Cincinnati.

Major Amos Morrill, of Epsom, who died in St. Albans, Vt., in 1810, and several others from this state, joined the Massachusetts society.

It is said that Freemasonry was an important factor during the Revolutionary struggle. Sullivan Lodge, which held meetings at Nottingham or Deerfield, was formed by returned officials in that vicinity.

In this connection, is it not pertinent to ask, Is there not a serious deficiency in our state histories? Where can the average reader find in accessible books a connected or detailed account of the men and events during the stormy times of the Revolution?

While New Hampshire furnished the largest percentage of men, officers, means, of any state to prosecute the Revolutionary War, how little is made of these facts in any general history. For instance, but little is known of Dr. Henry Dearborn, who with fifty-six notable patriots gathered, as a horseman galloped on Nottingham Square tooting a horn April 20, with the news of the fight at Lexington and Concord, and that they made the remarkable march on foot to Cambridge, seventy-two miles, in seventeen hours, and paraded on Cambridge common at sunrise on the morning of the 21st "spiling for a fight," and his future eventful career to commander of the American army in the war of 1812. Then among the heroic families that have characterized the state, "the family of governors," orators, soldiers, and statesmen, "the silver-tongued Sullivans." Who rendered more efficient service, either as soldier or statesman, in the formation of the state and national government than Maj. Gen. John Sullivan, or is more entitled to a statue in the state house yard? Then the McClarys, four of them state senators; and no monument to mark the burial place of Major Andrew McClary, the highest officer killed at Bunker Hill, who, with two hundred New Hampshire soldiers, was buried at Medford, Mass. The eight Cogswell brothers deserve to be remembered. Their united service in the army was over thirty-eight years, and each won a commission. The Gilmans, the Cilleys, the Harveys, the Gookins, Reid, and others who rendered meritorious service to the state and nation should not be forgotten. Two prominent officers who did not survive the war should be kept in memory.

On that memorable occasion, the most notable soldiers' reunion ever held in the state, that at Concord in 1825, General Lafayette, with French accent and voice tremulous with emotion, offered the sentiment, "Here is to the memory of Yorktown Scammell and Light Infantry Poor." It is not fair to assume that he deemed these officers best entitled to mention. He for the first time informed the soldiers that Gen. Enoch Poor was killed in a duel by a French officer (Adjutant-General's Report), and that a monument had been erected at his grave in Hackensack, N. J., which he had recently visited. Where can we find so prominent illustrations of the saying that one's name and fame depends upon his biographers, as in the case of our most popular officer? The biography of the chivalrous, accomplished, and beloved Alexander Scammell has not been written. With youthful ardor, he was one of the bold patriots that floated down the river on a gondola from Durham to Fort William and Mary, capturing and returning with the powder and small arms December 14, 1774, "making war inevitable," and opening the Revolutionary War. He was promoted for merit, became associate confidential private secretary of General Washington, adjutant-general of the Continental army, and was barbarously slain at Yorktown at the age of thirty-three. He left no family, no property, and has had no biographer to send his "name and fame down the ages." His name was honored and fondly cherished by his comrades, but it is seldom found in history, while the name of the adjutant-general of the British army, Major André, is mentioned even in school histories, and a monument erected to his memory in Tappan, N. Y.

In fact, a full, connected history of New Hampshire in the Revolution has never been written, and only those who have made researches from numerous sources have a correct idea of the important services of the few sturdy, determined New Hampshire patriots in molding the destinies of the state and nation. There is plenty of historical data, reminiscences, legends, traditions, which, with copies of official records, town histories, manuscripts, sketches, and scraps contained in the useful and honored repository of the New Hampshire Historical Society and elsewhere, should enable one with a genius like Sir Walter Scott to compile and weave most interesting volumes covering a space of two hundred and fifty years; or some painstaking Belknap to write a history of our state worthy of the material now at hand, especially of its most progressive, prosperous, and eventful period, from 1760 to the adoption of the federal constitution and formation of the republic in 1797.

If this crude communication furnishes information or suggestions to any one interested in this line of local historical matters, I shall be duly grateful.

MANCHESTER, January 2, 1893.

# GRACE FLETCHER.

CONTRIBUTED TO MANCHESTER HISTORIC ASSOCIATION BY
JOHN C. FRENCH.

While volumes have been written concerning the greatest statesman and orator of the English language, Daniel Webster, little has been published in regard to his first wife, "Beautiful Grace Fletcher," and nothing of her brief life in Pittsfield, New Hampshire. Some facts, corroborated by official dates and records, may be of local interest, in this attempt to rescue them from oblivion by printed mention.

Grace Fletcher passed some seven years of girlhood life in Pittsfield, and ever after retained an attachment for that picturesque town, and was later an occasional visitor to her sister and friends residing there. She was born January 16, 1781, in Hopkinton, the fourth child of the Rev. Elijah Fletcher, the Congregational pastor in that town. Her father died in 1786; her mother married the Rev. Christopher Page, who succeeded Mr. Fletcher as preacher. Mr. Page was induced to leave Hopkinton and accept the following proposition to settle in Pittsfield in 1789, when Grace was eight years old. The following, from the town records of Pittsfield, illustrates the method of settling ministers of " the standing order " of that period:

COPY OF THE VOTE, 1789.

*Voted*, To give Mr. Christopher Paige a call to settle here as a minister in gospel order in this town.
*Voted*, To give Mr. Page sixty pounds as a settlement, the one half in materials to build with, the other half in labor at three shillings per day.

*Voted*, To clear up five acres of land on the parsonage yearly until we have cleared twenty acres, and for Mr. Paige to have the improvement of the parsonage during his ministry in said Pittsfield.

*Voted*, To give Mr. Christopher Paige sixty-six pounds yearly as a salary, the one third part in cash, and one third part in corn at three shillings per bushel and good rye at four shillings per bushel, and a third part in good beef at twenty shillings per hundred, during his ministry in said town.

Mr. Page built on the minister's lot a quite pretentious house for the time and place, employing and boarding in his family, to superintend its construction, Abram French, a young and skilful carpenter, who had been engaged in finishing the interior of the first meeting-house. The house is now owned and occupied by Capt. Asa W. Bartlett. Here was born James W. Page, who became an eminent merchant, and was for many years the head of the great commission house of James W. Page & Co., of Boston. He was an intimate friend of Webster, and one of the trustees under his will of the Marshfield estate.

The "Fletcher girls" were prominent among the rustic youth of Pittsfield. The oldest sister, Bridget, married Josiah White, of a worthy family, located on a small farm and reared a family of children. She lived to old age and died in Pittsfield.

Grace Fletcher was described by those who knew her well during her life in Pittsfield, as the youngest and brightest of the "Fletcher girls," with winning ways, beautiful features and complexion, and sparkling eyes, leading an active life as she joined in the rough sports or ran and romped with bare head and bare feet over the new fields, in search of wild flowers and berries.

In 1796, by reason of want of harmony, the Rev. Mr. Page asked for a dismissal from the church at Pittsfield; afterwards preached in Hopkinton, Deering, Washington, and Roxbury, and finally located at Salisbury. He died in that town in 1822, and his wife in 1821. Grace was fifteen years old when the family left Pittsfield. The deed, signed by Christopher Page and his wife Rebecca, conveying his real estate to Abram French, in 1796, is still in existence. Mr. French married at that time, — one hundred years ago, — Hannah Lane, and their married life continued fifty-four years, rearing to maturity eleven children, and maintaining a home of industry, thrift, and hospitality.

Grace Fletcher had the facilities for acquiring a good education, her school days ending at Atkinson Academy, at the age of eighteen.

This institution was one of the academies that early admitted both sexes as students. A manuscript book containing several poems written by her, showing her penmanship and literary ability of that date, has been preserved.

While making her home with her sister Rebecca, who had married Judge Israel W. Kelley, of Salisbury, a town famous for noble men, she met Daniel Webster. While this was a sparsely settled farming community, here were born some of the famous sons of New Hampshire of that generation, among the number Ezekiel and Daniel Webster, Joel Eastman, Ichabod Bartlett and his four brothers, and across the town line in Boscawen, John A. Dix, Nathaniel and Charles G. Greene, William Pitt Fessenden, and others, coming statesmen and authors.

In view of the numerous fairy stories and conflicting dates surrounding her courtship and marriage only one brief quotation is here given. Lanman, in his "Private Life of Webster," states that on his last visit to his birthplace Webster pointed out to him the spot in Boscawen where, at the age of fourteen, he attended school, and where subsequently he first became acquainted with Grace Fletcher. The acquaintance was mutually pleasant, and ripened to reciprocal love. They were married in Judge Kelley's parlor, June, 1808, she at the age of twenty-seven and he at twenty-six. Trained in similar surroundings, religious faith, tastes, and ambition, their married life of twenty-one years was one of peculiar affection and domestic happiness. At the time of their marriage Webster was tall and ungainly, inheriting the complexion of his father, which was said to be "so dark that it could not be soiled by gunpowder." In that community he was often called "Black Dan." His future greatness was not even predicted; the commanding presence, the noble physique, were not yet his; such titles as the

"Immortal Daniel," the "Great Expounder," "The Black Giant of the East," the "Godlike Daniel," "The Greatest Man of the Age," had not been applied.

The following is copied from the large and valuable published "History of the Fletcher Family": A letter now in the possession of a granddaughter of its writer has the following: "She gives as a reason why she has time for letter writing in the evening that Cousin Grace Fletcher is trying to entertain a young man by the name of Daniel Webster by playing checkers. Father and Uncle Chamberlain think him a young man of great promise, but we girls think him awkward and rather verdant." Probably "we girls" changed their minds before they died.

Immediately after marriage they established a home in one of the historic colonial houses in the prosperous town of Portsmouth, where they at once gained popularity and prominence. Mrs. Webster, with her superior grace and beauty, inherited ability and intellectual accomplishments, was equal to all occasions, never discouraged, proud of her husband's success, but not unduly elated. Queen at home, or in the public drawing-room, she met the most distinguished men of her time.

Their first son, Fletcher Webster, was born in Portsmouth in 1813. He was a graduate of Harvard,— a lawyer, traveler, and author. He was killed at the second battle of Bull Run in 1862, while serving as colonel of the Twelfth Massachusetts Regiment of Volunteers,— known as the Webster Regiment during the War of the Rebellion.

Grace Webster was born in 1815, and died of consumption at an early age. With all their progress and popularity, the fond parents were called to deep sorrow by the death in 1817 of this precocious daughter.

Webster was first chosen a member of the national House of Representatives from New Hampshire in 1813, and was re-elected in 1815. After their residence in Portsmouth of nine years, said by Webster late in life to be "nine blessed years," they removed to Boston in 1817, where greater honors were in store. In 1818 another daughter, Julia, was born. She inherited her father's intellect and her mother's grace, and on reaching maturity married Samuel Appleton, a wealthy merchant of Boston. In 1820 Edwin was born, a graduate of Dartmouth, who died in Mexico in 1848, at the age of twenty-eight, while serving as major in the U. S. army. In 1821 another son, Charles, was born, who died in 1825. The deep sorrow of the parents was nearly inconsolable. Brief extracts from two letters follow, which indicate their feelings and grief at that time, as expressed in verse, as their darling boy was of rare beauty and promise:

EXTRACT FROM LETTER FROM WEBSTER, WRITTEN IN WASHINGTON TO HIS WIFE ON HEARING OF THE DEATH OF THEIR SON.

"My son, thou wast my heart's delight,
  Thy morn of life was gay and cheery;
That morn has rushed to sudden night,
  Thy father's house is sad and dreary.

"I held thee on my knee, my son,
  And kissed thee laughing, kissed thee weeping;
But, ah! thy little day is done,
  Thou'rt with thy angel sister sleeping.

"Dear angel, thou art safe in heaven;
  No prayers for thee need more be made;
Oh! let thy prayers for those be given
  Who oft have blessed thy infant head.

"My father! I beheld thee born
  And led thy tottering steps with care;
Before me risen to Heaven's bright morn,
  My son! my father! guide me there.

"The staff on which my years should lean
  Is broken ere those years come o'er me;
My funeral rites thou shouldst have seen,
  But thou art in the tomb before me.

"Thou rear'st to me no filial stone,
  No parent's grave with tears beholdest;
Thou art my ancestor — my son;
  And stand'st in heaven's account the oldest.

"On earth my lot was soonest cast;
    Thy generation after mine;
Thou hast thy predecessor passed,
    Earlier eternity is thine.

"I should have set before thine eyes
    The road to heaven and showed it clear;
But thou, untaught, spring'st to the skies,
    And leav'st thy teacher lingering here.

"Sweet seraph, I would learn of thee,
    And hasten to partake thy bliss!
And, oh! to thy world welcome me
    As first I welcomed thee to this."

FROM MRS. WEBSTER, REPLY.

BOSTON, Saturday morning, January 22, 1825.

"*My Dear Husband*: I was sitting alone in my chamber reflecting on the brief life of our sainted little boy when your letter came inclosing those lines of yours, which to a "mother's eye" are precious. Oh, my husband, have not some of our brightest hopes perished! "Our fairest flowers are, indeed, blossoms gathered for the tomb." But do not, my dear husband, do not let these afflictions weigh too heavily upon you; those dear children who had such strong holds on us while here, now allure us to heaven:

"On us with looks of love they bend,
    For us the Lord of life implore;
And oft from sainted bliss descend,
    Our wounded spirits to restore.

"Farewell, my beloved husband! I have not time to write more, only to say I regret you have lost the pleasure of Mr. and Mrs. Ticknor's society, which you so much need. I fear Mrs. Dwight is not much benefited by her voyage, so the last accounts appear, though at first they thought her better.

"The children are tolerably well, though not free from colds.

"Your ever affectionate
"G. W."

During the last of her life Mrs. Webster was afflicted with a tumor, and although in delicate health, attempted a tedious journey with her husband to Washington, but before reaching New York city contracted a severe cold, and lingered in that city at the home of an intimate friend for nearly six weeks, daily attended in the most affectionate manner by her large-hearted and devoted husband. She died January 21, 1828, at the age of forty-seven, deeply lamented by friends and the nation. Her body was placed in the tomb belonging to her husband, beneath St. Paul's church, Boston, and the remains of her two deceased children brought to the same resting place.

Mrs. Webster was much attached to the picturesque town of Pittsfield, and both before and after marriage made long visits to her sister, Mrs. White. Mr. Webster sometimes accompanied her, and while in town called on some of the hardy farmers for a social chat, and in accordance with the custom of the times accepted a draught of cider or a glass of grog.

Mrs. Webster's last visit to Pittsfield was in the summer of 1827, requiring a long tedious carriage drive from Boston, while suffering from an incurable malady. On reaching the home of her girlhood she remarked that she had cherished a strong desire to see the town of Pittsfield once more and visit her old home and friends.

The fact that Daniel Webster, the great expounder, once owned a farm in Pittsfield has not before been mentioned in print; the circumstance had long been forgotten and is not now known to the townspeople. The fact is in evidence by the county record of deeds, where it appears that Daniel Fogg and others gave Daniel Webster a warranty deed, December 6, 1825, of the premises occupied by Josiah White. In December, 1838, Webster transferred the same premises by deed to Alfred Marston.

The possession of this farm came about in the following manner: Mr. White, a worthy man, was not financially prosperous. His neighbors talked that he was "kept poor by the pride and extravagance of his wimmen-folks." Webster, in his characteristic prodigal generosity, contributed liberally from time to time to aid the family of his brother-in-law, and eventually was obliged to assume ownership of the place. The farm is situated on the north side of the road leading from the White dam to Shaw's pond, near the Barnstead town line, and now owned by Martin Sanders. A good field on a fine ridge of land is still cultivated, but all traces of the buildings formerly receiving as guests the most celebrated man of the age, with his family, have long since been obliterated, and no vestige of their historic interest remains.

Gone long since her relatives, but the place and romantic scenery remain, the charming features of which were so familiar to "Beautiful Grace Fletcher."

JOHN C. FRENCH.

MANCHESTER, N. H. Rewritten January, 1897.

# AUTHOR OF "THE SWEET BY AND BY."

At the quarterly meeting of the Manchester Historic Association, March 18, 1896, Orrin H. Leavitt of this city, being introduced with appropriate remarks by S. C. Gould, presented the Association with a gavel made from the wood of an apple tree which grew on the land of Joseph P. Webster, who was a native of this town and believed to have been the author and composer of the beautiful hymn, "The Sweet By and By." Mr. Leavitt opened his presentation speech by reading the following sketch from the Concord & Montreal Railroad Pathfinder for 1895:

"Three miles in a southerly direction from the passenger station of the Portsmouth branch of the Concord railroad at Massabesic, high above the graceful curve of the white sand beach, stand six pine trees, each of them more than a yard in diameter, and probably more than 150 years old. They have outlived all their contemporaries on the shore of the lake, and now remain landmarks of the primeval forest, and of a time when their locality was one of the beauty spots of the earth. As long ago as when slaves were held in Massachusetts, one Harvey, a sea captain of Salem, brought to that town on one of his voyages a negro, to whom he gave the name of Cæsar. This negro ran away and came to live near these pines in a hut near the lake, and from him the strip of white sand shore has taken and retained the name of Cæsar's beach. Sloping back to the south is an open field, in the foreground of which are the ruins of an old cellar grown over by lilacs. Here Joseph P. Webster was born, who was the composer and author of that inspiring hymn, 'The Sweet By and By,' a hymn which has been a consolation to many wearied souls, and will be still to thousands yet unborn. Doubtless the vision of that beautiful shore of 'the land that is fairer than day,' was but a reflection of this picture of his childhood. For many years there was a hotel there, which was burned and built and burned again. It was known as the Island Pond, but the present owners deeming that name inappropriate, have named it Idolia, in honor of the beautiful butterfly, *Argynnis Idolia*, which is found in great abundance at this place. The butterfly was named after Idolia, the fabled home of Venus."

The reading of the above clipping calling up some discussion in regard to the real authorship of the song, at a special meeting, May 5, Mr. Gould again referred to the matter, saying that since the last meeting his attention had been called to an interview in the Louisville "Post" with Dr. Samuel F. Bennett of Richmond, Ill., who claims to be the author. The "Post" says:

"The author of 'The Sweet By and By' was Samuel Fillmore Bennett, M. D., a graduate of Ann Arbor University, Mich., living in Richmond, Ill., and now about sixty years of age; that the immortal hymn was the single song of his life, and written at the age of thirty-one; that he was a newspaper editor on 'The Independent' at Elkhorn, Wis., prior to the civil war; that Joseph P. Webster, a musical composer, was then living in the same town, and they were warm friends and collaborated together. The war intervened and called Mr. Bennett as colonel of the Fortieth Wisconsin Volunteers. He returned from the service, opened a drugstore at Elkhorn, and resumed verse writing. He and Mr. Webster, in 1867, began work on a Sunday school song book, which was called 'The Signet Ring,' and afterwards published."

The "Post" says that not long ago Mr. Bennett related the details of the hymn to an interested audience, with his eyes filled with tears as he spoke of his friend Webster.

"I am thankful to do justice to one of the noblest men who ever lived, a fine, sensitive soul, with the true artistic feeling. It has been said that we are both infidels, and that the song was the ribald jest of a carouse. As to my religion, that is my own affair; but the hope and longing of every immortal soul as expressed in that song was the faith of both of us. To us creation would have seemed a farce if infinite love and immortality had not overshadowed us and promised a life of bliss beyond the grave.

"Mr. Webster, like many musicians, was of an exceedingly nervous and sensitive nature, and subject to times of depression. I knew his peculiarities well and when I found him given up to the blues I just gave him a cheerful song to work on. One morning he came into the store and walked to the stove without speaking. 'What's up now, Webster,' I asked. 'It's no matter. It will be all right, by and by,' he answered. The idea of the hymn came to me like a flash of sunshine. The sweet by and by. Everything will be all right then. 'Why wouldn't that make a good hymn?' said I. 'Maybe it would,' he replied, gloomily. Turning to the desk I wrote as rapidly as I could. In less than half an hour, I think, the song as it stands today was written. Here it is:

## THE SWEET BY AND BY.

" There's a land that is fairer than day,
    And by faith we can see it afar;
For the Father waits over the way,
    To prepare us a dwelling-place there.

CHORUS,—

" In the sweet by and by,
    We shall meet on that beautiful shore,—
In the sweet by and by,
    We shall meet on that beautiful shore.

" We shall sing on that beautiful shore,
    The melodious songs of the blest;
And our spirits shall sorrow no more,—
    Not a sigh for the blessing of rest!

" To our bountiful Father above
    We will offer our tribute of praise,
For the glorious gift of His love
    And the blessings that hallow our days.

"In the meantime, two friends, Mr. N. H. Carswell and Mr. S. E. Bright, had come in. I handed the verses to Mr. Webster, a little tremulous with emotion. As he read it, his eyes kindled. Stepping to the desk he began to jot down the notes. He picked up his violin and tried them. In ten minutes we four gentlemen were singing that song. Mr. R. R. Crosby came in, and with tears in his eyes, said: 'Gentlemen, that hymn is immortal.' We were all elated and excited. Within two weeks the children of Elkhorn were singing it on the streets.

"In 1868 'The Signet Ring' was published, and the publishers distributing circulars to advertise it, and on the streets was 'The Sweet By and By.' On the strength of that one song nearly a quarter of a million copies of the book were sold. The song was afterwards brought out in sheet music, and it has been translated into a number of foreign languages. Mr. Bright of Fort Atkinson, Wisconsin, and myself are the only living witnesses to the origin of the song."

# OLD DERRYFIELD AND YOUNG MANCHESTER.

CONTRIBUTED BY DAVID L. PERKINS TO THE MANCHESTER HISTORIC ASSOCIATION.

There is an apt analogy between our little town republics associated together under one state government, and our grand national system where the states themselves are so associated, and our little town republics came first. The savant and historian may well have recourse to this fact. It is also true that ours of New Hampshire was the first written constitution among the states, or colonies, and it was her ninth vote that ratified the federal constitution. It was her general, John Stark, who turned the adverse tide of the Revolution at Bennington, and her matchless son, Daniel Webster, fashioned the bulwarks of the constitution. Thrice glorious little state, she is ever proud of her children,— John Langdon, Samuel Livermore, John Stark, John Sullivan, Daniel Webster, Lewis Cass, Levi Woodbury, Franklin Pierce, Salmon P. Chase, Horace Greeley, John P. Hale, Benjamin F. Butler, William Pitt Fessenden, Henry Wilson, Joel Parker, John A. Dix, Nathan Clifford, Marshall P. Wilder, Ichabod Bartlettt, Mark Farley, Charles A. Dana, Zachariah Chandler, Gilman Marston, Fitz John Porter, Lydia Maria Child, Edna Dean Proctor, Celia Thaxter, Constance Fennimore Woolson, and others of her family.

About the year 1750, many of these little democratic townships were incorporated into the body politic in this section of New Hampshire by the royal governor, Benning Wentworth. It was the day of the backlog, the flintlock, and the tinder-box.

In this year the settlers in the vicinity of Amoskeag upon ungranted lands petitioned for a charter, but the territory of Harrytown did not exceed three miles in its widest part, comprising in all about eight square miles. The earliest settlements here were made under a Massachusetts charter when that state claimed all this territory, including, of course, Tyngstown and Harrytown. That the new town might be of respectable dimensions, a movement was set on foot to add the then southwest section of Chester and a segment from Londonderry, and the petition was so ordered.

The time was opportune, for since 1730 there had existed in Chester a feeling of unrest between the English Congregationalists and the Scotch-Irish Presbyterians over the question of settling a minister. In this connection it may be observed that preaching was provided at the town meetings, and the gospel so ordered was paid for out of the general tax list. The Baptists were the first to rebel against this relic of the old world union of church and state, and in good time they won the day. The Congregationalists of Chester seem to have been in the majority, and as many of the Scotch-Irish minority were domiciled in the section that was sought to be disannexed, they were the more willing to rid themselves of their persistent co-religionists. The Londonderry people yielded with less alacrity, but in time they fell into the movement, and, as we conjecture, partly out of fellowship with their coadjutors of the Scotch-Irish faith. September 3, 1751, the charter was granted under the name of Derryfield, including about eighteen square miles of Chester territory and nine square miles from Londonderry, thus giving to the new town an area of thirty-five square miles, irregular in shape and diversified in soil. Along the river bank sand dunes were conspicuous, while back and under the compact part of the city of today, there was an almost endless network of springs. Much of it was pine land. John McMurphy of Londonderry was commissioned by the royal governor to warn the proprietors, freeholders, and inhabitants qualified to vote, to assemble in town meeting September 23, 1751, " to chuse their town officers."

Accordingly the yeomen of Derryfield made choice of five selectmen, of whom John Goffe was first, a town clerk, two commissioners to examine the selectmen's account, a constable, two tithing men, three highway surveyors, two invoice men, two haywards, two deer keepers, a culler of staves, and a surveyor of boards, planks, joists, and timber. The duties of the deer keepers must be left largely to conjecture, but let us hope that they were faithful to their trust, for old Derryfield must have been a famous trysting place for deer.

November 16, at an adjourned meeting, it was "Voted to rase twenty-four pounds old tenor, to be rased to paye for priching for the present year," the "old tenor" having reference to the depreciated bills of credit that had been issued by the province. This was a good beginning, however, and whatever may be said of the subsequent history of the town, it should be remembered that the marvelous fishing facilities at Amoskeag had ever been a source of contention among venturesome spirits, and it is therefore no tax upon our credulity to believe that they came hither at stated periods to fish, to drink, and to fight betimes if need be. It should be borne in mind that the drink habit was then well-nigh universal, and even the minister could not be entertained with becoming hospitality without a mug of flip or a noggin of rum. Like all communities, there were the ne'er-do-wells among them, and an occasional specimen who was afflicted with a moral obliquity by reason of which he sometimes failed to distinguish his own from the chattels of others. Instances might be related, but after the lapse of these many years the task would be ungracious, for the poacher and the mutton no longer vex the vicinage. But the men of Derryfield were of sturdy stock, and it need not be said of them as a class that as pioneers and makers of history they were inferior in natural ability and general integrity to any class of people who came to these shores in pursuit of civil liberty. And there was royal blood among them, too, but royal blood is of little account in a new republic where every man is a sovereign, except for family use.

Several highways were at once projected or completed, and it is hinted in Potter's history that an element of Scotch thrift entered into the fact that John Hall's hostelry at the center of the town was a converging point. He had been the agent of the town in procuring the charter. At all events the roads were built, and it is reasonable to presume that they conserved the convenience of a sparsely settled community, for some of them are still used.

It is said that the annual supply of lamprey eels salted for family use by the farmers of Derryfield and adjacent towns, were equal to three hundred head of beef cattle, and it is therefore no cause of surprise that the fishing privileges at Amoskeag and on Cohas brook were of great value to the early settlers. There was little or no currency or coin to be had, and trade was largely carried on by a system of " truck and dicker," or by an exchange of commodities, and the taxes were paid, in part, at least, in produce, a liberal discount being made for cash. Some of the more venturesome spirits made periodical excursions into the wild northern territory, where they engaged in trapping fur animals, the pelts being a source of revenue. It was on one of these expeditions that John Stark was captured by the Indians in 1752 on Baker's river in the territory now known as Rumney. There were no newspapers here, and marriage banns, advertisements, and legal notices were recorded and posted, mayhap at the tavern, the store, or on some one's barn door where the town meetings were held. It was an early cause of complaint that cattle were brought hither to feed upon the Derryfield commons, and I infer from the following notice that one's neat stock was not always safe from a general mixing up with foreign herds at the autumn round-up.

"ARTIFICIAL MARK.

"Benjamin Baker's artificial mark fore nete cattle and shepe — his — the tope of the right ear cropet, and a hapiney out of the under sid of the left ear."

The fifth article in the warrant of February 12, 1753, was " to see what method the town will take to prevent stray cattle being brought into the town to eat up our feed on the common land or unfenced land." Cattle were frequently taken "damage fesant;" and on one occasion Archibald Stark took three colts which were duly prized and sold at auction for the cost of poundage. The record is quite voluminous, technical, and exact as to form.

At the annual March meeting in 1752 it was "voted that ther be three selectmen for the year and now mor," from which we infer that the Derryfielders were not in favor of multiplying offices. The same old difficulty of settling a minister served as a bone of contention in Derryfield, and seems never to have been settled. As early as March 5, 1752, it was "Voted, to give Mr. mcDouell a Cauell to the ministry, Eather to Joyen with Bedford or by our selves. Voted, John Ridill, Alexander McMurphey, John Hall, a Comitey to prosequet the given of Mr. Mcdoul a Cauell to the work of the minestery to Joyn with the town of Bedford or seprat and Distink by our selves," but nothing came of it. A pound was also voted to "be built at Moses Willes," but the pound was a long time in coming. Indeed, for many years the pound and the meeting-house were fruitful subjects of contention, and considering the temporal drift of affairs, it is safe to presume that the pound, fully equipped, came first. As late as 1764 we find it "Voted, John Goffe have Libberty to Buld a Pound for the town at hies own coste and charges near the Brig at hies House;" but as the pound had been provided for in many previous town meetings, I am by no means sure that this was the end of it. Indeed, at the annual meeting, March 3, 1800, it was voted to build a pound thirty-two feet square and seven feet high, on a lot adjoining the never completed meetinghouse, and this pound was used until about 1830.

At a meeting held February 2, 1753, it was "Voted, that Benjamin Stevens barn and William McClintos barn be the tow placeses of publick worship till the money voted at the last March meeting be expended. Voted, that the minister should be keep at William McClintos."

March 4, 1754, they "Voted one hundred and fifty pounds,

old tenor, for this year for preeching, and charges arising thereby, and that John Goffe Esq$^r$ is chosen to obtain preeching till said money is Vie," for likely enough by this time the "old tenor" bills of credit had so depreciated that, like the Confederate money in the late war, it took a large sum to procure a little comfort.  An article in the warrant of August, 1754, was "to see what spott they will Pick upon to Sett there said meeting House upon betwixt y$^e$ fore mentioned Will$^m$ Mac Clintock and James Umphrey;" and it was voted September y$^e$ 5$^{th}$ "that y$^e$ meeting House for Publick worsep in Derryfield be bult upon the Publick Road as is mentioned in y$^e$ Second article of y$^e$ warrant," but at a meeting March 1, 1755, the above vote was reconsidered.

Derryfield was the victim of untoward events, and as a community they can hardly be said to have been prosperous or progressive.  They were heroes together in the wars, but they were no less contentious among themselves in time of peace.  Even their local advantages seem to have involved them in misfortune, for many of them devoted their time to the fisheries at the expense of their farm work.  While other towns flourished Derryfield languished.  The Scotch-Irish Presbyterians and the English Puritans were uncongenial, and a bitter feud grew up among them over the location of a meeting-house that lasted for many years, and gave the town an unsavory reputation.  To this fact, and their lack of zeal for the public school, may be attributed nearly all the evils that afflicted the town for more than a half century.  If a meeting-house site was chosen by these militant heroes, it was soon revoked.  If the money was voted, the vote was rescinded.  First one party prevailed, and then the other. As early as 1754 it was voted to build a meeting-house near Lieut. John Hall's tavern.  Then thirty voters petitioned the selectmen for another meeting, and this being denied, they appealed to Joseph Blanchard and Matthew Thornton Esquires, two justices of the Province, who righted their wrongs.  At a meeting September 2, 1758, in John Hall's barn, it was voted to build a meeting-house on John Hall's land, and John Hall was placed on the building committee.  They proceeded far enough to erect a frame, but the opposition became so bitter that taxes and labor were withheld, and they proceeded no further. July 15, 1759, money was voted to board and shingle the house, and November 15 an examination of the committee's account was ordered. It was also " Voted not to underpin our meeting hous at present, but to make one door this year." December 3 it was " Voted not to co'lect any more money from the town this year towards the Meeting House;" and it was also voted to borrow money to pay off the committee, which was afterwards rescinded. It was voted to use the meeting-house money for town purposes. In August, 1760, the selectmen were authorized to underpin the house and put doors in the same. In December, 1761, a committee was chosen " to call John Hall to account for the money that he received." This controversy resulted in a vexatious law suit, in which our protean friend Lieut. John Hall seems to have had the best of it. In 1764 the controversy was carried to such a pitch that no money was raised for preaching; but in the following year the opposition rallied and carried things with a high hand. March 31, at an adjourned meeting, the Hall party elected town officers before their rivals came upon the scene, aided, it was alleged, by the votes of minors and others not qualified to vote. John Hall was chosen moderator, town clerk, and selectman. An adjournment was then had to John Hall's tavern. The opposition then held their meeting, and chose a rival set of town officers. Finally the legislature interfered, and the tangle was unraveled. June 27, 1766, it was " Voted to Repear the meeting House in part theis year." It was also " Voted to Lay a good flor in the Meeting House and make three Good Dores and Hinge them one Said House and Shout upe the Under Windows and a Commadate the Meting House with forms Suitable for to Sit on." Yet from this ebulent spirit little was done to render the meeting-house habitable against wind and storm until after the Revolution, when in 1790 the pew ground was sold at vendue. And after all it may not be accurate to say that the people of Derryfield were irreligious above other communities, for those in the south part of the town who felt the need of religious service worshipped in Londonderry, and those of like mind along the river front fellowshipped in Bedford. As regards the meeting-house and the public school it need not be denied that the men of Derryfield were remiss. Yet preaching was supplied in an itinerate or desultory way. We may at least console ourselves with the thought that religious feuds, unaided by race prejudice, have wrought more havoc in the world than fell to the lot of Derryfield. But even if these men were not intensely religious, they were at least intensely patriotic, and from no town in New England did there go forth to the French and Indian wars, and to the war of the Revolution, more men in proportion to their population than from old Derryfield. All but two men capable of bearing arms followed Stark to Bunker Hill, and there was not a Tory among them. Any town might well felicitate itself on a list of heroes such as Col. John Goffe, Capt. John Moore, Benjamin Kidder, Sergt. Ephraim Stevens, William Gamble, Michael McClintock, John McNeil, Archibald and John Stark, Judge Samuel Blodget, and others of like character. The environments of this people were vastly different from our own. They were pioneers in a new country, inured to the hardships and privations of frontier life, and to the perils of war, and far removed from the arts and allurements of civilization. The conditions were not calculated to propitiate the graces. The fishermen at Amoskeag and the flatboat rivermen were no carpet knights. There were no vicarious warriors among them. This much may be conceded. Yet it is a source of regret that the sturdy, virile, self-reliant men of Derryfield had not given more of their attention to the practice of religion and the encouragement of education. But who can say with complacency that we of today would have been more circumspect if our conditions had been reversed.

With reference to schooling little is found in the early records until the warrant of February 16, 1757, when the fifth article was, " to see if the town will raise any money for scholling, or how much," and at the March meeting it was "voted to dismis the fifth article and not to use eaney money for scollen for this year." We need not criticise the orthography, and if the spelling book had been more in evidence these quotations would have been less quaint. If there was a lack of facility there was at least a directness of statement that is refreshing in this age of subterfuge and inordinate conceit. Evidently the epigram of Talleyrand, that language was invented to conceal thought, was not known to their moral code. With all their faults we believe that a renascent spirit was a part of their quality. We find that in 1783 the town was divided into four school districts "for the benefit of scooling their children," and doubtless other, though scant provision had been made at earlier meetings for the meager education of the young. It has been said "that for nearly a century after the settlement of the town, there was neither lawyer, physician or minister among its permanent inhabitants," and it may come near the truth to say that the schoolmaster should be added. And yet there were educated men in Derryfield. The first schoolhouse, the little black wooden one on the old Falls road near the Amoskeag bridge, is said to have been built by private subscription in 1795. Frederick G. Stark of the West side, of the Stark lineage, and born on the old Stark homestead on the north river road, remembers to have heard John Stark, Jr., his grandfather, and Abby Stark, relate their experience in attending school over the hill, out Lake avenue, but whether it was a public school, *query.* There were other schoolhouses here, ordered by the town, about 1798.

And now as tending to show the solicitude of these stern men of war for their individual, corporate, and political rights, I will submit a few extracts from the early records which will perhaps be worth the perusal. From the following protest we may be assured that elections did not always satisfy the defeated electors even in the good old times.

" We the subscribers making a demand that non but qualified voters as the law directs should votte in the choise of town officers, and such as was not worth one shilling besides the poll of rateble estate had the privilage of votting. We enter our desant against the procieding of their choice. Witines our hand March y^e 5, 1753. John Goffe, Archibald Stark, Benjamin Hadley, Moses Welles."

As has been heretofore observed, the fisheries were of great importance to the early denizens of Derryfield. The first menace in this section to the unimpeded run of salmon, shad, alewives, and lamprey eels from the sea to our inland waters was in Cohas brook, and it was probably the dam of a saw or grist mill that evoked the action of the town. As this was the forerunner of conditions that resulted in the Manchester of today, the narration may be of interest. I have abridged the record so as to retain the gist or gravamen of their plaint. At a town meeting as early as March 4, 1754, it was set forth that obstructions existed in Cohas brook, so called, "whereby the elewives are much hindered in their passage into Massapissack Pond," and it was voted to remove them, and "if some method be not speedily taken in order to remove and amend such incumbrance, it is altogether likely it will wholly stop the corse of said fish, which will be a vast damage, not only to s^d Derryfield but to all the adjacent towns." . . . . Then the penalty, for if any person or persons shall refuse or neglect to remove said obstructions in said brook while the elewives are running they shall forfeit and pay the sum of forty shillings for every day, "one half moiety to the use of the poor of the town, and the other half to the complainant." . . . And all persons were forbidden to fish with nets in said brook within fifteen rods of the Merrimack river. There were other grievances somewhat ambiguously set forth in a town meeting held April y^e 20, 1758, when it was "Voted on the forth article in the Waront to take the Waront and List out of Benjamin Hiddaley's hand for the falling reesings—that some Pipeal are Deed, and some removed out of the town, & others come into the town that would enjoy Privigles wothout Piayen their equeall Preporeshen."

That a public office was held to be a sacred public trust, and not to be wantonly declined is clearly set forth March 5th, 1759, when it was "Voted that Thomas Russ shall peay the fienn as the law Diriecks for not quilifien him self a cording to law to serve a Connstable in the town acording to the Vote of s^d town." After that I am inclined to exclaim, "happy land of Derryfield where the office-seeker's itch was unknown." Oct. 29, 1764, it was "Voted, John Goffe and John Stark to setel the accoumptes thies year that is Betwixte Constable James Peteres and the inhabitants of Derryfield," and in the absence of light, we refrain from drawing an inference not creditable to the integrity of said Peteres.

If the men of Derryfield were warriors in time of war, it may also be said of them that they were statesmen in embryo in time of peace, as witness the following: In the warrant for town meeting of August 29th, 1783, it was provided "$1^{ly}$ to choos a moderator to regulate said meeting. $2^{ly}$, to see if the town will vote to except of the Plan of Government especially that Part that is not yet Confirmed by the Convention, or what vote they will Pass. 3, to see if the town will Vote to give their Representative instructions in an especian manner with respect to the Eighteth Article in the Confederation of the United States, and whether the town will vote to comply with the recommeration of Congress for altering the same." At the meeting September 16th, it was " Voted, General John Stark, Esq$^r$, moderator. Voted to choose a Committy to Consider of the Plan of Government. Voted that said Committy consist of seven. Voted that General John Stark, Major John Webster, Lieut. John Hall, John Goffe, Jun$^r$, Lieut. John Perham, Ensign Samuel Stark, James Gorman be said Committy. Voted to refer the consideration of the third article of the Warrant respecting the 8th article of the Confederation to said Committy before mentioned. $5^{thly}$, Voted to adjourn this meeting to Tuesday the 23$^d$ Day of this instant at one o'clock, afternoon." At the adjourned meeting the report of their " Committy " was accepted, and it was "Voted that the clause in the Eighth article of Confederation stand as it now is." It will be observed that the warriors of Derryfield were the leading civilians.

I would like to say something of the vernal maids and prolific mothers of Derryfield, but it must suffice that they were given in marriage, and that their progeny speaks for them in many a thrifty and honored family, for the descendants of Stark, Goffe, Stevens, Kidder, Huse, Dickey, Webster, Harvey, Walker, Merrill, Weston, Hall, Nutt, Gamble, and many others still abide among us.

For Derryfield it may well be said that "The stone that the builders rejected has become the head of the corner." As with communities so with individuals, for in a republic like ours, the children of strong, rough sires often become gentle, cultured, and honored citizens. At this late day we need no Talmud, or astral rays, or visual shekinah in order to estimate these men of iron blood. We need not claim that Derryfield was a Nazareth or a Valhalla. Her sons did not set themselves to extirpate sin, but they were shrewd enough to know their rights and brave enough to fight for civil liberty. The town seems not to have suffered very extensively from the Indians. John Stark suffered a term of captivity, and Ezekiel Stevens was scalped and left for dead, but he recovered and lived to a good old age. John McNeil and Archibald Stark are believed to be the first of the Scotch-Irish stock to take up their abode in the vicinity of Amoskeag. The name of Derryfield was changed to Manchester in 1810. The first child born in the new town was Rodnia Nutt, and he was the father of the famous dwarf known on both sides of the Atlantic ocean as Commodore Nutt.

After the Revolution signs of prosperity began to dawn, and in 1792 the Amoskeag bridge was built, probably at the foot of Bridge street. In the olden time the designation of "Amoskeag Falls" included the river bed from Merrill's falls at the site of the old locks south of the Granite bridge, to the present dam at Amoskeag.

There is a conflict of authority as to the location of General Stark's historic sawmill, the one that he abandoned so abruptly on hearing of the battle at Lexington. In Potter's history we find it stated, p. 419, that Stark was at work in his sawmill at the head of Amoskeag Falls when he heard the news, and without a moment's delay he shut down the gate of his mill. . . .

He also mentions, p. 528, a "sawmill at the head of the falls which stood just above the Amoskeag bridge," owned in common with Judge Blodget, which was built prior to the Revolution. Query, was this the Amoskeag bridge at the foot of Bridge street? Col. Kidder recollects climbing over the decaying timbers of an old mill just below the bulkhead at Amoskeag Falls south of the gate house on the river bank. Just back of the mill a basin was formed by the angles of the rocks and probably fortified with human labor, where water was stored. From this basin came the hydraulic power for this mill. This was seventy-five years ago. Potter also mentions, p. 528, a saw and grist mill at this point, supplied with water power from a basin about ninety rods long and from four to six in width. It "was intended to answer the purposes of a canal and mill pond." *This* basin was a part of the Blodget canal, and the Blodget canal was not constructed until 1794 and after. There was an old mill on this site. Potter says, p. 663, that he had reason to believe that the second or third mill in this vicinity was built on Ray brook by Archibald Stark, probably in 1736, located a few rods west of the Hooksett road; that it was in existence in 1756 in a somewhat dilapidated state, and that " four years after, in 1760, Mr. Stark had built a mill at Amoskeag Falls."

Per contra, our esteemed fellow citizen, Henry W. Herrick, in a recent publication, gives us the benefit of his careful and painstaking research, as follows:

" Early in life he erected a mill for sawing lumber on Ray's brook at the present site of Dorr's pond, and it was this mill that was so suddenly stopped at the news of the battle of Lexington, and permitted to rot and rust during the eight years of the Revolution. The remains of the old dam are yet to be seen at low water. After the Revolution Stark, in common with Judge Blodget, erected a saw and grist mill on the east side of the Amoskeag Falls, near the present entrance of the company's large canal."

Some years since Mr. Herrick consulted those who were contemporary with Stark, those of the neighborhood and of the family guild, and they gave the Ray's brook location as the proper one. It seems strange to us that there could be even a suspicion, or a shadow of doubt, as to the identity or location of this historic mill. The weight of authority would seem to be with Mr. Herrick. Even if we take Potter's dates, the Ray's brook mill would have been but forty years old when the battle of Lexington was fought. It could hardly have been "dilapidated" twenty years before, in 1756, and we are confirmed in this view of the case when we consider the enduring fibre of the old growth timber of which this mill was doubtless built.

And now, after a lapse of years, let us enter upon a field of inquiry that more nearly concerns us. It is a trite saying among the cullers of historic lore that traditions and the quick early memories of the wise whose mental faculties are unimpaired, are important adjuncts in pacing out the lines of human progress. With this thought I have had recourse to Colonel John S. Kidder, who was born in Manchester May 31, 1811, a lineal descendant of General Stark, a resident within the limits of the ancestral estate for all but about twelve years of a thrice honored career, whose memory is clear, and whose genial personality and unspotted reputation are like the north star to all who know him. The interesting features with which this paper will conclude should, therefore, be accredited to Col. Kidder. First with reference to the freeholders and houses within a couple of miles of our city hall just prior to 1838, when the first cotton mill was erected on the east side of the river — for Amoskeag and Piscataquog were not annexed until 1853. We will begin, then, in the vicinity of Amoskeag Falls.

*Col. John Ray's* farm of about one hundred acres, including the Riverside or Col. Eastman estate, was originally a part of the Stark estate of about three hundred acres. The State Industrial school land was also a part of the Stark farm.

*Frederick Kimball* owned and occupied a small piece of land, including the old tavern stand on the north river road, a couple of acres or so, where he kept tavern at one time. The house still remains.

*John Stark, Jr.*, lived for a time, at least, in the little wood-colored house at the southeast end of Amoskeag bridge. It was built about the year of 1747, and is now one hundred and fifty years old. Frank Stark, the General's son, lived here at one time and here Abby Stark was born. The old house still remains to remind us of the past. Mr. Stark had about fifty acres (a part of the original Stark estate) extending back from the river nearly to Union street.

*Samuel P. Kidder.* The house of Samuel P. Kidder, the father of Col. John S., Samuel B., and our widely known fellow-citizen, Hon. Joseph Kidder, stood just over the Amoskeag upper canal of today, nearly opposite the Locomotive Works on Canal street. The farm of over one hundred acres extended back from the river to Oak hill. It was formerly known as Heathhen hill from the fact that a species of heath hens with tufted heads were plentiful there, and they annoyed the farmers by scratching up the early corn. The approximate bounds of the Kidder farm north and south were Harrison and High streets. The house was a substantial one of the colonial period, and is now known as the Campbell house. It stands on Canal street south of the Locomotive Works.

*Frederick G. Stark.* The house where Frederick G. Stark lived was erected and occupied by Judge Blodget while engaged in building his historic canal. It came to the possession of one James Griffin, of whom Judge Stark purchased it. It was on the west side of the old Blodget canal at the foot of the falls, by the present lower canal where the old locks were located. These old locks are now nearly or quite obliterated. The house stood within three or four rods of the lower locks of the upper canal, and was torn down many years ago. Judge Stark kept a country store here, and furnished meals and lodgings for the river men. He afterwards kept store in Piscataquog for many years.

*Jotham Gillis*, the father-in-law of Judge Stark, lived in a small house of F. G. Stark, near the old grist-mill on Mechanics row, so called, and long since gone. He was advanced in years and of feeble health. In 1810–13 he was clerk of the

Amoskeag Cotton and Wool Co., of which Judge Stark was afterwards the agent. He came from Woburn, Mass.

*Samuel B. Kidder's* house is still standing just south of the gate-house at Amoskeag Falls. It is reached by a little bridge that crosses the railroad track from upper Canal street. Mr. Kidder was for many years gate-tender and time-keeper at the falls, and there was no better authority as to high and low water marks and the flow of the Merrimack.

*James Ray* was just below the S. P. Kidder house, east side of the Blodget canal, and north of the old McGregor bridge. He had five or six acres near the corner of the old River road and Bridge, now Canal and Bridge streets.

*John Gamble* owned a house and country store near the junction of the old Derry River road, near the corner of Canal and Bridge streets of today.

*Henry B. Barrett* lived near the corner of Granite and Canal streets, about where the Concord railroad track now stands. He was a carpenter and farmer, and had a few acres of land where the Concord railroad station stands.

*Benjamin Stevens* was a farmer with about thirty acres, and his house stood a little this side, or north of the gas works, at a turn of the old River road and the Parker ferry road.

*Samuel Hall.* Next came Samuel Hall, a farmer on the old Ferry road between the Benjamin Stevens house and the river. He had charge of the ferry across the river to what is now known as Ferry street. There were from forty to fifty acres, and the house is probably no longer in existence.

*Hezekiah Young* lived in the large wood-colored house since occupied as "The Women's Aid and Relief Home," at the lower end of Elm street. It is still standing and is owned by the Amoskeag Company. The farm contained about one hundred acres and extended half way out to the Center.

*Nathaniel Baker* lived on the River road south, in what is now known as Bakersville. His farm extended back from the river, and the buildings are no longer standing.

*Joseph B. Hall.* The Joseph B. Hall house was on the Ferry

road to the Center, about half way from the river, on a farm of perhaps one hundred acres, extending out as far as Hallsville. The house is gone. Coming back to the Amoskeag bridge we find the little black-wooded schoolhouse on the old Falls road, on the bank of Christian brook near the bridge. It was the only schoolhouse along the river.

*Andrew French* occupied the little house on the bluff at the intersection of the old Falls road and Elm street, where Judge David Cross now lives. He was a farm hand and river man. The house is gone.

*Job Rowell.* The Job Rowell farm of about one hundred acres from the river back included the present site of the Governor Straw estate, at the corner of Elm and Harrison streets. It was bounded north by the Christian brook and south by land of Samuel P. Kidder.

*Daniel Rowell* owned a small place near the corner of Pearl and Union, of the Rowell farm, an acre or so, and he was a farm hand, and perhaps a river man.

*John Hall* was on the brow of the hill up Bridge street on the old road from the Falls over Bald hill to the turnpike. It was a little black-wooded house where N. J. Whalen now lives, corner of Bridge and Hall streets. It was under the shade of two mammoth willow trees. The farm contained from seventy-five to one hundred acres, extending as far south as Lowell street, and north to the S. P. Kidder land. The west bound was near the foot of the hill, and it extended east to the Moses Davis land.

*Moses Davis.* The Moses Davis house, painted red, was on the same road east of John Hale's, and in later years it became the pest-house. There were about seventy-five acres.

*David Stevens.* Next east was the David Stevens place on the old Bridge-street road, near the Mammoth road, where Hiram Turner lives. The old house is no longer there.

*Capt. Ephraim Stevens.* South of that and on the Mammoth road was the Capt. Ephraim Stevens place of about two hundred acres. It is now known as the poor-farm, and is owned by the city. A famous hostelry flourished there after the Mammoth road was built. Capt. Stevens was the father of our esteemed fellow-citizen, Joseph L. Stevens, who served as postmaster in Manchester from Feb. 21, 1870, to May 15, 1886.

*Robert Stevens.* Then came the Robert Stevens farm, near Hanover street, between the Mammoth road and the old road. The house is still there and is occupied by his son, Robert I. Stevens.

The *James Hall* house is still standing on the old road leading to the Center south of the Robert Stevens place. He was a farmer and had thirty or forty acres. The house stood near the Robert Wilson place, from whom Wilson's hill derived its name.

*Daniel Hall.* Next south came the Daniel Hall place at the corner of the Candia road and the Derry road, just north of the present residence of Isaac Huse at the Center. There were a few acres.

*Samuel Jackson* lived on the premises where Isaac Huse now lives at the Center, and the postoffice was located here for many years. The fine old house is still standing.

*Quimby & Dwinnells* kept a tavern stand on a small tract at the Center, and south of the Jackson place. The house was burned down years ago.

*Gilbert Greeley* lived in the house where George Porter lived and died at the Center. It was a milk farm of about fifty acres, and at one time Mr. Greeley kept a country store there.

*Philip Stevens.* Let us now return to the vicinity of the McGregor bridge, and we find that Philip Stevens lived just back of Smyth's block of today, then on the Derry road from the bridge to the Center. He had about one hundred acres from the River road southeast, as far out as the Ryefield, bounded north by the S. P. Kidder land to the Sam Hall place.

*Jesse Saunders.* Next on the Derry road southeast was the Jesse Saunders house. He had an acre or so south of Massabesic street, or south of the brook where the old mill way stood. It was near the point where the Portsmouth Railroad crosses the Derry road. He had no stated occupation.

*Lizzie B. Stark* lived on the North River road and the house is still there. It was formerly owned by John Stark, Jr. She was a great grand-daughter of the general, and has but recently deceased. There was a small group of houses near the Jesse Saunders place, including one or two small country stores. There were also other ancient houses here and there of which no trace is left, but the foregoing practically includes all the houses within two miles of the city hall on the east side of the Merrimack river at or just before 1838, when the future city of Manchester was laid out by the Amoskeag Company.

Colonel Kidder and a comrade named Harwood were accustomed to fish at Amoskeag, and upon one occasion they took upwards of seven hundred lamprey eels in a night. This great take was made at a place called "the eel gut." Originally, and before the water was held back by the dam, there were three streams below the bridge, and the "eel gut" was on the east stream. It is said that the eels would sometimes fasten themselves to the rocks in the river by their mouths, and they were then taken in great numbers by hands covered with woolen mittens. The east stream is now blocked by the wall south of the east end of the stone dam. One result of the dam was to obliterate many famous fishing-places, and there is no visible sign of the "eel gut." It was just south of the bridge and is probably covered by twenty feet of water. The fishing season was from the last of May and extended into July. Some of the fishing stands were owned by individuals, and others, open to all, were formed by the angles of rocks and by eddies in the stream. There was a place called "the slash hole," where many salmon were caught. It was on the east side of the center stream a few rods below the bridge. Another valued place was on the west side of the center stream where eels were taken, known as "the Dalton place." Salmon and shad were also caught in great numbers between the "Dalton place" and the bridge. At the Dalton place an eddy was formed by the water into which nets were cast. A platform was built out twelve or fourteen feet, and the privilege of the platform was often held, night and day, for two or three weeks before the fish began to run. It was an unwritten law of the platform that if the holder abandoned his possession for ever so brief a time, a new comer acquired the right by turning a plank or slab, and of course frequent contentions arose over their respective claims. One might hold the right in person or by an agent, but there must in either case be a continuing personal presence on the platform night and day. On the west stream there was a desirable spot called "the eel trap." Its location was on the rocks or ledge on the east side of the west stream below the dam, and about half way to the eddy. Just below the "eel trap" was "the salmon rock," where that succulent fish was taken in great abundance. The fishermen scooped them with strong nets. Another desirable place was just below, or south of the P. C. Cheney paper-mill plant, where salmon and shad were caught, called "the setting place." It was a shelving ledge to the water of some ten feet or more, on which there was a solitary point where one could sit and fish. The first comer was entitled to the privilege until he caught a fish, when he was expected to yield to the next one in waiting, and there were often a dozen or more anxious waiters who took the right in the order of their coming. This law of the rock was well understood and was strictly observed, though we may easily conjecture that many disputes were liable to arise over the question of priority. The old rock doubtless still holds its place as in the olden time. A few rods south of this was a famous place called "the maple stump," for at one time there had been a maple tree there. It was several feet up from the water, and from this vantage-ground the salmon were taken with dip nets. Old Mr. Hardy usually held this place, for he was a famous fisherman of that day, and his son Reuben followed in his footsteps. At the eddy on the west side they drew seines for shad and they were caught almost by the ton.

Philip Stevens was widely known for his success in snaring pigeons at the corner of what is now known as Beech and Merrimack streets, near the present location of the free mission church. He had another stand near his house, probably near the

Universalist church on Lowell street. They were baited with oats and rye, or still better with buckwheat. The grain was scattered over a bed about fifteen feet square, and a large net was so arranged that when the birds were busily feeding he pulled a rope that drew the net over them. It was supplied with hooks that held to the ground, and in this way they were made captive. They were sold for a shilling per half dozen, tied together in half dozen bunches through the natural holes in their bills. Great clouds of these birds filled the sky in the harvest season, and there seemed to be no end of them. William Parker of Merrimack accumalated a snug fortune in this way, and for many years he was familiarly known as Pigeon Parker. James Harvell of West Manchester, who died about 1870, claimed a record of twenty-eight and one half dozen at one pull of the net.*

Before the Mammoth road was built the main thoroughfare from points north to Boston passed down the Merrimack valley through Hooksett, Amoskeag, Piscataquog, Merrimack, and Nashua, then known as Dunstable. Those were lively times indeed, for the turnpike was full of teams laden with all kinds of country produce, fish, game, and peltry for the Boston market, and return loads were brought from thence to supply the up-country trade. There were often from fifteen to twenty double teams together, and four and six horse teams were on the road continually. The inevitable tavern-stand dotted the way on an average of about two miles, and many of them were full of guests overnight. There were two of these hostelries in Hooksett. The Farmer stand at Amoskeag is still remembered, and is still standing. Then there was the McGregor tavern on the Butterfield place on the west side, where the Amoskeag stable now stands. There was one in Piscataquog on the rising ground south of the A. C. Wallace lumber mill and the Chandler hostelry on the River road in Bedford. There were two or three in Merrimack, one just outside, or north of Nashua, the Riddle place at Souhegan, and one at Bean hill. Another at Reed's Ferry was kept by Pigeon Parker. There was one at Thornton's

-----
*So stated by John K. McQuesten.

Ferry and another just below. Joe Mitchell kept a place on the west side of the river in Hooksett, and so on through the entire country.

We may be sure that there were innumerable rollickings, and jousts, and piquant stories without end around the old open fireplace, with plenty of flip and grog to cheer them on that we wot not of. I wish some one could give us a vivid picture garnished with stories that were rich, rare, and racy, and with incidents of that period. Col. Kidder is the oldest fireman in Manchester, for as early as 1829 he belonged to a hand-tub company in Piscataquog, handled by eighteen men ; John Parker was foreman. The little red engine-house stood about where West Hancock street intersects with South Main. In 1831, at the age of twenty years, Col. Kidder kept a country store on the site of the A. C. Wallace mill, in which he succeeded Gen. William P. Riddle. He was appointed postmaster by Gen. Jackson in 1834 and held the office for about six years, and he was also a member of the first city government in 1846. " Squog " was then a hamlet of considerable importance, for there was a tavern there and four country stores, and it was the head of navigation on the Piscataquog river. For many years there were from one to three lawyers located there, notably James McK. Wilkins, John Porter, and Jonas B. Bowman. In 1836 Hon. George W. Morrison opened an office on the west side in a small wooden schoolhouse near where the Amoskeag new mill now stands. There were locks in the river, remnants of which may still be seen near Riddle's island, and boats came up as far as the Wallace mill, where goods were unloaded into Mr. Kidder's store. These old river boats were sixty-five feet long, seven and one half feet wide, and three feet deep at the mast-board. By these boats a vast amount of merchandise came from Boston and was distributed in Bedford, Goffstown, Derryfield, Merrimack, Dunbarton, Weare, Hooksett, Hopkinton, Haverhill, Chichester, Bow, Concord, Sanbornton, Salisbury, Boscawen, Chester, and other points both near and remote from the river. A boat with a crew of three men made a round trip each week, carrying about fifteen tons, and the down cargoes were largely made up of choice lumber for the Boston market. Frederick G. Stark, Esq., has a valuable official record of the river traffic at this point as early as 1816-17, giving rates, cargoes, owners of boats, consignees, and other valuable information. We may well believe that the sturdy rivermen were no enthusiasts on the subject of the iron horse propelled by steam.

Remnants of the old canal, where these boats came to and from the locks, may still be seen on the east side of the river along the west wall of the Print Works.

# MANCHESTER SEMI-CENTENNIAL.

CONTRIBUTED TO MANCHESTER HISTORIC ASSOCIATION BY
H. W. EASTMAN AND FRED W. LAMB.

One of the most interesting features of the semi-centennial celebration of the incorporation of the city of Manchester, held on September 7, 8, and 9, 1896, was an historic and industrial exhibition held in The Kennard under the joint auspices of the Historic Association, the Art Association, and Electric Club. The exhibition was free to all, and thousands of visitors availed themselves of the rare opportunity to inspect an elaborate collection of relics, household utensils, and various articles, ancient and modern, illustrating the progress of Manchester during its fifty years of existence.

The Manchester Historic Association accepted an invitation from the city authorities to join in the exhibition, and its display was especially interesting and instructive.

Under the direction of President John C. French, E. P. Richardson, David Perkins, George F. Willey, and John Dowst, committee on exhibit, the loan of historic curiosities was solicited, and a generous response resulted. The committee appointed Mr. F. W. Lamb as general clerk and representative of the Association, who was ably assisted in the work by President French, H. W. Herrick, E. P. Richardson, F. B. Eaton, and others.

LIST AND DESCRIPTION OF ARMS ON EXHIBITION, BY FRED W. LAMB.

1. The "Molly Stark Cannon." This cannon is of brass and was cast at Paris, France, in 1747. It was brought to America as a part of the armament of the French army in Canada, commanded by General Montcalm, and it was captured at the battle of Quebec on the plains of Abraham by the English under General Wolfe. When General Burgoyne invaded the Colonies in 1777 the old gun was a part of the field artillery taken along, and when he sent Breymann to the aid of Baum at Bennington, the cannon was taken with him. When Breymann surrendered at Bennington, August 16, 1777, the gun came into possession of General John Stark. By him it was presented to the New Boston Artillery Company, then attached to the Ninth Regiment, New Hampshire Militia. It is a four-pounder and is three and one fourth inch bore. The following is the inscription on the gun. "Taken at the Battle of Bennington, August 16, 1777. Presented to New Boston Artillery Company, Ninth Regiment New Hampshire Militia, by General John Stark."

2. The "Old McGregor musket." This musket is exactly six feet long and was carried in the siege of Londonderry, Ireland, in 1688, by the Rev. James McGregor, the first pastor of Nutfield.

3. S. B. Kidder exhibited a cannon ball picked up at Fort Ticonderoga, N. Y.

4. Harrie M. Young exhibited a powder and ball pistol for percussion caps, a flintlock pistol, a Colt's navy revolver and a pirates boarding hook.

5. A. D. Scovell exhibited an old knapsack of horsehide captured from the British in the war of 1812.

6. Among the relics of General John Stark were a pair of saddle buckles worn by him at the Battle of Bennington, a powder horn presented to him by one of his soldiers and handsomely engraved, four old order and field accounts, a flask picked up on the battlefield of Bennington by him, a large iron camp kettle and a flintlock musket captured by him at the old French and Indian war.

7. George Emerson exhibited an old flintlock musket captured at Crown Point, November 7, 1760, by Jonathan Emerson.

8. John K. McQuestion exhibited an old sword captured in the French and Indian war by Mr. McQuestion's greatgrandfather.

9. Joseph Sawyer had a six-pound cannon ball that was plowed up at Bemis Heights.

10. H. O. Dudley exhibited the revolver, holster, and belt which he took from Major-General Roger A. Pryor when he captured him on the picket line, November 26, 1864. Also the sword he wore at the time.

11. Harrie M. Young exhibited the sword, scabbard, and flintlock pistol used by General Wilkinson during the Revolutionary war. He served under Arnold in the North, was at Trenton and Princeton and was appointed by Gates adjutant-general in 1777. In 1778 he became secretary of the board of war presided over by Gates. He resigned in 1779 in consequence of a quarrel with Gates, but was soon appointed clothier-general of the army. In 1791 he was appointed to the United States infantry and led an expedition against the Wabash Indians. He commanded Wayne's right at Maumee Rapids and was appointed general-in-chief in 1796. He was governor of Louisiana in 1805 - 06, given command of the Mississippi department in 1808, three years later he was court-martialed, but acquitted of complicity with Aaron Burr and of being in the pay of Spain. In 1813 he was made a major-general and sent north. His campaign was unsuccessful, mainly on account of Hampton's disagreement with him, and he was superseded. A court of inquiry exonerated him in 1815. The same year he was discharged from the army then being reorganized. The rest of his life was spent in Mexico.

12. John J. Bell estate of Exeter exhibited the pistols and holsters carried through the war of the Revolution by Major-General John Sullivan. He was a member of the first Continental Congress and through the darkest periods of the Revolutionary war he ranked among the ablest leaders of the American

armies. In the siege of Boston he was next in command to General Lee. When in the battle of Long Island, in 1776, General Greene was disabled by sickness, Sullivan was selected to command his division of the army. Serving afterward under the immediate supervision of Washington, General Sullivan was distinguished for his discretion and valor in the battles of Trenton, Princeton, Brandywine, and Germantown. In 1778, Washington and Count D'Estaing arranged for the French fleet to attack the British near Rhode Island, and Sullivan was sent with a large force to co-operate in besieging Newport. On the day appointed for the combined attack, a violent storm so shattered the French vessels that they withdrew from the contest. After defeating the English in one engagement, the American forces retired from Rhode Island. In 1779, Sullivan was sent with a large force into western New York, to take vengeance upon the hordes of Indians and Tories, who, besides other atrocities, had massacred the inhabitants of Wyoming and Cherry valleys. The savages were dispersed, many were killed, and their villages destroyed. In 1780, Gen. Sullivan resigned his commission, and returned to New Hampshire. He was afterwards governor of this state. He died at Durham.

13. D. Breed exhibited an ancient revolver.

14. Mrs. Luther S. Proctor exhibited a sword carried through the Revolutionary war.

15. H. W. Herrick exhibited the bugle of the First N. H. Light Battery, which was used through the civil war.

16. John H. Cilley exhibited the handsomely engraved sword used by Col. Cilley during the Revolutionary war, and also the elegant pair of flintlock pistols presented to him by vote of the New Hampshire legislature, for meritorious action during the war. I append a few extracts from his life by Gov. William Plumer, and published by Bradbury P. Cilley in 1891.

"In 1758 he enlisted as a private soldier under Captain Neal, who was attached to Major Rogers's battalion of Rangers, and marched to the northern frontier and Canada, and was then appointed a sergeant. He continued in the service more than a year.

"In 1774, when the political controversy between this country and Great Britain ran high, he publicly and zealously espoused the cause of his country ; and in the close of this and the beginning of the succeeding year, before the British had actually commenced hostilities, but after it was reduced to a moral certainty that the contest would terminate in war, he, with a number of others, went to the British fort in the harbor of Portsmouth, dismantled it, and removed the cannon, arms, and ammunition to places of safety in the country, which afterward proved of great value to the American army.

"As soon as intelligence reached him of the skirmish at Lexington of the 19th of April, 1775, he marched at the head of one hundred volunteers to headquarters at Cambridge, and promptly tendered his services to his country. He was appointed lieut.-colonel in the Revolutionary army, and in April, 1777, colonel of a regiment, and held the command during the war. Though he was a strict disciplinarian, his constant, unremitted attention to the comfort and care of his soldiers secured him their confidence and esteem. He was with the northern army, and fought bravely in the actions of the 19th of September and of the 7th of October, 1777. In the battle of Monmouth, in August, 1778, he displayed such bravery as merited, and he received, the approbation and thanks of the commander-in-chief. He distinguished himself in the perilous action, under Gen. Wayne, in storming and taking Stony Point. On the 20th of March, 1779, the New Hampshire House of Representatives unanimously presented him with an elegant pair of pistols, *as a token of the intention of the state to reward merit in a brave officer*, and on the 19th of June, 1781, the legislature appointed him a commissioner in behalf of New Hampshire, to repair to Rhode Island on the 25th of that month, to meet such commissioners as might be appointed by the other New England states, to agree upon a method of regularly sending supplies to the army during that year.

"After peace was established in 1783, he returned to his fam ily, and was afterwards appointed first major-general of the militia. He died in August, 1799.

17. Hiram Forsaith had a powderhorn dated 1763.
18. S. L. Flanders had a handsomely engraved powderhorn.
19. H. W. Herrick had two powderhorns of the dates of 1843 and 1845.
20. Ex-Gov. Frederick Smyth exhibited a small powderhorn.
21. Geo. W. Wilson had an old powderhorn which was carried through the French and Indian war.
22. Mrs. E. P. Richardson exhibited a powderhorn which was carried by her grandfather, James Harradon, at the battles of Lexington aud Bunker Hill. This horn has attached to it a broken suspender, used as a string to hold it in place at the wearer's side, and was attached to it on that morning in the long ago when James Harradon, a lad of sixteen, secured his father's musket, powderhorn, and bulletpouch, and left his home without his parents' knowledge, to take part in the battle of Lexington. He afterwards joined the Continental army in Boston, and assisted at the Battle of Bunker Hill.
23. W. L. Spaulding had one-half of a barshot picked up on the battlefield of Wilmington, South Carolina.
24. Miss Martha Poor Cilley exhibited the camp chest used by Col. Cilley at Valley Forge for medicines, etc., and carried through the Revolutionary war. Also, the orderbooks of Col. Cilley and Brig.-Gen. Enoch Poor at Valley Forge, and a small silver cup presented to Brig.-Gen. Enoch Poor by Lafayette. Enoch Poor was one of the foremost of the patriots of the state of New Hampshire during the dark days of the Revolution. He was appointed to command one of the three regiments sent out by the colony, joining the Continental army shortly after the battle of Bunker Hill. He took part in the Canadian movement in 1776, and then joined Washington with the main army in New Jersey. In 1777 he was promoted to the rank of brigadier-general. He took part in the battle of Stillwater, and led the attack at the battle of Saratoga. After the surrender of Burgoyne, he joined Washington near Philadelphia, and took part,

the next summer, in the battle of Monmouth. He was chosen, just before his death, to command one of the two light infantry brigades under Lafayette, but he died in September, 1780.

#### EXHIBIT UNDER CHARGE OF CAPT. J. N. BRUCE.

1. Capt. John N. Bruce exhibited his army sword, belt, sash, and hat with two bullet holes through it just where it came above his head, and his modern Templar sword.
2. Dr. C. W. Clement exhibited a flintlock gun, A. D. 1728.
3. J. R. Bruce exhibited three guns, among them being a Springfield and an Enfield rifle, one pistol, sword, and spear, used during the Mexican war, war club, two haversacks, two canteens, and a cartridge box.
4. E. P. Richardson exhibited a rebel lieutenant's sword and belt. The belt was made of card clothing, which shows how badly off the Confederacy was for leather.
5. H. W. Herrick exhibited one old gun, one powderhorn, and a surgeon's dress sword used during the civil war.
6. J. G. Lane exhibited Capt. Anderson's sword, dated 1840, belt, silk sash, and a flintlock gun of 1812.
7. Herbert Dunbar exhibited a Colt's cavalry revolver carried from 1861 to 1865.
8. Adjutant-General Ayling exhibited the Krag Jorgenson rifle, which is the new rifle just being issued to the United States army. Its caliber is 30, and it is adapted to the use of the new smokeless powder and a steel jacketed projectile. This projectile, when fired from this rifle with service ammunition, develops a speed of 2,000 feet per second, and its trajectory is so flat that for practical use as a military arm, no change in sight is necessary up to 400 yards. Its range is 2,000 yards, and with other explosives than a smokeless powder, the excessive fouling of the bore makes the arm unreliable, if fired without cleaning. In appearance, the weapon is unwieldy and awkward, and being of the bolt breech mechanism and box magazine type, has not yet, nor is it likely to, become a favorite with the infantry of the United States.

9. F. G. Walker exhibited an old flintlock gun, an old flintlock pistol, a pistol of five barrels, a canteen, powderhorn used in the Mexican war. Also, the sword used by Dick Barnes.

10. W. A. Spaulding exhibited one old Harper's Ferry flintlock gun of 1822.

11. William Heath exhibited one old Mississippi flintlock fowling piece.

12. Louis Bell Post, Grand Army, exhibited a large case of relics of the civil war, collected by members of the post.

13. Abner Hogg exhibited an old Revolutionary flintlock musket of 1776, and a bayonet of 1779.

14. The War Veterans exhibited guns and pistols.

15. Geo. W. Webster exhibited one of the 40,000 army muskets made at the Amoskeag shop in 1863, and also one of the two pistols made there.

16. Joseph B. Sawyer exhibited a machete, a knapsack saved from the fire when the old town house burned, and which belonged to the famous Stark guards, a belt, bayonet, and cartridge box.

17. Edward I. Partridge exhibited a Sharp's rifle.

18. S. H. Perry exhibited a knapsack used during the civil war.

19. W. H. Carpenter exhibited a Murland magazine rifle firing 18 shots.

20. Arthur C. Moore exhibited a Sharp's rifle, two spurs found at Gettysburg, two bayonets, two pistols, and a magnificent collection of 17 swords, embracing cutlasses, hangers, claymores, rapiers, cut and thrust and dress swords, and a fine specimen of the old Roman short sword, the use of which made the name of the Roman soldier feared throughout the then civilized world.

21. A. M. Scott exhibited a small piece of a silk flag carried through the war by him as sergeant and color-bearer in a Maine cavalry regiment. The battle-scarred piece of silk, bearing the colors of "Old Glory," was carried through many a hot action by Mr. Scott, and, as he says, he held it aloft on two different

occasions in passing across the city of New Orleans, La., during the dark days of '61 to '65.

22. There was also exhibited the flag which Ex-Gov. Smyth hung out in front of Smyth's block when Abraham Lincoln came here.

### INDIAN RELICS, ARMS, AND IMPLEMENTS.

1. Will H. Heath exhibited a fine collection of Indian relics, consisting of a large board, about two by three feet, completely covered by small arrow and spear points, one glass case of very small points, an obelisk covered with imperfect points, and a number of loose stone implements in another case, among which were two very fine totems, or charms, scalping knives, and tomahawks, gouges, and skinning tools, and a very fine, large black polisher.

2. S. B. Kidder exhibited a very fine collection of small arrow points on five large cards, an Indian bow and two arrows, and an Indian bowl.

3. Ex-Gov. Frederick Smyth made a very fine exhibit of arrow points, implements, and pottery, picked up at the "Willows." His collection is very rich in Indian pottery, there being many fine specimens on exhibition.

4. E. P. Richardson made a magnificent display of Indian relics, etc. This collection was picked up around Manchester, and embraces many fine specimens of pestles, war clubs, axes, hammers, polishing tools, etc. There was one very fine Indian pipe in this collection. He also exhibited two old Indian corn mills of stone. One is very large, being about a foot in diameter.

5. Nate M. Kellogg exhibited a very fine war club eighteen inches or more in length, which was plowed up on North Union street a few years ago.

6. W. H. Huse exhibited one small glass case containing some very fine arrow points.

7. The John J. Bell estate, of Exeter, made a fine exhibit, con-

sisting of six cards of arrow and spear points, and several large axes, war clubs, chisels, etc.

8. Gertrude H. Brooks exhibited an Indian pipe and six colored Indian drawings.

9. Mrs. Grafton had an interesting exhibit, consisting of a gun cover which belonged to Chief Joseph, and several poisoned arrows from the Custer battlefield.

# NEW HAMPSHIRE ELECTION SERMONS, 1784-1861.

Contributed to The Manchester Historic Association
by S. C. Gould.

| YEAR. | PREACHER. | DEGREE. | RESIDENCE | TEXT. |
|---|---|---|---|---|
| 1784 | Samuel McClintock, | D. D. | Greenland, | Jer. xviii. 7-10. |
| 1785 | Jeremy Belknap, | D. D. | Dover, | Ps. cxliv. 11-15. |
| 1786 | Samuel Haven, | D. D. | Portsmouth, | Matt. xxiv. 45-47. |
| 1787 | Joseph Buckminster, | D. D. | Portsmouth, | James i. 5. |
| 1788 | Samuel Langdon, | D. D. | Hamp. Falls, | Deut. iv. 5-8. |
| 1789 | Oliver Noble, | | Newcastle. | |
| 1790 | John C. Ogden, | A. M. | Portsmouth, | Neh. v. 19. |
| 1791 | Israel Evans, | A. M. | Concord, | Gal. v. 1. |
| 1792 | William Morrison, | D. D. | Londonderry, | Rom. xiii. 3. |
| 1793 | (No sermon preached). | | | |
| 1794 | Amos Wood, | A. B. | Weare, | Isaiah ix. 7, |
| 1795 | John Smith,* | A. M. | Hanover, | Isaiah xlvii. 8. |
| 1796 | William F. Rowland, | A. M. | Exeter, | 2 Sam. xxiii. 3. |
| 1797 | Stephen Peabody, | A. M. | Atkinson, | Ex. xviii. 21. |
| 1798 | Robert Gray, | A. M. | Dover, | Gen. xii. 2. |
| 1799 | Seth Payson, | D. D. | Rindge, | Eccl. ix. 18. |
| 1800 | Noah Worcester, | D. D. | Thornton, | Judges iii. 11. |
| 1801 | Jacob Burnap, | D. D. | Merrimac, | Ps. lxxxvii. 4-6. |
| 1802 | Joseph Woodman, | A. M. | Sanbornton, | Hosea, vii. 9. |
| 1803 | Aaron Hall, | A. M. | Keene, | 2 Chron. xix. 6. |
| 1804 | Nathaniel Porter, | D. D. | Conway, | 1 Chron. xii. 32. |
| 1805 | Reed Paige, | A. M. | Hancock, | Rom. xiii. 4. |
| 1806 | James Miltimore, | A. M. | Stratham, | Job xxix. 14. |
| 1807 | Nathan Bradstreet, | A. M. | Chester, | Luke vii. 4-5. |
| 1808 | Asa McFarland, | D. D. | Concord, | 2 Peter i. 19. |
| 1809 | William F. Rowland, | A. M. | Exeter, | Gal. v. 14. |
| 1810 | Roswell Shurtleff, | A. M. | Hanover, | Rom. xiii. 1-5. |
| 1811 | Thomas Beede, | A. M. | Wilton, | John vii. 1-5. |

* The sermon preached in 1795 was never printed.

| | | | | |
|---|---|---|---|---|
| 1812 | Moses Bradford, | A. M. | Francestown, | 1 Tim. i. 15. |
| 1813 | John H. Church, | D. D. | Pelham, | 2 Chron. xv. 2. |
| 1814 | Peter Holt, | A. M. | Epping, | Dan. ii. 44. |
| 1815 | David Sutherland, | | Bath, | Rev. i. 7. |
| 1816 | Pliny Dickinson, | | Walpole, | 2 Chron. xxiv. 2. |
| 1817 | Daniel Merrill, | A. M. | Nottingham W. | Matt. vi. 10. |
| 1818 | William Allen, | A. M. | Hanover, | Joshua i. 8. |
| 1819 | Nathan Parker, | D. D. | Portsmouth, | John viii. 12. |
| 1820 | James B. Howe, | A. M. | Claremont, | John ix. 29. |
| 1821 | Ephraim P. Bradford, | A. B. | New Boston, | Isaiah xxi. 11. |
| 1822 | Jonathan French, | A. M. | No. Hampton, | 2 Chron. i. 10. |
| 1823 | Daniel Dana, | D. D. | Londonderry, | Prov. xiv. 34. |
| 1824 | Bennet Tyler, | D. D. | Hanover, | Gen. xx. 11. |
| 1825 | Phineas Cooke, | A. M. | Acworth, | Matt. xxii. 21. |
| 1826 | Ferdinand Ellis, | A. M. | Exeter, | Ps. lxxxii. 6-7. |
| 1827 | Nath'l W. Williams, | A. M. | Concord, | Matt. vi. 10. |
| 1828 | Nathaniel Bouton | A. M. | Concord, | Luke xix. 13. |
| 1829 | Humphrey Moore, | A. M. | Milford, | 1 Cor. xii. 21. |
| 1830 | Jaazaniah Crosby, | A. M. | Charlestown, | Deut. xxviii. 1. |
| 1831 | Nathan Lord, | D. D. | Hanover, | 1 Cor. xiii. 5. |
| 1861 | Henry E. Parker, | A. M. | Concord, | Jer. xviii. 7-10. |

No sermons were delivered between 1831 and 1861, and none after 1861.

## CORRIGENDA.

The names of three men in the foot notes, page 34, of the address delivered by George C. Gilmore, were accidentally omitted in copying, viz.:

McGilvary, William, Merrimack.
Moore, James, Merrimack.
Hutchinson, Alexander, Londonderry.   Transferred to the artillery, June 7, 1775.

# HON. SAMUEL BLODGET.

## THE PIONEER OF PROGRESS IN NEW ENGLAND.

A SKETCH BY GEORGE WALDO BROWNE READ BEFORE THE MANCHESTER HISTORIC ASSOCIATION, JUNE 16, AND DEC. 15, 1897.

Samuel Blodget, or Bloggett, as the name was then spelled, was born in Woburn, Mass., April 1, 1724, at a time when the American colonies, in addition to the privations and hardships of founding their scattered homes in the wilderness of a new country, were entering on the last half of what might not inappropriately be styled a Hundred Years' War, covering the most eventful period in the history of New England from the supremacy of King Philip, in 1662, to the Conquest of Canada, which ended the French and Indians Wars and brought the Peace of Paris, in 1763.

The old house in which his parents lived was torn down years ago, and no sign is left to tell where it stood, though there are sufficient records to denote nearly the site, which was on what is now known as the "Dow Farm," situated on the north side of Railroad Street, easterly from the central point of the city and a little more than five minutes' walk from the Public Library building. The Blogget estate at that time consisted of between thirty and forty acres of fertile land.

If one's progenitors count for aught the subject of this biography was especially fortunate, for it is difficult to find stronger branches of ancestry than those forming the tree of

## THE BLODGET GENEALOGY.

1. Thomas Bloggett, who is the first of the family of whom we have a clear record, was born in Western England, probably in County of Cornwall, in 1605, married Susan or Susanna ———, born in 1598, and came to America in the "Increase from London," 1635, with his wife and two sons, Daniel and Samuel. He was a glover by occupation and settled at Cambridge; died in 1642, leaving, besides the sons named, a daughter Susanna, born June 1637, and a son Thomas, b. 7th August, 1639.*

2. Samuel Bloggett, 2d son of Thomas, was born in England, in 1633, and was brought to this country by his parents when he was 18 months old. He married, Dec. 13, 1655, Ruth Iggleden, of Boston; died July 3, 1687, and his wife d. Oct. 14, 1703. Their children were (1) Ruth, born Dec. 28, 1656; (2) Samuel, b. Dec. 10, 1658; (3) Thomas, b. Feb. 26, 1661, who married Rebecca Tidd, Nov. 11, 1685; (4) Susanna, b. ——— — ———, m. to James Simonds, Dec. 29, 1685; (5) Sarah, b. Feb. 17, 1668; (6, 7) Martha and Mary, twins, b. Sept. 15, 1673. Martha m., in 1696, Joseph Winn.

3. Samuel, Jun., b. Dec. 10, 1658, m. April 30, 1683, Huldah, daughter of William and Judith (Hayward-Phippen) Simonds, b. Nov. 20, 1660. (Huldah was a sister to the James who married two years later Susanna Bloggett.) Samuel, Jun., who became known as Ensign Bloggett and who represented Woburn in the General Court, in 1693, died Nov. 5, 1743, and his wife died March 14, 1745-6. Among their children was

4. Caleb, b. Nov. 11, 1691, m. (1st) Sarah Wyman (3), b. Jan. 17, 1690-1. She was a sister of Ensign Seth Wyman, who was in "Lovewell's Fight" and in command of the company after Captain Lovewell was killed. Their children were (1) Seth S., b. Feb. 20, 1718; (2) Caleb, b. Dec. 1, 1721;

---

* His widow married James Thompson, of Woburn, 15th February, 1643-4; and his daughter Susanna m. Jonathan, son of the above-mentioned James Thompson, sen. Jonathan died 20th Octobor, 1691, and his wife 6th of February, 1697-8. (?) This couple had eight children, the 2d, Jonathan, Jun., b. 28th September, 1663, m. Frances Whittemore, by whom he had nine children, the 6th being Ebenezer, b. 30th March, 1701, m. 27th September, 1728, Hannah Converse. They had four children, the eldest being Benjamin, b. 27th November, 1729, who married Ruth Simonds of Woburn, whose son Benjamin, b. 26th March, 1753, became in after years widely known as Sir Benjamin Thompson and Count Rumford. The father of Sir Benjamin died 7th November, 1755, in his 26th year, while he (Sir Benjamin) died at his villa in Auteuil, near Paris, August 21, 1814, in his 62d year. James Thompson was a member of the first board of selectmen of Woburn.

(3) Samuel, b. April 1, 1724; (4) Susanna, b. June 19, 1727. Caleb m. (2) Elizabeth Wyman,* 2d cousin of Sarah, by whom he had a daughter, Elizabeth, b. Oct. 27, 1744.

## MEMORANDA OF THE WYMAN FAMILY.

1. Lieut. John Wyman was born in England, but was a subscriber at Charlestown to Town Orders for Woburn, Mass., Dec., 1640, and was taxed at Woburn, 1645, married Nov. 5, 1644, Sarah, daughter of Myles Nutt, dying May 9, 1684. Among their children was
2. Seth, born August 3, 1663, m. Dec. 17, 1685, Esther, daughter of Major William Johnson (3). He, who was known as Lieut. Seth Wyman, d. Oct. 26, 1715. Among their children was†
3. Sarah, born Jan. 17, 1690-1, who m. Caleb Bloggett (4) and was the mother of Samuel Blodget.

## MEMORANDA OF THE JOHNSON FAMILY.

1. Captain Edward Johnson, born in England, 1599, married Susan, or Susanna ———, who was b. in England, in 1597. He died at Woburn, Mass., April 23, 1672, and she in 1690. Among their children was
2. Major William, born in England, 1629 or 1630; died at Woburn, May 22, 1704. He m. at Woburn, May 16, 1655, Esther, daughter of Thomas Wiswall, a ruling elder of the church at Newton, Mass. They had
3. Esther, born April 13, 1662; m. Dec. 17, 1685, Lieut. Seth Wyman (2) she being Samuel Blodget's grandmother. She died March 3, 1742.

(*Note.* Authorities consulted for these genealogies : Sewall's History of Woburn; Wyman's Charlestown Genealogies and Estates ; Woburn Records.)

The heroic part, performed by the Wymans in the early history of the colonies is too well known to need mention here, while the Johnsons were not less distinguished for their bravery and mental capacity. It was to one of them, Edward Johnson, belonged the authorship of that notable narrative, "Wonder-Working Providence of Zion's Savior in New England," which

---

\* Daughter of Thomas Wyman (2) and granddaughter of Francis Wyman (1) who was a brother of Lieut. John.
† Ensign Seth Wyman, as he became known, was a son of this couple, b. Sept. 13, 1686; died in September, 1725, from effects of blood poison. (See Kidder's History of Lovewell's Fight.)

has been so frequently quoted by the writers of colonial days. He was a representative from Woburn for twenty-seven years, and a Speaker of the House in 1655. Nor were the Bloggetts behind these families as earnest and efficient defenders of the settlements against the depredations of the prowling beasts and savage denizens of the wildwood, or as upright, far-seeing citizens in those brief intervals of peace, which came so rarely like rays of sunlight struggling through the clouds on a rainy season, helping to lay the foundation and rear the pillars of that self-government which was to be the strength of a nation in after years.

Ensign Samuel Blogget was a man of prominence in the affairs of his time, having served one year in the General Court, as has been mentioned. One of his sons, William, an uncle to the subject of our sketch, was a soldier under Major William Tyng in his expedition to Canada during the summer of 1709.* Caleb Blogget, the father of Samuel, was a Captain of the Militia and a man of importance in town, which is shown by his appointment as one of the three trustees chosen by Woburn to receive and portion out its share of the $60,000 loan raised by the State to remedy the scarcity of money then prevailing. Captain Caleb Blogget was active in securing grants allowed by the Massachusetts court in New Hampshire and he was among

---

\* Mass. Archives, Military, 1704-1711. Vol. 71, page 635.
Received Sept : 25, 1709, Twenty Shillings of Mr. Samuel Blogget of Woburne onaccount of his son William Blogget who lay sick in the Queens Service at the house of Mr. Bond in Watertown under the command of Major Tyng. I say received by mee. PHILIP SHATTUCK,
Physician.

Mass. Archives, Vol. 71, page 735.
To his Exelency The Governour, Her Majesties Councill and Representatives in General Court assembled.
The petition of Samuel Blogget of Woobourn Humbly Sheweth that your petitioners son of William Blogget was taken Sick at wattertown while he was in Her Majesties Service under command of Majr: William Tyng in the Expedition for Canada ye last sumer, Viz 1709 and after he had lain Sick sum time there, Majr Tyng was pleased to order me to take my son whome to my house : and thinking he might be better lookt after there than where he was :, so J took him whome And found nursing and watchers for him for the space of three weeks and J paid Doctor Philip Shattuck twenty shillings for Physick for my said son while he was Sick at water Town ; for which J have had no Consideration, as yet, which is the Occasion of my moving at this time for such allowance as may be thought proper for me in the Matter the which being Granted will ingage me as J am in duty bound to pray &c. : for you
Your humble petitioner and servant SAMUEL BLOGGET.
June ye 7th 1710
This May Certify whome it may Concern that William Blogget a souldjer De-

the grantees of the township of Washington, which, however, failed to prove very profitable to the early proprietors. He was also concerned in the claims of a grant of land in the Merrimack valley partly covered by Tyng Township, and he was afterwards prominent in the affairs of this unfortunate grant.*

Coming of such stock and reared amid the rugged scenes of those trying times, it is little wonder that Samuel Blodget gave early promise of those sturdy qualities which were to make him an important factor in the development of the natural resources not only of his native town but of that belt of productive country from whence the busy Merrimack receives its vast power, and which it has returned to its employers with wonderful increase, largely due to his inventive genius and untiring energy. August 23, of the year of his birth, that memorable assault was made by the colonists of northern New England under the leadership of Captains Moulton and Harman, of York, Me., upon the Jesuit stronghold at Norridgewock, when Pére Rasle, the priest, and 80 of his Indian followers were killed and the mission destroyed. Though the Indians continued their predatory incursions against the settlers, often with fatal results, for another year, this overthrow of the Jesuits, followed by Lovewell's expedition against the Indians and rout of the Pickwackets, culminated in the treaty of peace signed by the Abnaki chiefs at Boston on December 15, 1725,† thus giving to the overtried colonists the longest interval of comparative rest from contest that they knew during that century of conflict.

It was during this period of cessation from hostilities that

---

tained in Her Majesties Service, under my Command in ye year 1709 being Sick at Watertown, was by my orders Comitted to his father Samuel Blogget of Woburn; who Carried hime whom to his house, and provided a nurse and watcherst for him for the space of three weeks.
    June ye 8th 1710                                                          Wm TYNG.
                                  [Endorsed.]
Jn the House of Representatives June 28: 1710. Read and Comitted & Jn answer to the within Petition.
    Resolved That the sum of fiffty Shillings be Alowed and Paid out of the publick Treasurey to Samuel Blogget the Petitioner
        Sent up for concurrence
Jn Councill                                                     JOHN CLARK Speaker.
June ult. 1710.
    Read and concur'rd                                   JAS ADDINGTON Secry.

\* State Papers, Vol. XXIV, page 158; Proprietors' Records of Tyng Township.
† Mass. Archives.

young Blodget passed his boyhood days. For the first time the inhabitants of Woburn had been able to give thoughtful attention to the matter of schools, and he received the rudiments of his education while the moving school system of the town was in its most popular stage, if a method intended to satisfy all and meeting the full expectations of none could be called "popular" at any period of its existence. But it was the best that could be done under the times and circumstances, and by its arrangements the town was enabled to have an average schooling of about two months in each of its half dozen districts. Samuel, when in his teens, was thus brought under the instruction of those well-known and popular Masters of the Three Rs (to say nothing of the fourth, the Rod), James Fowle and Ebenezer Flegg.* The latter was afterwards the noted pioneer minister of Chester, N. H. There can be no doubt of his aptness as a scholar, or that he improved every opportunity to acquire an education, thus obtaining more than an average knowledge of mathematics and philosophy, with a proficiency in penmanship that few could equal. Naturally of a studious, speculative bent of mind his application to study did not cease with the passing of his school days but continued through life, his text-book the great volume of observation and his master that stern disciplinarian—experience.

If the treaty of the Abnakis remained inviolate by them— and who knows of a covenant that they broke — the trouble between the English and the French began to foment, breaking out afresh in 1744, in what became known as "King George's War," during which the New England colonists, on June 17, 1745, won that remarkable military surprise the capture of Louisburg, that French stronghold on the island of Cape Breton styled respectively by friends and enemies as the Dunkirk and Gibraltar of America.

In this active campaign the name of Samuel Blodget appears for the first time in public papers, though until the rolls of the

---

* With the Chester records the spelling of this name, which had been Flegg until then, became Flagg, and has so continued since. He was settled in Chester as minister, June 23, 1736.

## HON. SAMUEL BLODGET. 127

gallant men who conceived and carried out the audacious undertaking have been found and consulted, the capacity in which our hero served must remain in conjecture.* It seems to be the impression of those who have written of him that, judging by his subsequent career, he was connected with the commissary department.† As he was never what could be strictly termed " a fighting man," this deduction seems very plausible. Still it should not be forgotten that he was barely past his twenty-first birthday, with the " fire of youth " in his veins, and that he was not lacking in those qualities which would incite him to more active duties and the storm of battle, that taking into consideration the fact that thirty years later he stood musket in hand with the bravest of the brave on the sanguinary field of Bunker Hill,‡ is it not more than probable that by the side of his friends he scaled the ramparts of Louisburg?

Upon his return from the Louisburg campaign, having then reached his majority, he naturally looked for some means by which to earn his livelihood. He was not needed at home, and seeking the excitement of new fields, he went to Haverhill, Mass., where he engaged in traffic on the Merrimack between that city and Newburyport.

Samuel Blodget's business must have proved quite profitable, for at the last sale of land lying between what is now Water Street and the river, in 1751, he bought a lot for a wharf. The same year he also bought a farm in what was then Goffstown, but which later became a part of Manchester, N. H. This farm, which contained 317 acres, was situated on the south bank of Black Brook and about two miles west of Amoskeag village, between the Dunbarton and Goffstown roads. The

---

* Several Woburn men, among them Jonas Wyman, a relative, who died during the siege of Cape Breton. were in the company of Captain ―― Stevens of Andover, 2d (?) Mass. Reg. commanded by Col. Samuel Waldo, and it seems very probable that Samuel Blodget was with them. This, unfortunately, is one of the companies whose records cannot be found. See Hon. Chas. Hudson's list of soldiers published in the N. E. His-Gen. Reg. XXIV, 357-380; XXV, 249-269. From Mr. Hudson's list I find that Samuel's brother Caleb belonged to the 9th Mass. Reg., Col. Joseph Dwight commander, 9th company, Gershom Davis, Captain. A Nathan Blodgett belonged to the 8th company of this regiment, Captain Peter Hunt.

† An idea originating with Judge Potter and adopted by others.

‡ Chase's History of Haverhill, Mass.

house was one of the first built in town, and was a large, old-styled farmhouse standing under a row of stately elms in later years. This historic residence eventually became a prey to fire, and the second dwelling raised over its cellars was also burned, July 6, 1885. The site of these houses are still plainly seen, though the old elms are gone. Just what attracted him to this place is not known, but no doubt his speculative mind had anticipated the profit likely to accrue from dealing in the pine lumber which grew so bountifully in this vicinity. There was no mill in Goffstown at that time and we soon find him planning to have one constructed.

December 29, 1748, he married Miss Hannah White, daughter of Nicholas White of Plaistow, N. H., but then situated in the Haverhill District. Mr. White had served in the Louisburg expedition, and was a man of considerable prominence at the time. His brothers-in-law, Obadiah and John Ayers were among the proprietors of early Concord, N. H.

### THE WHITE GENEALOGY.

1. William White, b. in England in 1610, came to Ipswich, Mass., in 1635, moved to Newbury the same year. In 1640 removed to Haverhill, being one of the first settlers of that town, and was one of the grantees of the Indian deed of Haverhill, dated November 15, 1642, said instrument it was said was both written and witnessed by him. He married Mary ———, who died February 22, 1681. He died September 28, 1690.
2. John, only child of William and Mary White, was b. 1640; m. in Salem November 25, 1662, Hannah French. He died January 1, 1669. She m. (2) Thomas Philbrick of Hampton, N. H.
3. John, Jr., only child of John and Hannah (French) White, was b. March 8, 1664 ; m. October 24, 1687, Lydia, dau. of Hon. John and Elizabeth (Treworthy) Gilman of Exeter, N. H., and a granddaughter of Edward Gilman, who came from Norfolk, England, 1638, with five children, to settle first in Hingham, Mass., second in Ipswich, and then, 1650, in Exeter. Captain John White owned and commanded a garrison house in Haverhill, Mass. He died Nov. 20, 1727.
4. Nicholas, the sixth of the 14 children of John, was b. in

Haverhill, Mass., Dec. 4, 1698; m. (1) Hannah, dau. of Samuel Ayers, who was killed by Indians in 1708. She d. January 25, 1732. He m. (2) Mary Calfe of Ipswich, and d. April 7, 1782.

5. Hannah, 2d child of Nicholas and Hannah White, was b. in what is now Plaistow, N. H., September 8, 1726, m. Samuel Blodget December 29, 1748.

With their second child a baby of a few months of age, he and Mrs. Blodget moved to their new home in a comparative wilderness soon after its purchase, though he did not abandon his interests in Haverhill. This was about four months before the granting of the Derryfield charter, though his farm did not come within the territory of the new township.

It soon proved that he had chosed an unpropitious time to begin farming, if he had any serious intentions of making that his occupation, for he had barely got his family settled here before the period of peace the pioneers had been enjoying ended, and what became known as the French and Indian War began.

Always among the first to offer his services he joined the New Hampshire regiment of five hundred men under Colonel Joseph Blanchard of Dunstable, and upon the organization of the expedition against Crown Point in 1755 he became sutler. In passing it is worthy of note that this regiment consisting of three companies commanded by Captains John Goffe and John Moore of Derryfield, and Robert Rogers of Starktown (now Dunbarton) was raised in this vicinity. The last named company, in which John Stark was a lieutenant, was chiefly employed in ranging and reconnoitring and soon became known as "The Rangers," being the original of what evolved into that redoubtable battalion of Indian fighters widely known as "Rogers' Rangers," and without which a different fate must have awaited the New England colonists.

While this expedition through a series of singular circumstances failed to accomplish the object of the campaign, the gallant defense against the attacks of the French and Indians under Baron Dieskau on the shore of Lake George and the complete tout of the allied foes, raised the sinking hopes of the colonists and revived the courage of the English at home.

In the autumn Colonel Johnson, after having erected what was called Fort William Henry, disbanded his forces, with the exception of 600 men retained to guard the works, Rogers and his Rangers being among them.

The battle between the English and the French took place September 8, and it would seem that Samuel Blodget must have come home soon after, for we then find him engaged in trade in Boston, as well as the projector of a little enterprise connected with the recent engagement at Lake George. In the issue of *The Boston Gazette, or Country Journal* of December 22, 1755, we find the following advertisement:

### THIS DAY PUBLISH'D,

And sold by SAMUEL BLODGET, at the South End of *Boston*, near the Sign of the Lamb, and opposite to Capt. *Smith's*. A prospective plan of 2 of the Engagements the *English* ha with the *French* at *Lake George*, on the 8th of *September*, 1755; exhibiting to the Eye a very lively as well as just Representation of them; together with a Part of the Lake, the Camp, the Situation of each Regiment, with the Disadvantages attending them: The Appearance of the *Canadians, Indians* and Regulars, as they made their Approach to the Brest-works; the Form of the Land and the Enemy; together with the Advantage they had in their Ambuscade against Col. *Williams*. As also a PLAN of *Hudson's River* from *New York* to *Albany;* with such Marks as will be of great Service to *Navigation:* Likewise the River and Waggon Road from *Albany* to *Lake George*; together with a plan and Situation of each of the Forts that have been lately built. All which is carefully and neatly struck off from a large Copper Plate.

N. B. There will be sold with each Plan a printed Pamphlet with Explanatory Notes, containing a full, tho' short History of that important Affair from the Beginning to the End of it.

☞ The above Map, together with the Pamphlets, may be had of the Printers thereof.

The pamphlet referred to was a quarto of six pages, entitled "A Prospective Plan of the Battle near Lake *George*, on the Eighth Day of *September*, 1755. With an Explanation thereof;

Containing a full, tho' short History of that important Affair. By *Samuel Blodget*, Occasionally at the Camp, when the Battle was fought. Boston; New England. Printed by *Richard Draper*, for the Author. MDCCLV."*

An edition of this pamphlet was brought out in London by T. Jefferys in 1756. But it must soon have become scarce here, for in Thomas' "History of Printing" (second volume, second edition) it is stated that "Blodget's plan is rarely met with."

A second expedition being planned for the capture of Crown Point in 1757, Mr. Blodget again enlisted and was attached to the New Hampshire regiment under Colonel Goffe, who, after making his memorable march through the wilderness by the way of old Number Four (now Charlestown, N. H.) to join General Webb at Albany, N. Y., was stationed at Fort William Henry under the command of Colonel Munro of the British regulars and the Provinicial troops. The important duty of sutler of the garrison was assigned to him immediately upon his arrival, and he held the position until the unfortunate closing of the defense of the garrison.

The importance of possessing this post, which was the key to the battlegrounds of that part of America, had already awakened the Marquis de Montcalm, commander of the allied forces of the enemy, to active plans in that direction. The winter before an unsuccessful attack had been made, its failure being due to the alertness and effective action of Rogers and his Rangers. But Lord Loudon had so far withdrawn his troops from the proper defense of the colonists that the auspicious time for the French commander to act seemed to have come. Quick to improve an advantage he proceeded up the lake toward Colonel Munro's little garrison. With the customary pusillanimity or cowardice of the British commanders in America at that time, General Webb, who then commanded the army in the region of Lake George, actually retreated to Fort Edward, leaving the objective point of the French and their allies,

---

\* A copy of this rare pamphlet is now in the possession of the Massachusetts Historical Society, which also has another pamphlet with a *fac simile* of the plan and explanatory remarks by Samuel A. Green, M. D., to whom I wish to acknowledge my indebtedness for these facts.

both numbering fully eight thousand men, defended by less than one-fourth of the number of the enemy.

Still, with full confidence that Webb, who was less than fifteen miles away with 6000 men, would come to his assistance in ample time to save him, Col. Munro prepared as best he could for his defense. Montcalm came, and for six days the brave Scotchman in command of Fort William Henry made a resistance as only he could have done supported by such men as came recruited from the clans of the Frazers, McKenzies, the Campbells and Grants, with the heroic Rangers of the Merrimack under the lead of Rogers. Disheartened but not daunted by the prolonged failure of Webb to appear, the inevitable was submitted to with as good grace as possible, until the last grain of powder had been burned, cannon bursted and the fortress no longer tenable. Montcalm, with that gracious manner so natural to him, promised the broken spirited Munro that he should be allowed to depart in peace with his men, on the condition they should not take up arms for 18 months. Nothing else could be done, and the battle-worn veterans marched out of the garrison, stocked their guns, and in an orderly manner started toward Fort Edward to seek refuge with their unfaithful commander.

So far Montcalm had acted the part of a magnanimous commander, but even he had not counted on the result. He had gained the consent of his red allies to accompany him by promise of shares in the plunder. Then, the moment they saw they had been robbed of their reward, they began to manifest an uneasiness. One more greedy than prudent rushed forward to snatch a shawl from one of the women, and then another sought to get possession of a soldier's cap. Resistance was made, when in the midst of the struggle a painted chief leaped upon a stump in the centre of the clearing and gave the wild warwhoop of the Huron! Its echo had not died away on the distant hillsides before the unarmed troops were attacked right and left. In vain Col. Munro called and emplored for protection from his French conquerors. If Montcalm had acted a noble part in the terms of capitulation, he showed the opposite now. Perhaps he knew better than the others his helplessness to succor the hapless men and women, who were slaughtered like dumb creatures on every hand.

It so happened that the New Hampshire men were in the rear and thus received the brunt of the massacre, dying like the brave men they were. Of the two hundred eighty fell victims to this inhuman treatment. The stories of the escapes of those who were fortunate enough to save their lives equalled in startling interest the inventions of the boldest romancer.

Among the unfortunates was Samuel Blodget, and like his companions having no means of defense he improved an opportunity to break through the yelling horde and reach the shore of Lake George, when he concealed himself under a batteau, until he deemed it safe to leave his place of concealment. Silence had settled upon the awful scene, where the dead lay strewn like driftwood on the banks of some overflowing torrent, but it proved the cunning red men still lingered about the desolate grounds. It may have been in the hope of finding some of the fugitives, for the moment he showed himself he was pounced upon by several Indians and quickly overpowered.

In their eagerness for plunder the savages swiftly tore the clothes from his person, intending then to put him to the torture. But the captors had counted "without their host." The captive slipped from their clutches, and running swiftly to the edge of the lake sprang into the water before they could recover so as to give effectual pursuit. After swimming a long distance, and then making a painful journey through the forest, he finally reached Fort Edward on the third day.

One of Mr. Blodget's biographers,* who has been largely quoted by all others in speaking of him, was inclined to the belief that soon after his escape from "the Massacre at Fort William Henry" he established himself in business at Boston. He was there for a short time, but returned to the army the following spring, and he remained at Fort Edward for nearly a year, as witness the following order, the original of which is in Wo-

---

* Judge Potter.

burn, Mass., Public Library, contributed to it by Dr. Samuel A. Green, Librarian of the Massachusetts Historical society:

"Camp at Lake George,
" October ye 4th 1758

"Sir:

Pleas to Deliver to Ephraim Severns a soldier In my Company In Col. Nichols Regiment, to ye Value of four Shillings, Lawful money out of your Stores, which I Promise to Stop out of his Pay on the Rools for you, for which this Shall Be your Voucher.

"EPHRAIM WESSON, Capt.

"To Mr. Samuel Blodget, Qr. Master.
"195   (Endorsed)

" EPHRAIM SEVERNS."

This shows that he held the commission of Quartermaster at the time, while the following statement from the Diary of Lieut. Samuel Thompson and Woburn Men in the French and Indian Wars shows the esteem with which he was looked upon by his fellow men:

"I Isaac Merriam at Fort Edward fell in sick Some Time in July & had a permitt to Com Down to albany In Company with a Number of other sick and at my arrival Did Apply to Comasary of the Kings Hospital for my Self & others was Refused. But Mr. Blodget arrived at Albany we all apply to him who Supplied us with Nessariys we wanted to our Great joy & Satisfac'n and did continue so to do Till I Left albany the 20th of October and of the Opinion that Great numbers would have suffered had it not ben for Mr. Blodget Supply, their being for Sum Time Neither Doc or Officer to Do anything for us & the Sick Sent almost every week and in Great Numbers———& for Near a Month Before I came away had Recovered so far as to becom helpful for Coming Necesssry to the poor helpless Creatures and always found m Blodget Ready & willing to Supply me with sutch things as I went for.

" ISAAC MERRIAM.

"Suffolk SS. Boston March 14 1760.

"The above Named Isaac Marion Personaly appeared and made Solemn oath that the above declaration by him Subscribed is Just and True.

" Coram John Phillips
"Just. Pacis."

It is shown by the above papers that he was on the frontier as late as October, 1758, but it is probable that soon after he returned to his home, where he remained that winter. But the following spring he appears in Boston, engaged in the ready made clothing business, as shown by a receipt signed by Messrs. Chase and Russell, in May, 1759.* December 10, 1759, from an advertisement in the Gazette we learn that he was a trader on Marlborough Street, where he sold English goods, sugars, hats, etc., and also where "Officers and soldiers who have lately been discharged, may be supplied at the lowest Price, till their Muster-Rolls are made up," proving that he had relations still with the army.

Having seen enough of military life to satisfy him for a time, at least, he now gave his undivided attention to business, entering at once upon that career of success which won for him a wide-spread acquaintance and confidence of people. Not satisfied with doing one thing at a time, with that versatile capacity of his which seemed almost unbounded in its scope, he started into other branches of business, starting in September of the same year that he went to Boston one of the first "pot and pearl ash works" in the country at Haverhill, Mass., on the bank of Mill Brook. Taking in as a partner Mr. John Greene, of Haverhill, and finding the works extremely lucrative, he extended the business to Goffstown, New Boston and Hampstead, N. H. Haverhill was becoming a trading centre and foreseeing the profit likely to come from furnishing supplies to his workmen, as well as to the public at large, in 1765 he established a general store at Haverhill, and placed it in charge of Mr. Nathaniel Walker, Jr. This store was continued for seven years, or until 1772. Already he had begun in the lumber traffic and finding that profitable, January 10, 1765, he built a saw mill at Black Brook so as to manufacture his lumber himself. Buying a little later in the year large tracts of timber land in Goffstown and Hooksett, he soon after opened a general store in the former town. Still retaining his clothing business in Boston he may be said to have been at the height of his success as a business man.

At this time we find that he had interests and influence in

---

* Potter.

still another direction, for in 1764 his name, with those of his sons, then all minors, Samuel, Jr., Nathan, Caleb, and William, were among the grantees of Franconia.

In addition to the branches of business already mentioned he entered quite successfully into the fur trade, making large and frequent shipments to London of furs, pot and pearl ashes, Sir William Baker, Lord John Havergal and others of equal note being among his customers. His merchandise was exchanged for these commodities and thus he realized a double profit on all he handled. His lumber found a ready market in Haverhill and Newburyport, whence he moved it by river transit, running it over the falls at high water, or drawing it past those places by team. At this time, bearing the extra cost of this way of transport, he doubtless foresaw the great benefit likely to come from a system of canals on the Merrimack, though there is nothing to show that he contemplated then that which was to prove the master work of his long and energetic life.*

Speaking of him at this period Judge Potter said: "He became widely known throughout the country as a merchant of energy and great probity,—and by means of such extensive acquaintance was able afterwards to accomplish undertakings beyond the means of ordinary men. The people of Boston placed great confidence in him, and he was on terms of intimacy with some of the most distinguished citizens."

The truth of this wholesome flattery was borne out by the fact that he was chosen chairman of two committees of importance at a meeting of its voters of Boston, in Fanueil hall, March 14, 1768.

In 1769, after ten years of business in Boston, with the exception of about ten months in 1764 when he was in Medford, he sold out there and moved his family back to Goffstown, where he continued to carry on his other enterprises with renewed vigor. It is easy to imagine that he at once obtained a high place in society, and from his genial, courteous, enthusias-

---

* Mr. Everett, in his sketch of Samuel Blodget, says: "The idea once grasped by him became the ruling passion of his later years. But the breaking out of the Revolution prevented the consummation of his scheme at that time, though it was simply postponed, not abandoned."

tic manner became very popular. He was among the richest, if not the richest man, in this vicinity, and with interests so broad and widely scattered, for those times, took his natural position as a leading citizen.

In 1770 the governor appointed him Collector of the Excise of the Province of New Hampshire, and notwithstanding the general disfavor from the people that these officers met elsewhere, he retained the confidence and friendship of the public through two terms of the ardous duties of the position. Some thing of the straightforwardness of his character, as well as his method of procedure, is illustrated by the following petition, the original of which is still among the state papers :

Province of New Hampshire.

To his Excellency, John Wentworth, Esquire, Captain Genera and Commander in Chief, in and over His Majesty's Prov ince of New Hampshire, and to the Honourable, his Ma jesty's Council for said Province :—

Humbly shews Samuel Blodget collector of the Excise of the said Province of New Hampshire for the present year. That during the last year he was collector of the Excise and that sundry persons who had sold spirituous liquors, drew out their Accounts in a very loose uncertain manner and made application to Richard Jenniss, Esquire, who administered oathes to them in such a loose way that the oath only included what they had sold during eleven months of the time without mentioning what had been sold by other persons by and under Them, and afterwards deducted Twenty per cent. out of what they had sold which makes near Eighty per cent. allowance for wastage, &c. instead of the twent per cent. allowed by law ; and one of these persons so sworn before said Jenniss and paid the Excise accordingly : by means of all which, Your Petitioner Humbly apprehends if the said Jenniss is suffered to continue swearing Those Sellers of Spirituous Liquors that his Majesty's revenue will be greatly Diminished and the Excise of the Government Rendered of very little value, wherefore your Petitioner most Humbly prays that your Excellency and Honors would take the matter under your wise consideration and Recommend to said Jenniss not to administer the oath to any person respecting their Excise for the present year, or to make such other order or determination thereon as to your Excellency and Honors in

your great wisdom, shall seem best and your petitioner will ever pray, &c. SAMUEL BLODGET.
Portsmouth, March the 13th 1771.

Governor Wentworth carrying into effect, in 1771, his plan of dividing the province into five counties, named Rockingham, Strafford, Hillsborough, Cheshire and Grafton, all so called in honor of dignitaries of the old country, Samuel Blodget received a commission as Justice of the Inferior Court of Common Pleas for the County of Hillsborough, which he held until the end of the king's power over the province and the consequent dissolution of the provincial courts of justice. At this distant day it is difficult to realize the feeling of prejudice the colonists were then beginning to bear against those who held offices under the crown, and therefore we cannot fully appreciate the generous conduct of him who could treat both sides with such fair mindedness as to retain their respect and confidence. Judge Blodget did that, even accepting a more perplexing trust and discharging its arduous duties with that never failing tact which always gave him friends and ardent supporters.

The following letter was written by him about this time, the original of which is in the possession of the Woburn (Mass.) Public Library—1—97 :

    Inscription    JAMES FOWLE, ESQR.
                         in Woburn.

                          Goffstown, Aug. 26, 1771.
Sir—

My uncle Benj will shortly pay you a visit. You must not expect me to pay anything for him ; as he has left me and has Reported abought this Town that I had agreed to Give him Large wages—-But poor old man will shortly feel the effect of his Ingratitude and abuse of my family ; he might have lived with me to the end of his life, provided Truth and Gratitude had been his guid ; this he is a stranger to, you are not a Stranger to occasion of my Taking of him—paying his Debts &c but more of this when J have the pleasure of seeing you in meen time J am your
                friend and humble Servant
                          SAM'L BLODGET.

This James Fowle will be remembered as one of his schoolmasters, and shows that he had kept in touch with him through all of those years. It also gives us a glimpse of the kindness and solicitation of his nature. We come now to one of the most trying situations of his life.

Benning Wentworth was succeeded as Governor of the Province of New Hampshire by his nephew under an appointment of August 11, 1766, and in addition to his commission of the office of his predecessor he was made Surveyor of the woods in North America, with the object of putting into execution the acts of parliament for the preservation of "the king's woods from trespass & waste and for the additional raising of revenue." This proved one of the most unpopular acts of the old country and tended to stir up contention wherever it was attempted to be carried out. Governor Wentworth chose his deputies wherever pines abounded, and these officers were the source of trouble and bitter feeling on every hand. Under the provisions of this act the owner of land growing pines must have one of the deputy surveyors survey his trees and mark all reserved for the king before he could fell one! The royal totem was a broad arrow carved in the bark of the tree or blazoned on the log if found cut down. Inability to meet the expense of this marking was no excuse, and whoever was found guilty of this offense had his logs confisticated immediately. Be they still in logs at the mill, hewn timber for house or barn, the deputy placed the king's mark upon them, when no one dared to touch them! The property was advertised and sold at public auction, the proceeds going into the royal treasury. All white pines ranging from fifteen to thirty-six inches in diameter were included in this reserve for the English navy.

Seizures were of common occurrence wherever pines abounded and mills had been built. In the winter of 1771-2 intense excitement was caused in this vicinity by an extensive visitation from the governor's deputies, nearly all of the mill yards on the Piscataquog being found with logs coming within the sizes of the king's reservation. The broad arrow was blazoned on every one claimed by royal authority and the natural owner notified to appear in court and show if he could why he should not forfeit them. The citation at this time was published in the New Hampshire Gazette of Feb. 7, 1772, and read as follows:

All persons claiming property in the following WHITE PINE LOGS, seized by order of the SURVEYOR GENERAL in Goffstown and Weare, in the Province of New Hampshire, may appear at Court of Vice Admiralty to be held at Portsmouth, on Thursday the 27th instant at Ten of the clock a. m and shew cause why the same should not be declared forfeited, agreeable to all information filed in said Court.

200 White Pine Logs from 15 to 30 inches diameter lying at Richard's mill in Goffstown.
250 Ditto from 15 to 35 inches diameter at Patty's mill.
35 Ditto from 36 to 20 ditto at Dow's mill.
140 Ditto from 30 to 18 ditto at Asa Patty's old mill.
270 Ditto from 36 to 17 ditto at Clement's mill in Weare.
154 Ditto from 36 to 15 at Job Rowell's mill.
Also 74 bundles of Clapboards at Merrimack River.
Portsmouth, Feb. 5, 1772.
       JOHN SHERBURN, D. Rr.

Finding themselves in this unpleasant situation, and knowing that their chances would be improved by having some influential person confer with the governor's officers, Samuel Blodget was unanimously selected for the purpose. Accordingly he went to Portsmouth and succeeded in effecting a compromise, whereby the offenders were to pay a moderate compensation for the transgression of the law, when information against them was to be withdrawn. Judge Blodget was appointed the agent by the governor to settle with the offenders. At the same time he was appointed Deputy Surveyor for 34 towns in the Merrimack Valley. The following is a transcript of his commission:

    To Samuel Blodget of Goffstown, in said province
(L. S.)   Esq.

Whereas, His Majesty, by his Royal Commission, dated the 16th day of July, 1766, hath been graciously pleased to appoint me Surveyor General of all His Majesty's woods, in North America, with power to appoint deputies and under officers, to carry the said service effectually in execution;

I do, therefore, by virtue of authority vested in me by said commission, appoint and depute you, to preserve the King's woods from trespass or waste, and to put in execution all the acts of Parliament, and Statutes enacted for that purpose, and to do and perform all acts and things whatsoever, to the said office appertaining, in the following Districts, viz: — Goffstown, Bedford, Weare, Pembroke, Allenstown, Bow, Dunbartown, Merrimack, Amherst, Litchfield, Chester, Concord, Boscawen, Hopkinton, New Boston, Sanbornton, New Salisbury, Canterbury, Methuen, Wilton, Peterborough, Temple, Plymouth, New Chester, Alexandria, New Britian, Meredith, Lyndborough, Henneker, New Amesbury and Camden, all in the aforesaid province, and also Haverhill, Andover, Dracut, Chelmsford, and Ipswich, in the Province of Mass. Bay; Hereby authorizing and requiring you, the said Sam. Blodget, to forbid and prevent, by all lawful means, to violation of said acts, and to seize and Mark for his majesty's use, all pine timber that you may find cut and hauled from the King's woods, without license first had and obtained from me, and all offenders aforesaid, to prosecute and to punish, as to law and justice appertains. And you, the said Sam. Blodget, are hereby required to return to me an exact account of your proceedings herein, quarterly, from this date, or oftener, if occasion shall require, and for your encouragement to exert yourself with diligence and fidelity in the duties of the said office, you will receive such compensation for your services, as your merit shall appear to me to deserve, out of the fines and forfeitures only, that may accrue or be levied by your means. This warrant to be in force during pleasure only. Given under my hand and seal, at Portsmouth, the 11th day of February, 1772.

J. WENTWORTH.

Samuel Blodget, Esq.
To be Assistant Deputy Surveyor of the woods.

Upon his return from Portsmouth, Mr. Blodget sent a copy of the following letter to each of the offenders:

Goffstown, Feb. 24, 1772.

Sir;—The late seizure of White Pine Logs, has caused me a disagreeable journey to Portsmouth, at the special request of a number of my friends, to solicit the Governor in the behalf of them who have unnecessarily trespassed in cutting the King's timber, &c. His Excellency thought fit to deputise me one of his Majesty's Surveyors of the King's woods in this Western District, thereby authorizing me to carry The King's laws into execution. As they are very severe, I shall be very loath to prosecute unless obstinate or notorious offenders force it upon me; of which I give you this early notice, at the same time, acquaint you his Excellency has pleased to put it in my hands to make the matter easy to you.

SAML BLODGET.

Mr. Blodget's efforts were rewarded by a speedy settlement with all of the trespassers, who then obtained possession of their logs, with the exception of the owners of the logs at Clement's mills in Weare, at what is now called the Oil Mills. These parties resisted and when the sheriff came to serve a warrant on them he and his assistants were routed after being unmercifully beaten by the indignant inhabitants of the vicinity! Of course this conduct was rank treason and the affair produced extreme excitement far and near. Again Judge Blodget was called upon to use all of his persuasive powers to conciliate matters. Future events proved, if his conduct did not then, that his sympathies were with the oppressed colonists. It is true they were defying the law, but it was a law without reason or justice. As iniquitous as were the stamp act and the duty on tea, this was equally so, and though bearing it as well, or better, than might be expected, it served to get the province into a turmoil. Governor Wentworth soon saw his mistake in trying to enforce such an odious measure, but not till the seeds of discontent had been sown which was to bring a harvest of patriots of the pines which became whirlwinds to the red-coated soldiers of King George on the battlefields of Bunker Hill and Bennington. A writer[*] in speaking of this matter has said: " It is strange Mr. Blodget should have accepted an office to which was attached such disagreeable duties; stranger still that he could perform such duties and still retain the respect and esteem of his neighbors as he seemed to do." He was conversative enough in his views and aims to realize that an obnoxious law could be administered by kindly argument where a more arbitary officer would raise fierce dissension, by which nothing could be gained by precipitation; and they knew it was the law and not its upholder in this case which was wrong. When the

---

[*] Henry Everett.

struggle came, as it did in a short time, he was found among
the first with the loyal sons of the Merrimack valley at the
front.

At the time of the battle of Lexington, his term of offices
under the king having expired, he was engaged in trade at
Goffstown.\* But no sooner had the news of this opening of
hostilities reached him than he again entered the service of his
country. He was actively engaged in the Battle of Bunker
Hill,† though belonging to the commissary department of the
Continental army, later being appointed sutler of Gen. Sullivan's brigade, stationed upon Winter Hill. Mr. Blodget was no
alone caterer to the common soldiers, but the following items
selected from the accounts of the Commissary General Trumbull we find :

April 1, 1776, By Bread to Brig. Maj. Scammons,   435
            General Sullivan's Table   249
            B'g Q. M. G. Frazier   156
            Genl Lee's Table   96

Upon the removal of General Sullivan's Brigade from Boston,
Judge Blodget returned to his interests in Goffstown, having
concluded that he had seen enough of conflict. He was then
in his fifty-third year, and though not an old man by any means,
nor broken in health, had less desire for the stirring scenes of
war than in his younger years. But he never hesitated to lend
his assistance in every other way to the cause and his pocket
book was always open to its benefit. If he was not in active
service the family was certainly to do its part, for he had two
sons at the front.

At the raising of the three Continental Battalions his second
son, Samuel, Jr., volunteered his services and November 7,
1776, was commissioned Captain of Company 8, in Colonel
Enoch Poor's regiment. Nathan Hale of Rindge having been
Colonel at time of muster, Colonel Poor afterward promoted. These were three years' men, but in December, 1777, for
some reason unknown, Captain Blodget resigned, and went in-

---
\* Potter.
† Chase's History of Haverhill, Mass.

to trade in Exeter, which proved a failure the following year, by which his father was involved to the extent 4219lbs-8s-2d. This amount Judge Blodget afterward paid with his usual good grace, the following statement being found at the front of the page containing his son's accounts :

"Boston, Oct. 11, 1788. This act, though attended with great loss is given up and a receipt given in full discharge; it being consented to by the children then present, viz.: Nathan Blodget, Abigail Stickney, Polly Gilman and Caleb."

Caleb, the second son, only sixteen, was appointed an ensign in the Continental Army in 1779, and promoted to Lieutenant and Quartermaster in 1781. He was described in the enlisting papers as Caleb Blodget of Goffstown, light complexion, blue eyes, 16 years old, 5 ft., 6 inches tall.*

Something of Judge Blodget's generosity and public spirit may be learned from the following proclamation issued by him in 1777, for the purpose of encouraging the growth of wool and flax in town :

ONE HUNDRED DOLLARS REWARD.

March the 1st, 1777.

Whereas Wool and Flax are scarce articles amongst the Inhabitants of Goffstown they not raising a quantity equal to their own consumption, and is probable theire wants will Encrease; as a small Incouragement to sd Inhabitants; I do promise to give the following bounty on the above articles of flax; and on Lambs for the increase of wool, and I do promise to give Every Freeholder and an Inhabitant of Goffstown in the State of New Hampshire the Following bounteys upon the Following condition; that is to say; two pence per head upon any number between ten and Twenty, and three pence per head upon any number between Thirty and forty, provided the Lambs survive the first day of next August, at the which time the bounty will be paid with this proviso; that they neither Kill or suffer to be Killed, any sheep or Lambs either for sale or private consumption, between the last day of May and the first day of the aforesaid August; the breach of this last proviso; will be considered as a bar against the above bounty; and

---

* War Rolls, Vol. I, p. 552. Ditto, p. 664, Vol. III, April 5, 1780, Captain Blodget attests to a soldier's certificate as a substitute in the sum of 200 lbs. for Mr Moses Eastman.

as Bears in this quarter; often destroy the sheep and Lambs, the aforesaid Inhabitants are Intitled to twenty shillings per head for every grown Bear they shall kill within the bounds of said Goffstown between the month of April and the month of October following; provided the head of sd Bear or bears be presented and delivered to me at my house in Goffstown within twenty-four hours after sd Bear is killed;—also a further bounty on Flax; that any Inhabitant aforesaid shall be Intitled to two pence per pound upon any quantity of well dressed flax above five hundred pounds; that he shall raise this present Season and upon his own farme within the Town aforesaid; provided he apply between the month of November next and the first day of March following;—be it Remembered, in case the several number of Lambs, the Quantity of Flax; and the Beares, according to the several Bounteys, shall not exceed the sum of one hundred dollars; the First applyance will have the preference—N. B. the donor Excludes himself from any part of the aforesaid Bounteys.

As the above Bounteys are given with a Real design to Encrease the growth of wool and flax amongst us, the donor hopes no one will apply unless he is really Intitled to some of the aforesaid Bounteys according to the true intent and meaning of this Instrument, and willing to answer any Reasonable Question on oath that may be asked.

Dated March the 1st, 1777.

N. B. The Flax is expected to be dressed according to the usual custom of this place.

We have found no records to show who competed for these prizes. If none did so, or if he paid the full amount stipulated, it shows the generous nature and the public spirit of the man. That his popularity was general is shown by the fact that at the first session of the Honourable House of Representatives held at Exeter on the third Wednesday of December (16), 1778-9, Judge Blodget represented Goffstown and Derryfield, which were classed together.*

In 1780 he served as Town Treasurer of Goffstown, and the year following he was elected one of the Selectmen, and during his remaining stay in Goffstown he was continually in office, serving as Moderator several years. Besides being called up-

---

\* From original volume in Secretary of State's office labeled "Members, etc., 1775-81." State Papers, Bachellor, Vol. VIII, p. 820.

on to do the business at home he was often appealed to from
all over the county, was often the referee in important cases,
Judge of Probate, before the County courts or the Legislature.
A man of energy and character he was looked up to by every
one. This may truly be said to have been the most prosperous
period of his life, and quite as certain the most happy one.
Those giant schemes which were to be productive of so much
good and make his name more widely known, but which were
to despoil him of his well earned fortune and break him down
in health still slumbered in the chambers of his mind. But it
must have been soon after, it not at that time, when he was
studying upon his invention for raising ships or sunken bodies
from the bottom of rivers, seas and other parts of water. His
friends tried to discourage him in what they considered a fruitless expenditure of time, and his enemies poohed at the visions
of an old man. (He was then 58.) But his nature was not
one to be turned from its purpose, and laboring night and day,
with such anxiety as only an inventor can know, he completed
his "diving tongues," as the machine was called, in 1782. It
would seem as if the golden opportunity to test the work was
at hand, for the following year a vessel went down off Plymouth
with a valuable cargo.

Judge Blodget lost no time in entering into such preparations
as were necessary to test his invention. Reaching the spot in a
small vessel he for the first time put his machine to use. After
some delays and vexations he succeeded in raising the sunken
ship intact! Besides receiving a good sum as reward he at
once put himself in a way to insure a handsome competence.
But he was not one to be satisfied with ordinary success. It
was not enough that he should command. "A common man,"
says Judge Potter, "at the age of nearly three scores years,
would doubtless have been content with a first success, particularly when favored with a competence; but Judge Blodget was
an uncommon man, and at his advanced age of life he determined upon visiting Europe, to bring the value of his invention
before the people of the old countries."

Accordingly he began to arrange for a trip across the ocean

at once. The better to carry out his plans, he formed a partnership with Mr. John Stoughton of Haverhill and Mr. John Codman, Jr., of Boston, Mass., furnishing one-half of the capital himself, the first of his partners one-third, and the other one-sixth. He had heard of a Spanish government ship which had been wrecked off the coast of Portugal, having for a part of its cargo a large amount of coin, he resolved to seek the opportunity to put his diving tongues to another test. Accordingly armed with papers of recommendation from the most distintinguished men of New England, among them the Governor of Massachusetts, he set forth on his uncertain voyage, accompanied by Mr. Stoughton. Upon the margin of his passport, bearing date of June 20, 1786, was written in the governor's own hand the following:

I do hereby certify that the said Blodget is by good Judges, reputed to have great knowledge in ye mechanical powers, and he has distinguished himself by recovering from vessels wrecked, and sunk in deep waters, the goods and cargo with which they were laden, and that he is a gentlemen of good education and character.
JAMES BOWDOIN.

Leaving Boston on the 25th, he and Mr. Stoughton eventually arrived at Lisbon, to find that they were too late to display their invention upon the Spanish government ship, as its treasures had been mostly recovered and the ship "gone to pieces." But upon being advised of a vessel having sunk off the Spanish coast, going down with a cargo of bars of copper, they resolved to repair thither, under the direction of General Munzo, to whom they had been introduced by the Ambassador of Spain. Here they would have been successful but for a quarrel among their Spanish helpers, and desertion of a part of their number. Finding that their efforts were likely to go unrewarded if successful, the two men then returned to England, out of the pocket and with but poor promise ahead. However, Judge Blodget soon conceived the idea of raising the English naval ship Royal George, which had gone down with such dramatical effect several years before. His invention had met with a favorable report, and finally successful in bringing the matter before the Lord Commissioners of Admiralty, he received the courteous invitation:

Admiralty Office, 23d Nov. 1786.

Sir: — Having communicated to my Lords Commissioners of the Admiralty, your letter of the 13th inst, informing them of your having discovered a mode of applying fastenings to bodies under water, by which means you can take up ships from any depth, not exceeding twenty five fathoms; I am in return commanded by their lordships to desire you will attend them at this office next Tuesday at 12 o'clock.

I am, Sir:
Your very humble servant,
P. H. P. STEPHENS.

To Samuel Blodget Charlton St.

At this meeting Judge Blodget was shown every respect possible, but his offer to raise the hulk of the Royal George was refused upon the rather peculiar ground that "she was not needed." A new vessel already christened by that name was in process of building, and it would be awkward to have two Royal Georges on hand. As there was no other opportunity for the inventor to prove his claims, he was forced to retire, his experiment having proved a costly venture. Unwilling to return under the cloud of his failure, and somewhat broken in health, he spent the following seven months in sight-seeing, visiting many parts of the Kingdom. It was during this, the first and only vacation of his life, that he wrote home the following memorandum:

MEMORANDUMS FOR S BLODGET JUNR CONCERNING THE EDUCATION OF HIS CHILDREN.

London, May 16, 1787.

Hon Sir

Please to write as often as may be convenient & to be very Particular respecting my children.*

If Billy should be in Boston when you arrive there Please to advise his being sent to me as soon as may be convenient, tak-

---

* Judge Blodget's grandchildren and his wards.

ing the necessary care in providing for him every essential to make his voyage comfortable.

Also I am sure everything will be done by M Gilman to forward the Education of my litttle Girls. Yet I should like to have your opinion of the Genius, situation & the Progress they make in Learning to read, write, draw, Dance, &c., &c.

Dancing I believe to be very essential to give them confidence and a graceful deportment, as well as to their health. Therefore I wish they may be sent to the Best schools in Boston. In short I would have no reasonable expense saved for in comparison with the general advantage which may be gained. By their constant application to useful Learning, a little money can be no object.

& Pray let their day be divided into Particular hours so as to allow a sufficient time for each employment. They may work with their needle 2 hours, write 2 hours, dance 2 hours, play on the Guittar or piano forte 2 hours, & so on through the day & let their hours be fixt by a weekly arrangement, so that they may know what to do before their time comes. — In fine weather let all the little children that may be in Town go into the common together either early in the morning or in the afternoon. This will give them a free enjoyment of the air & contribute much to their health. I would have the Children dressed neatly & clean, but not fine. I mean not in Rich or Gaudy colours. In London the Girls all wear white with Blue or Pink sashes & have no other Colours in their dress — Boys are dressed in Green or Scarlet & this method of Dress pleases extremely.

I am an advocate for particular attention to Children & wish my little girls to be treated as if they were women and never to have them Punished if it is Possible to flatter them or reason them into their duty, nevertheless I am willing to leave Mrs. G. to her own method, which I dare say will be in most respects similar to mine.

Above all things I would have them love each other & consider Betsey Gilman & the Little Stickneys as Brothers and Sisters for this must be of great Importance at some future time. Therefore anything that may tend to increase their affection & friendship for each other must not be neglected.

I have no particular directions for the Boys, but to have them employed every hour at something, when they are not at school. Pray insist on their Playing, but do not be very rigourous in anything except when you command them not to be idle. You may let them choose their employment whether at

work or play as often as may be proper for them they will see
that they are among friends & contract a degree of love and respect for you.  Pray don't neglect to make all the Children
sensible that their own good is the Principle or only object in
all your conduct toward them, for if they are fully convinced of
this Important truth, they will (by Imitation) contract the
most amiable habits & be forever what we all must wish they
will be Beloved and respected by every one who may be hon-
oured with their acquaintance.

You will please not to mention any thing you have seen or
that I have told you respecting our embarrassments to any Body
(Caleb & Mr. Gilman excepted)  It requires but a small extra
exertion to relieve me & they surely will not neglect me when
they know our future fortune depends on their exertions.

This memorandum may be shown to Mr. Gilman Mrs. Gilman & Caleb if you please but not to nobody else ———

It will be a great mistake if I am not Immediately relieved in
the manner pointed out ——— Nothing but absolute madness can
Prevent my being placed in a very different situation from that
I have remained too long ——

But as I know Mr. Gilman has done everything he thought
Prudent, I bear every disappointment patiently for I consider the
evils I have suffered as unavoidable — But they may be prevented in future, & will be I am sure, as I know Mr. Gilman
will not fail to exert himself to the Purpose ———

Tell Mr Gilman that my health is much better than for 18
months Past that I hope soon to be Intirely recovered ——

I wish you to send a few foxes flying & Gray Squirrels, yel-
low Birds & wood Ducks, &c., &c.— for which I will pay
whatever they may cost in trouble, &c., as several Persons who
have befriended me in my distress have a right to expect some
return, and I am very anxious to make them a present as soon
as I have an opportunity.  I should like to begin by Presenting
them with some Curiosity of our Country.  Cushing, Davis, Barnard or any friend of ours will bring them for me.

Pray let your letters to me be as full as Possible as the smallest occurrence whether Political or of whatever nature — the
smallest trifles are Important to me.  In Particular remember
all our domestic concerns of every nature.  If you should write
Nathan remind him of his neglect to write me or remit me —
ask him what I have done to forfeit his friendship.

After giving an estimate of a bridge across the Merrimack
River at Haverhill to Newbury, and a few minor items refer-

ring to accounts with others, he closes his Memorandum with the following :

With respect to our American Paper I should be glad to hear from time to time of its value & with you to have the opinion of Mr Gilman on the Propriety of a considerable speculation. I wrote to Mr. Gilman on the Subject but told him not to mention it to any Body. He may how ever consult who he Pleases as I mean to be entirely governed by him in all the measures I take ———*

Returning from his trip abroad in the summer of 1787, he opened a general store in Haverhill, Mass., Sept. 1, 1787, soon after supplying his son William, who was still running the store at Goffstown, with a bill of goods. He continued in this store for three years, though his active mind would not allow him to confine himself exclusively to trade. In 1788, he established a stage line between that town and Boston, which was run regularly for two or three years, under his control. This appears to be the first coach line in that vicinity and one of the first in the country. Meeting with good success in that venture, he with others established another line, connecting Haverhill with Concord this state, though this did not become permanent.

In the three years in trade there he had so far recovered his shattered fortune as to start a duck manufactory in 1790. That was the same year that Slater and his company of pioneer manufacturers were establishing their cotton mills at Pawtucket, though little dreaming of the countless number of men, women and children their industry was destined to give employment. It is worthy of note that it was this year, 1790, that the invention by the English divine, Dr. Cartwright, of the power loom, which was to be such a potent factor in the development of Manchester, was first tried in that city for which it was named, and the invention destroyed by an exasperated mob, but labor saving machinery was sure to come, and the power loom foremost in the list.

Judge Blodget was successful with the making of duck, and respected by the people at large, he was elected representative

---

* The original of these memorandums is now in possession of Mrs. Eunice K. Brown a descendant.

to the legislature from Haverhill in 1791. He was again at the height of prosperity, but his restless, ambitious spirit was not satisfied. The proposition of the Middlesex canal, which had originated with Hon. James Sullivan, was an absorbing theme of conversation everywhere in business circles. That was a period of rapid improvement. Boston was becoming a thriving town of twenty thousand inhabitants, and there were suburbs that only needed the stimulus of trade to give them place and power. The valley of the Merrimack, far up into New Hampshire, even the country into Vermont, if sparsely settled, promised a rich harvest of trade to the centres which could draw it. Better means of communications was thus the great question of the day. Turnpikes, under the control of corporations, were the main arteries of business. Moved by slow-going ox-teams, over these priced highways, the transportation of the country produce, lumber, firewood and building material became at once tedious and costly. Once such a maritime highway as the Merrimack offered was opened and producer and the consumer must both be benefited by the result. Judge Blodget realized that the Middlesex canal was a foregone conclusion, and he believed it was time for him to carry out the pet project of his life. Though he had arrived at that age when most men are laying aside the cares and responsibilities of business, he formed his plans with the sanguineness of a young man with the world all before him. In fact it was his happy belief that he was yet in his prime. He had lived a perfectly abstemious life, and with a careful husbanding of his strength he confidentially looked forward to a hundred years of activity.

In 1793 he moved back to Amoskeag, taking up his residence on the east bank of the Merrimack. He purchased the land about the Falls and laid every calculation toward performing his herculean task, confident it could be done within his own means.

May 2, a date worthy of remembrance, along with that of another May-day thirteen years later, he opened work upon his canal, making considerable progress during the season in blasting and constructing a dam to afford a pond. Work was not begun upon the Middlesex canal until September 10th, of the same year, so he was over four months ahead of Sullivan's enterprise. In September of 1794, he leased his "Duck Factory standing in a lane near Kimball Carleton's in said Haverhill to David Blackburn of the same town, weaver, James Alexander late of Newburyport, weaver, and Isaac Schofield of Newburyport, weaver." This lease was for two years, but he continued to let this property until 1799, when his affairs became so deeply involved it was set off on execution in favor of Samuel Parkman of Boston. With the leasing of his business in Haverhill Judge Blodget may be said to have concentrated all of his energy and capital in pushing the work on his canal. On May 18th, 1795, he had so far advanced with the stone work that Colonel William Adams of Londonderry, a skilled carpenter, was employed to begin upon the woodwork.

### WINNEPESAUKEE TRIP.

During the year of 1795, with every prospect of a successful ending to his work on Amoskeag canal, Judge Blodget proposed the scheme of making the Merrimack navigable to Lake Winnepesaukee, thus preparing a direct highway, or rather waterway, of commerce through the then most populous section of New Hampshire, affording a direct intercourse with Boston. The plan seemed to meet with favor wherever it became known, and it was so far developed that Col. McGregor of Goffstown, and Major Duncan of Concord consented to construct the locks and canals around Hooksett Falls, while other equally reliable men of this state and Massachusetts were to complete the work above that place. In order to satisfy himself of the perfect feasibility of the project and to prove the same to others, accompanied with two or three others, he made a trip of examination. Happily he kept a journal of the journey, with his deductions of same, of which the following is a copy:

### BLODGET'S JOURNAL TO WINNIPISSIOKE POND, 1795.

Oct 4th 1705, Began my Journey to Winnipissioke Pond from Canal at Derryfield.

From S B Canal to Isle Hooksett is 8 miles the fall is 40 Rods about 20 feet fall, to be Canal'd by Esqr. McGregor and

Majr. Duncan. To the next falls, which are called Garvins falls is 4 mills, 80 Rods in length & 25 feet falls, must be canal'd. Turkey River fall is ½ mile above but need no Canalling. From thence to Concord is 4 miles and Smoother water; from Concord to the Crotch of the River, is 18 miles, but two pair of falls in this distance which will need no canaling. From this Crotch of the River we ran up the East Branch towards Winnipisioke Pond — the First Mills we came to was a grist and saw mill ½ mile from said Crotch, on the north side of the stream the property of Jeremiah Sanborn and others; their dam Extends but half across the stream which is about 3 mill water running in it, and about 6 Rods wide, so that a sett of mills and the canal may be placed on the south side of the stream & do excellent service without doing any damage to these other mills —— by the advantage of a canal running up the stream fifteen or Twenty Rods fifteen feet head may be obtained. Here is a long fall of water for more than two miles & is by far the greatest on this stream. In this distance I presume the distance is near 100 feet fall — here I remark that whether I have Judged well on the fall of water or not — yet I am well assured of some very good privileges — there is 3 or 4 hundred acres of land well cloathed with Tall White pines & to be sold lay adjoyning to these Rapids — the proprietors of it are Capt. Clark, his Brother and others; they are very urgent that this canal should be opened & as an Incouragement, offer to give gratis five Rods of their land on each side of the stream for the use of the canal, this I find is the case with many others.

At the head of these falls is still water for one mile which reaches within a few rods of Hancock's and other mills, they consist of one grist and one saw mill standing on the south side of sd stream, the Priveledge good but the mills bad.

About ¼ mile above Handcocks mills & on the north side of the stream stand a grist and saw mill, the property of Ebr Morrison and others. Both mill and Privieledge are poor.

Half a mile Farther up stands on the south side of the Stephen Chace's Fulling mill. He offers his landing freely for the use of the canal, which adjoins to Sandborn Bridge the stream continues the same.

4 miles further up stands Jacob Burfords & other Grist, saw, and fulling mills. They stand on the north side of the stream, about one mile of this is shole & small rappids the other is a Bay. These mills have from 7 to 8 feet head and fall. About half a mile up the stream stands Smarts Grist & saw mills with

the same head & fall, & on the same side of the stream — between Bumfords & Smarts mill, the bottom smooth, graveley Bottom Interspersed with Loose stone ——— all these mills are poor things scarce worth owning ; here I observe on the south east side a canal may be opened without doing any damage to the above mill & their owners ——— and take advantage of 13 or 14 feet fall for a valuable set of mills, the land on the east side being the property of Gen'l. Badger, who I presume will cheerfully give the land for the use of the canal.

Smart's mill dam flows and mostly covers the rocks and sholes of $\frac{1}{2}$ mile till it reaches Sandbornton Bay which is very large and spacious — $5\frac{1}{2}$ miles across the south end of this Bay brings us to the narrows and rappids, on which stands a Grist, saw and fulling mills, the property of Collo. Sam'l Ladd all standing on the south side of the stream. From sd mills to the before mentioned Bay, is about 60 Rods, a smooth, Graveley Bottom, a few small loose stones, a gradual descent of abt 8 feet fall & 1 to 2 feet deep. About 80 Rods above these mills is another large Bay between which and the aforesaid mills is Rocky & shole ground, but the dam may be flowed so as to cover these Rocks I observe.

The canal may be carried very easily by Colo Ladd's mills (which by the way are miserable) without doing him the least damage & make a very good sett of mills. He is the owner of the land but seems to be disposed on the whole to Incourage the business.

One mile and a half above said Rocky shole, carries us across the sd Bay to the narrow stream again, & Rappid, for $\frac{1}{4}$ mile, on the north side of which stands a Grist mill & saw mills the property of Abm. Foulsom & have abt 8 feet fall. These Rapids have a smoothe graveley Bottom interspersed with loose stone — here a canal can be opened on the south side without doing any damage to the owners of these mills.

One mile and a half from these Rappids, brings us cross another Bay to another and last Rapid being abought $\frac{1}{4}$ mile more brings us into Winipisioke Pond — these Rappeds are a descent about 5 feet & 12 to 14 Rods wide from 1 foot to 18 inches deep. The Bottom graveley & considerable stony, but few of them large, not more than two of them will require power to move them. I rode my Horse across stream at the out let of the Pond — it appears by the large rock in the pond that the pond does not at the highest water exceed two feet. —

I farther observed that by the banks of the stream at any place the highest water does not exceed 3½ Feet.

In a summary he estimates the distance in an entry in the journal as follows:

Octr. 4th 1795.
A 6 days Route to examine the River from my Canal to Winipisioke Pond.

|  | miles |
|---|---|
| From S. B Canal to Isle Hookset | 8½ |
| From Isle Hookset to Garvin | 4 |
| From Garvin to Turkey R fall | 0½ |
| From Turkey R Falls to Concord | 4 |
| From Concord to the Crotch of the River | 18 |
|  | 35 |

From Merrimac River up The East Branch into Winipisioke Pond.

| From the Crotch of the River to J Sandborns mill |  | 0½ |
|---|---|---|
| From Sandborns mill to Handcocks mills |  | 3 |
| From Handcocks to E. Morrisons | do | 0¼ |
| From Morrisons to Chases | do | 0½ |
| From Chases to Jere Bumfords | do | 4 |
| From Bumfords to Smarts | do | 0¼ |
| From Smarts to Colo. Ladds | do | 5¼ |
| From Ladd to Abm. Foulsoms | do | 1½ |
| From Foulsoms to the Pond |  | 1¾ |
|  |  | 17½ |
|  |  | 35 |
|  |  | 52½ |

The following is the association paper, with the list of subscribers:

We the subscribers agree to associate for the Purpose of clearing the Fall upon the Merrimac River from Isle of Hooksett Falls to the entrance of the east branch of said River and from thence to construct such Canals up the East Branch of said River to Winnipissioke Pond, as shall make the Navigation for Boats and Rafts safe and convenient from said Pond to Isle of Hooksett Falls aforesaid. The Fund for the Undertaking to be divided into three hundred shares, & subject to such Regulations as the Company of associates shall hereafter

agree upon. And we reciprocally promise each to the other to take Respective Shares annexed to our names.
May 4
  1795.

| | |
|---|---|
| Saml Blodget fifty shares | 50 |
| Saml Phillips Kidder Ten Shares | 10 |
| William Blodget Ten Shares | 10 |
| Benjm. Blodget Ten Shares | 10 |
| Peter Gilman, Twenty Shares | 20 |
| His Honor Moses Gill Esqr five shares | 5 |
| Thomas Russell Twenty shares | 20 |
| William Tudor Ten Shares | 10 |
| James Sullivan twenty shares | |
| Abiel Smith fifteen shares | |
| Perez Morton Twelve shares | |
| Nathan Bond Ten Shares | |
| Wm. Harper Esq Sandbornton Five shares | |
| Nathan Hoitt, Esq. — Moultonborough one share | |
| Joseph Barrell twenty five shares | |
| Willis Hall three shares | |
| Robert Fletcher Five shares. | |

According to this paper two hundred and thirty one shares were sold, or within sixty nine of the full number desired. But as his work at Amoskeag soon demanded all of his attention and means, Judge Blodget was obliged to abandon the project. As he was the soul of the enterprise nothing further was done, except that a few years later the river was rendered navigable for boats as far north as East Concord. At that time the matter of opening the way as far as Judge Blodget had planned was discussed, but sufficient funds were not forthcoming and the project again collapsed.

According to Judge Potter, in his biographical sketch, " A line of dams were constructed from rock to rock, upon the east side of the channel of the river, from a point about fifty-seven rods above Amoskeag bridge, down the river, very near upon the line of the stone dams and bank wall of the stone basin of the Amoskeag Company, a distance of about thirty-three rods below the Amoskeag bridge to a point nearly opposite the house now occupied by Samuel P. Kidder, Esq.; thence it was extended east to the shore, making a basin about ninty rods in length, and from four to six rods in width. This basin was intended to answer the purpose of a canal and mill pond. On the west bank of the basin, and about half-way of the same, stood the mill 'Industry,' having a grist mill below it, and above it a saw mill belonging to William Blodget. Out of the southwest corner of the basin, the water passed through a slip of three hundred feet in length by twenty feet in width, to the lower canal, commencing above, and running immediately west of the 'Blodget house,' which part of the canal is now entire — to a point just below said house. From thence the canal followed the shore of the river down to a point just above the 'boiler shop' of the Amoskeag Company, where it passed into the river. The west embankment of the canal from the Blodget house downward, was of cobble work, filled with stone and covered with a spiling of plank. At convenient distances along this canal check gates were placed, so as to raise the water above them, a foot or so, making as many slight reservoirs as there were check gates."

Here comes in the invention of the judge's which cost him in its failure a sheer twenty thousand dollars and the labor of four years, but for which he might then have seen his way clear to a success which would have won him a good return for his expenditures and accomplished the dream of his life. Rather than blame him, however, we should admire him for the resolute energy which could rise above such a disappointment as few men meet, and in his old age cause him to begin anew. But for the explanation rather than the anticipations. These check gates described were fastened by a hasp and opened down stream. He had calculated that the raft or boat passing through the stream from the reservoir would gain a velocity sufficient to open the gates and pass on through the entire length of the canal unaided. But the project proved a failure. The velocity which he had counted upon as an assistant was his destroyer as well. The speed attained by the rafts or boats was such as to smash the one and "stave up" the other. The merchandise on the boats was scattered along the banks, while the logs had to be re-rafted. It was decided that the trouble lay in the great velocity of the courses. To remedy that two locks were to be made where there had been but one, and another season occupied in doing the work. "The upper one, of one hundred and fifty feet in length, was built upon the surface of the ground. The posts at the sides were tenanted into the cross sills, while their tops were held together by cross cap-timbers, and were still farther secured in their places by braces, extending from near the top of each post to the cross sill beneath." Confident that the extra precaution would insure them success this time, the projector and his engineer, Colonel Adams, announced the day for the trial, when a large crowd of spectators gathered to witness the novel sight. But again man had erred. The water now entered the canal with a power which tore the locks from their fastenings and tossed them on its foaming current! Worse than before, the work of a year was a wreck! This was late in the autumn of 1798, and the following June, an unusually high freshet completed the ruin of nearly five years' labor and the loss of $20,000 by washing off the canal below the locks.

His own fortune now depleted, and his years of anxious planning and working come to naught, Judge Blodget must have been an uncommon man to have found the heart to still persevere. But he was not one to give up. It was the ambition of his old age, stronger perhaps than it would have been in the prime of his manhood, when it was not too late to seek some other enterprise. In December, 1798, after the destruction of his locks, he obtained a charter for his canal, in order to more readily dispose of stock to secure the necessary capital to go ahead. He also employed a surveyor to select the most feasible route and to estimate the cost of completing the work. Colonel Loammi Baldwin, who superintended the construction of the Middlesex canal, made the survey, and evidently in sympathy with the project made a favorable report, placing the prospective cost at $9000. He recommended a route farther removed from the river's bank, in order to escape the high freshets, and what was of equal importance, if something of a sting to the man in his disappointment, that "there were certain established principles which it would be well not to depart from, nor presume much on new theories, or to introduce works of speculation into canalling."

Judge Blodget published the report of his surveyor, and immediately began to try and raise the money to proceed. He was so successful that he sold of stock and raised from other sources $7000. In December he had secured from the legislature of New Hampshire the power to raise $9000 by lottery for the purpose of completing "Blodget's canal," on which he raised $5000. These amounts making $12,000 he expended in work on the canal, without being able to finish it. In this dilemma he was granted in 1802 authority to raise $10,000 by another lottery. But the previous lottery, while it had been instrumental in raising him over half of the sum it was expected to afford, brought him trouble and embarrassment.

As has already been shown the temperament of Judge Blodget would not allow his ambition to be circumscribed. It was not enough that he should build a canal around the falls, but he must add to the enterprise with an invention of his own, which he fondly believed was to improve the situation. Even while working this scheme he was not so hedged by its accomplishment as not to foresee the broad and expansive result that it must in time bring. Not only would it afford an easy way of getting merchandise up and down the river, but it would assist in compassing the great hydraulic power afforded by the falls in the interest of man. "In his mind's eye, this site was destined to be the 'Manchester of America,' and he could see the brick upon the canal as plainly, if not as substantially, as we, who occupy his place half a century later." Proof of this is apparent in the fact that he bought at Hooksett a large lot of land containing clay beds, for the purpose of building factories at Amoskeag. It is still another curious fact that these clay banks have since furnished a large proportion of the brick used in the construction of our buildings.*

In 1795 he built him a fine residence, since known as the

---

* These clay banks were afterwards owned by Richard H. Ayer.

THE BLODGET HOUSE.
ERECTED IN 1795, TORN DOWN IN 1870.

Blodget mansion, and standing by the side of the canal in the rear of the Amoskeag Ax Company's buildings. It was a two story, old-fashioned farm house, with a front entrance on the east side, and a bulkhead on the south. In later years a barn, connected by a shed was built on the north end, and an open shed and one story building on the south. This last was the famous red store and was a scene of activity during the boating days. A highway at the time ran from the Falls road bending to southwest and after passing two houses, in one of which Mr. S. B. Kidder afterwards lived, came to the Blodget house, where the judge lived during his trying period of work on his canal, and where he died. It was also the birthplace of Samuel B. Kidder, December 26, 1806. The old house was torn down in 1870 by the Amoskeag Company, it being then occupied by the eccentric "Cy" Warner, who refused to vacate until the building was pulled down over his head. Judge Blodget had another house, which he called his sleeping house, and which he had probably lived in until his new one was completed. This stood a few rods east of the other, until it was finally moved to the bank of the canal and converted into a mill. Drinking water was obtained by this little group of houses from a spring bubbling up where the upper Langdon mill now stands, the water being carried to the dwellings in logs. A row of Lombard poplars stood in front of the house.

His speculation in clay beds, his acquisition of lands about the scenes of his operation and the building of this commodious dwelling gave those who were jealous of his possible success an opportunity to declare that he was using funds raised for another purpose and to his individual gain, that he was neglecting work on the canal and locks to advance his personal profit. Unfortunately the management of the lottery had fallen into unfriendly hands. As has been shown only $5000 had been paid him from its proceeds, where he had expected much more, and what was even worse the managers had paid this slowly and refused to explain why the rest was not forthcoming. Thus the legislature in granting him a seond lottery, 1802, appointed a committee to look after the settlement of the first, granted in 1798.

If the managers of the lottery and his enemies outside accused him off misappropriating the money that should have been applied to the furtherance of the canal, he as boldly and unhesitatingly charged them with gross mismanagement of affairs. He declared that, while the legislature had allowed them to receive "reasonable charges" for conducting the drawing of the lottery they had charged five dollars a day as their regular pay; that they had charged for expense during the drawing at the rate of three dollars a minute; that they had shown two sets of accounts differing from each other; that their lists of prizes were false and misleading; that they refused to let him see the books; that they had burned many of the books and lottery tickets, so as to make an investigation impossible. Serious charges in all truth, and warranting an investigation on the part of the state. But the committee chosen to look into the matter did not attend to that duty until a short time before the meeting of the legislature in June, and then while Judge Blodget was away from home, and without sending him notice of even their appointment. As a result they learned only one side of the question—that of the managers of the lottery, and their report accordingly did not afford the meed of fairness belonging to the defendant, who had ever desired a settlement by arbitration.

In reply to this report he repeated his grave charges, and on December 6, 1803, gave a public statement of the situation from his point of view, showing in detail the progress of work on the canal, using in part the following language:

"It has been a misfortune, that within a few weeks past, the interruptions by rocks and ledges, from the Head of the Falls to the Canal, has had such an effect upon strangers, that they dare not venture into it without the aid of a pilot. The proprietors have therefore been to an expense of cutting a new canal from the head of the Falls in the old canal, by the eastern bank of the river and nearly parallel with the same. This work is so well executed, that the waters shoot directly into the old

Canal; and such are the natural monuments on each side of this channel, that the stranger cannot fail, and will enter with ease and safety into the Canal.

"There has also been erected, at a very great expense, during the last season, below the second guard gate, a Basin to receive all loose logs, drift stuff, &c., so that a stranger, without the aid of a pilot, can pass from the head of the Falls directly into the Basin below the mills, without interruption, and in less than half the usual time. From this Basin to the lower Canal, are two locks of 100 feet each, through which we pass in twenty minutes. About thirty rods below these locks, there is a gate erected for the conveniency of stopping the water, by which we expedite the passage through the locks at half the usual time. By these alterations, business is done with great despatch, besides the saving of much labor, and the expense of a pilot. The last rafts that passed the Canal, have experienced all this. The Canal below the last mentioned gate is every way complete, as far as the slip through which the lumber passes in the Merrimack River again. From this slip to the river, requires four locks to be put down, of 9 feet lift, and 100 feet in length each, including that which must be placed in the river. Three of these locks are of 100 feet each, are framed, and have lain at the spot over two summers, and are unavoidably in a mouldering condition.

"At the time I petitioned to the Legislature of New Hampshire, for a Lottery, to raise nine thousand dollars, my sufferings proved much more: for by taking a new route, which was recommended to me, and complied with, out of this 9000 dollars, exclusive of necessary charges, I have received only 5000 dollars; all which; with many thousands more, have been actually expended on the Canal, besides 1300 dollars of toll received the last season: so the reports now circulating, of my being indifferent whether I complete the canal or not, and that I have made use of a Lottery money to build a house, &c., are both false and without foundation. So far from making use of the money I received from the Lottery, I have expended more than 7000 dollars upon the Canal, besides the 5000 dollars received by the Lottery. This I am ready to prove when called upon on."

Anxious to utilize the water power at the falls, he improved every opportunity to meet that object. He had built a saw mill in connection with John Stark soon after the Revolution, probably 1782, upon these falls just above Amoskeag bridge, the large rock or ledge there remaining forming a part of the western side of the canal, being the foundation of the west side of said mill. This mill was purchased by Judge Blodget and the privilege flowed out, in forming the pool or pond for his canal and for his "great mill, the Industry," which was located upon the river bank a few rods below the "guard locks" of the Amoskeag Manufacturing Company.

Judge Blodget's saw mill "Industry" ran three gangs of upright saws, circular saws being unknown then. William Blodget, his son, had built a saw mill about one hundred feet north of this, and nearly west of the house where Samuel B. Kidder lived so long. Near to his big saw mill on the south the judge had a grist mill.

At this time there was or had been on the west side of the Falls, in Goffstown, a mill owned if not built by a Mr. Patterson, and known as the "Patterson mill." This mill probably stood upon the same place where afterwards was built the Pollard or Harvey mill. It is not known which was built first the Patterson or the Stark mill. A man by the name of Whittaker erected the third mill at these Falls, long known as the Whittaker's saw mill, and which stood just below the Blodget house.

With the inevitable result that his far-seeing mind could realize he always had in view the future possibilities, and was impatient to see begun those enterprises of manufacture so soon to follow. He secured control of the land about his canal, and projected the establishment of a nail factory, and thought to use a building which he was then utilizing as a store house, and which was afterwards made into a barn. He tried to interest Boston capitalists in the scheme. Among others that he sought was the Hon. William Gray, better known as "Billy"

Gray. The following is the transcript of a letter to him.*

Haverhill, Sept. 24th, 1803.

Dear Sir:

I have never had the happiness of being particularly acquainted with you, if I had, I cannot say whether it would have been advantageous to both, or neither of us; but it does not follow but that even at this late hour of life with me, I may be able to show you some wordly good, or at least show you a project that if put into execution will terminate agreeably to your interest, if pursued on a large scale. It is a business which you are well acquainted with; it is the nailing business I mean. If you were here with me I should expect to be asked a few questions, and something like these. Where is the place you propose the nailing to be erected? At Amoskeag Falls, at the Canal. Have you a convenient place to set the slitting mill and other water works? A good fall and a plenty of water at all seasons of the year, with wood cheap and plenty. Have you ore in plenty in the vicinity of the place where these works are to be erected? What is the distance from Amoskeag to Boston? Sixty miles via Middlesex Canal. What vent do you expect for the nails? The traders and other inhabitants on the east and the west side of the Merrimack River, together with the inhabitants of a considerable part of Vermont state. Their pay will be in lumber, beef and other produce. Are there any nail works now erected in this great country? None of any consequence. It is presumed that nails can be transported by water from Amoskeag, *via* the Middle canal, to Boston, cheaper than they are transported from Bridgeport into Boston. But the wood at either of these places, costs more than three times the sum at Amoskeag. But it is not necessary to say much more on paper.

Sir, whatever has been my study and examination into the business, you are the only one that I have communicated it to in writing. If this sheet contains anything in worthy of your attention, I should be happy to hear from you, and meet with you upon the subject at Amoskeag Falls, upon the premises, which are twenty eight miles from Haverhill Bridge, laying in the town of Derryfield.

Yours, &c.

S. Blodget.

There is nothing to show that Mr. Gray took any notice of

---

* According to Potter.

this suggestion, and Judge Blodget's troubles pressing so thick and fast upon him, he was obliged to abandon all attempts of improving the water power, though he never lost a chance to expand upon the benefits likely to come to him who should do so.

From this plain statement it appeared that not only had he expended the $5000 afforded by the lottery, but he had actually used $7000 besides, which had been put in from his own property and the subscriptions of friends. If crippled in his own means and at odds with those who had in a considerable measure his fortune in their hands, the public was in sympathy with him In fact, however visionary his schemes may have seemed, however obstinate his enemies may have been againt him, and however straitened his circumstances, the common people were always his friends. They advocated his project now and everywhere sounded his praise. For him to fail would, in their minds prove a public calamity. If New Hampshire was indirectly against assisting him, the legislature of Massachusetts, realizing that that state was going to receive great benefits from trade through the completion of Blodget's canal, voted in March, 1804, the grant of a lottery to raise $10,000 to be expended under the direction of Colonel Baldwin, who had made the survey for the new route in 1798. The following June the New Hampshire legislature passed " An act to extend the time which was allowed Samuel Blodget for drawing a lottery," granted July 18, 1802. It now began to appear certain that Judge Blodget had fallen into the hands of those who hoped to profit by his failure, men who hoped through his age and many setbacks he would be obliged to give up his project, and leaving it in an unfinished condition, make the way for them to get possession at a low rate. They had misjudged their man. While the Massachusetts lottery gave slow and uncertain returns, allowing Col. Baldwin to make slow progress through the year 1805, the judge kept persistently and everlastingly at it. September 4, 1805, work had to be entirely suspended, but he roused new interest that winter by the publication of a document setting forth in convincing terms the good to result from the completion of his canal in the following comparison with the business of the Middlesex canal :

"It will be acknowledged by all enquiries into canaling business, that the canals are and will soon be of inconceiveable advantage to the public at large, especially when the Blodget Canal, so called, by his charter (but by an old Indian name Namoskeag) is completely finished; here are the locks that command an immense property of a great and a goodly country of many hundred miles in circuit, round the lakes and heads of streams, that empty into and form the Merrimack before they reach the locks at Blodget Canal ; this goodly country abounds with beef cattle upon a thousand hills and all kinds of produce, and lumber in abundance, with wealthy inhabitants suitably interspersed all over it, who wish a commercial intercourse with the prospering inhabitants of the commonwealth of Msasachusetts.

"As the committee of the Middlesex Canal has published the particular articles, that passed through their canal the last season the amount of which was 9405 tons of various articles, the toll of which amouuted to 11,832 dollars, it may not be amiss to inform the public the particulars and the quantity of each article that passed through the locks and slip at Blodget's canal t he last season, which is as follows, viz :

| | |
|---|---|
| 941,647 feet pine boards, | 1134 tons |
| 1,333 feet oak boards, | 3 " |
| 49,881 feet 2 inch oak plank, | 249½ " |
| 13,000 feet 5 inch pine plank, | 75 " |
| 13,800 feet 2 inch pine plank, | 38 " |
| 15,250 clapboards, | L-15 " |
| 343,500 shingles, | 68 " |
| 116,430 hogshead staves, | 204 " |
| 35,750 barrel staves, | 35 " |
| 122,578 hogshead hoops, | 245 " |
| 1,513 tons 3 feet oak timber, | 526 " |
| 1,434 tons 27 feet pine timber, | 1230 " |
| 62 tons 20 feet ash and elm timber, | 62 " |
| 240 empty hogsheads, | 12 " |

|  |  |
|---|---|
| 1,030 empty barrels, | 25 tons. |
| 294 shooks | 5 " |
| 2 empty boats for the Middlesex canal | 60 " |
| Amounting in the whole to | 3989 tons |

"Eighth tenths of the above lumber was carried through said canal and slip, in two months, viz., from the 5th of April to the 5th of June, 1805—after which a very small quantity of Lumber passed through the canal, owing to a failure of water and the Dam that is to be built to turn the water into the head of said canal not yet being erected—the Toll amounting to only 1082 dollars being fixed at the low rates of sixteen cents per ton for pine timber and other articles in proportion which, is done to encourage the business, the locks at the lower end of said canal, being yet in an unfinished state, those people who come down the river with lumber are obliged to break up their rafts in order to pass through the slip and then re-take said lumber, which not only subjects them to an extra bill of cost, but often detains them so long that they are obliged to haul up their rafts and wait until another rise of water, before they can proceed down the river to the Middlesex canal,—it is worthy of observation that the whole amount of every article that passed through the Middlesex canal both up and down the last year was

|  |  |
|---|---|
|  | 9405 tons |
| The whole amount of every article that passed Blodget's slip at Amoskeag the last season was | 3989 " |
|  | 5416 |
| Deduct the articles of wool and cider which was carried through the Middlesex in boats amounting to | 5405 |
|  | 11 |

Then there passed through the Middlesex canal only ten and a half tons more than passed through Blodget's slip the last season.—What may be expected when the Locks are completed at Blodget's canal—how must the merchants and the people of all descriptions in the country and in Boston and its vicinity rejoice to see that day?"

The result was most satisfactory. March 14, 1806, the Massachusetts legislature granted a second lottery in aid of the Blodget canal. Active men taking hold this time the avails of this summer were sufficient, with what had been raised by the New Hampshire lottery, to warrant the resumption of work in the latter part of the summer. Encouraged in every respect work was pushed with such vigor that a few days before Christmas, in December, 1806, Blodget's locks and canals were a reality! After twelve years and almost eight months of such trials, hard work, expenditure of money and disappointments as few men, younger than he, could have battled so bravely to the end Samuel Blodget had triumphed over enemies and such obstacles as must have crushed a less determined and enthusiastic spirit.

As it was then too late in the season to open the canal, May Day of the coming year was set for the happy affair. During the winter he busied himself with straightening his accounts and in preparations to meet the managers of the first New Hampshire lottery by a board of arbiters. Thus he was allowed no rest, though he was borne up by the thoughts of that day which was to witness the public acknowledgment of his triumph.

The morning of May 1st, 1807, the proudest day of Judge Blodget's long and eventful life, and the grandest day in the history of our proud city, came with the smiling sky and genial atmosphere of the fairest season of the year. At an early hour the people began to collect about the scene, eager, curious, expectant. Those came out of mere curiosity to see the man of whom they had heard so much for and against, those came to see the wonderful locks and the canal which he had devised to set at defiance the great laws of Nature, those came to scoff and to jeer at the visionary schemer who had squandered his own patrimony and sunk in an enterprise as vain as it was wild of conception the money of friend and stranger, those came to praise and admire the brave, courageous promoter of the public welfare and prosperity, and to laud his name to the sky should his dreams at last prove true, few came with a dim, vague gleam of the swift, marvelous transformation the matchless perserverance of one man was to bring to the unpromising scene about them, many came to cheer when convinced by their own eyes that it was not all some mad hoax, as many came to express their contempt in yells of derision should it after all prove a failure.

In the midst of the impatience of the spectators, the venerable projector of the great work, showing traces of the care and trouble through which he had passed, but with head erect and an eye undaunted, a man with a wonderfully vigorous bearing for one in his 84th year, Judge Blodget rode upon the scene in his old styled, two-wheeled carriage There was a general uncovering of heads, as he drove to the head of the canal, and alighted. Then, a deep silence fell on the crowd, while he stepped upon the raft with a few friends. The gate was opened, and while friend and enemy looked on with spellbound interest, the rude craft with its human freight glided safely down the passage-way and out upon the river below. The silence then was broken, tumultous applause rang on the air, the most adverse unable to withstand the happy outburst of spirit, until the huzzas fairly drowned the roar of old Amoskeag! Modest in his triumps, yet with a heart overflowing with thanksgiving, Judge Blodget rode down to his home, saying as he stepped down from his chaise: "I am well paid. My canal is complete. I have but one object to live for now. Let my difficulties with the managers be settled before the arbiters, and I die content."

The settlement of his accounts with the lottery managers was to take place in Haverhill, July 1, and until then he kept as busy as ever getting ready to support his claims. On that day he appeared before the arbiters as keen and firm in his manner as ever, to be met with the respectful attention that he deserved. But it was his last appearance in public. Riding home on the third, the weather being extremely cold for the season and he thinly clad, he took a severe cold, so that upon reaching his home he was obliged to seek his bed. As this was the first severe illness of his life, so was it his last, for on September 1, 1807, he sank into that sleep which he had so well earned. His funeral according to his own request was simple, after which he was borne to the ancient cemetery near the Falls, his grave marked by a plain headstone. Later,. when the encroachments of a growing city required it, the remains were removed to a place of sepulture in the south-west corner of the Valley cemetery, a plain, enduring granite monolith marking the spot. On its west face is this inscription :

To the Memory of
HON SAMUEL BLODGET,
Born at Woburn, Mass.,
April 1, 1724.
Died at Manchester,
(Then Derryfield,)
Sept. 1, 1807.

The north face has this : The Pioneer of internal Improvements in New Hampshire. The Projector and Builder of the Amoskeag Canal.

The south side has this explanatory note : Erected by His Great-Grandson, Joseph Henry Stickney, of Baltimore, Md., 1868.

The children of Samuel and Hannah (White) Blodget were an active and noted family.

Sarah, born in Haverhill, Mass , October 27, 1749, married Captain Stephen Perkins of Amesbury, where she lived and died.

Abigail, born in Haverhill, Mass., April 20, 1751, married Thomas Stickney, of Haverhill, where they lived and died. Their son, Thomas, managed the Blodget estate after the death of the judge, and no doubt would have carried out the business at the canal successfully had his health permitted.

Nathan, born in Goffstown, N. H., February 9, 1753, was for a time a merchant in Boston, in company with a brother-in-law, but afterwards went to Philadelphia, where he died.

Mary, born in Goffstown, December 1, 1754, married Samuel Gilman, who was in business with Nathan, 1780–90, in Boston.

William, born in Goffstown, July 6, 1756, died in infancy.

Samuel, Jr., born in Goffstown, August 28, 1757, married for his first wife Dorothy, daughter of Gen. Nathaniel Folsom. After a brief military career he went into business in Exeter,

N. H., but which did not prove successful. He next engaged in the East India trade in Boston, which proved profitable, and in 1789 he moved to Philadelphia, where his wife died the following year. Here he established the Insurance Company of North America, and in 1792, married Rebecca, a daughter of Rev. William Smith, D. D., Provost of the Philadelphia Univerith. In 1791-2, he bought a large tract of land in the future territory of Washington, D. C., building in 1795, at the same time his father was building his mansion at Manchester, the first house in Washington, and which was occupied for a time by President Adams and family while the White House was being completed. He also built another house of historical note, which he named the Union Pacific Hotel, which stood on the site of the present Post Office department, and which was bought by the government in 1810 and used as a "general post-office," until 1836, when it was burned. After the burning of the capitol by the British in 1814, Congress met in it for a time. He was interested in many schemes to benefit the National Capital and generously gave a large fortune to help build up the future city. He died in 1814, leaving a large property in trust for his family.

Caleb, born in Goffstown, August 17, 1759, served as Ensign in the Continental army in 1779, and Lieutenant in 1781; was lost overboard from a "Gunning float near Hogg Island,' August 9, 1789, and was buried in Boston. He was unmarried.

Elizabeth, born in Goffstown, January 12, 1761, died unmarried, December 23, 1778.

William, born in Goffstown, December 18, 1762, married Sarah, daughter of Major General John Stark.

Benjamin, born in Goffstown, July 6, 1768. He was concerned with his brother Samuel in the Washington purchase; died at Derryfield unmarried.

Upon the death of Judge Blodget, his grandson Thomas Stickney, a promising young man then living in Boston, came to Derryfield to complete the work of opening the river to better facilities for navigation. In 1810 the New Hampshire legislature granted a lottery for the benefit of the Blodget heirs that they might finish the work begun by him. Thomas Stickney started the first manufacturing industry, other than the saw and grist mills, on the Merrimack at this place, and in 1810 was chairman of the committee to change the name of Derryfield to Manchester, out of respect to the oft repeated prophecy of his grandfather that this would be the " Manchester of America." Had he had his health and lived to carry out his intentions, he might have realized some of the benefits likely to accrue from the efforts of Judge Blodget, but he was suffering from an acute disease which terminated his life in 1814, July 13, and he was buried in Granary Burial Ground in Boston. This left no one to look after the family interest, and the canal passed into the possession of the Merrimack Boating Company organized in Boston. Its first boat came up in October, 1814.

In summing up the life work and character of Samuel Blodget we must take into consideration, to do him entire justice, not only the result of his long and arduous toils and trials, but the peculiar condition and circumstances of his surroundings. Capital was not easily found to advance any enterprise of the most simple order, the spirit of progress had not been awakened in the hearts of a people which had not fully recovered from such a period of struggle for their civil rights as had necessarily put in the background all thoughts of bettering their financial condition. The art of mechanics was not understood and engineers were lacking to attempt a work of the kind. There had been no undertaking of the sort worth mentioning in the country, and those naturally looked with askance upon it who did not understand it. What modern resources, with modern knowledge of mechanics have done, with modern corporations to carry on the work, Samuel Blodget, alone and unaided, with such capital as he had individually accumulated in a time when big estates were unknown, set himself resolutely to do. If he was a visionary schemer, as his enemies delighted to style him, he was of that nature which has given us all of our great pioneers of progress. If a dreamer he was of the kind of Gouvernor Morris, who in 1806, suggested the Erie canal, scarcely of more importance than the Amoskeag canal, nor of greater magnitude of enterprise when the time of its construction and the wealth behind it are placed in comparison with Blodget's project. If he was ambitious of success, it was that ambition which made him a public benefactor without redounding to his personal greed or gain. In the light of later ideas of the fitness of things, some have tried to detract from his honor and the glory of his motives, by the means which were employed to procure the money necessary to accomplish his plans. Again must we place ourselves in the asssociations of that period. The lottery seemed the legitimate, and it might as truthfully be said, the only way of raising money for public enterprises. It had the sanction of church and state, and all classes of people patronized it. Says James Parton on this subject: "Chatham street, New York, was almost entirely occupied by lottery offices, the flaming bills of which made a great show on both sides of the way. Every device was employed to dazzle and lure the passer by. On certain days in the week, the drawing took place publicly in the space behind the front office, where a little girl, clad in spotless white, blindfolded, stood upon a platform, and drew forth the tickets in the presence of a breathless crowd." Every large city in America and Europe had at that time its Chatham street. In London, the sacred precinct of the west gate of St. Paul's cathedral was chosen as the place of drawing. The agent to do this was one of the smallest and prettiest of the Blue-coat School boys, selected from drawing to drawing, to remove the tickets, one after another, from the revolving wheel, and hand them to another little bright-eyed innocent, who passed them on to the manager, who announced their numbers in a high key of voice. There are plenty of instances to show how prevalent this custom was down to 1833, when Massachusetts abolished such methods and other states soon followed. The legislature of Massachusetts in 1786-7, in trying to encourage and stimulate the starting of the first cotton manufacturing in this country at Beverly, did not hesitate to resort to prohibitory duties, Eastern land grants, lotteries and the like, granting six tickets in the land lottery of 1787. Again in 1789 the legislature granted 500 pounds to be paid in eastern lands and invoked congress to assist by a national lottery. Nashua, this state, in 1745 or 6, petitioned to the General Court for privilege to raise money by lottery to build a bridge over the Nashua river. As late as 1811, the New Hampshire legislature inaugurated a lottery scheme to raise money to build the road through Dixville Notch. But Samuel Blodget needs no vindication of this kind. The record of his whole life is ample evidence that he never wronged any one. In fact if he had a fault, if that which borders upon a virtue can be styled a shortcoming, it was in placing too much confidence in others. In his own open, free-hearted, hospitable nature, he believed others to possess the honesty of purpose which was the ruling star of his life. He is described as having a sturdy figure, a little over five feet and nine inches in height, a full, round countenance inclined to floridness, blue eyes and brown hair, a fluent talker, genial in his intercourse and a man of strong personal magnetism, which never failed to draw about him a large circle of warm friends. He was rigidly temperate in his manner of living, using no ardent spirits, active in his pursuits, and usually lodged in a large room with windows open on both sides of his bed, regardless of the weather, and was always sanguine of success in whatever he undertook. By following these simple rules he believed he should live to be one hundred years old. No doubt they did sustain him through his arduous work, but that scantiness of clothing in which he believed was one cause of catching cold on his last ride from Haverhill, which in his over-taxed condition of body and mind, resulted in his death at a time when he was on the eve of seeing realized the prophecy of his dreams. But if others were to carry out the work he had planned, to reap the harvest of the field he had sown, it was his far-seeing brain, his long life of devotion to the laying of its foundation, his accumulated means, his undaunted spirit which made it all possible. The golden years of his life were a sacrifice for our beautiful city; his memory should be reverenced in every heart that has love for our growing institutions his name should be fixed imperishably with her history; and his sturdy figure in bronze or granite stand on one of our public squares as a perpetual reminder of him who has been fitly described as the Pioneer of Progress.

# INDIANS OF NEW HAMPSHIRE.

ETYMOLOGY OF THEIR LANGUAGE.

A PAPER BY HON. JOHN G. CRAWFORD READ BEFORE THE MANCHESTER HISTORIC ASSOCIATION, MARCH 17, 1897.

The origin of the American Indians has been a question of much doubt and speculation. The claim that they were of Asiatic extraction was strongly believed in by those who first landed on our shores. One reason for this belief was the similarity of the language spoken by the Aborigines to the Greek and Hebrew. More recent investigation has led to the belief that the primitive man had his abode on this continent.

Mexico and the South American states retain the evidence that at a most remote period in the world's history there existed in these countries a race of people whose records as shown on monuments and ruined temples antedate any records found in the old world

The discoveries recently made in Yucatan would indicate that the people of Asia were the descendants of the race that inhabited this country at the time, and long before the destruction of the continent of Atlantis. From this country, they emigrated to the east, and a portion of them in after years reached this country by way of the Behring straits and their descendants are the present native inhabitants of Alaska. Those who remained in Mexico and other southern countries, at the time of the eastern exodus, had a written language expressed in hieroglyphics which have been interpretated, and from these writing much has been learned of this, now almost extinct people.

From their ancient seat, they migrated to the north and east, and became the mound builders and cliff dwellers of other parts of this continent.

As they drifted away from their seat of learning they gradually lost their written language, and when the discoverers of America found the red man in New England, which for want of knowledge they called Indians, which name has been since retained to designate the Aborigines, it was found they possessed only a spoken language and that of a very limited character. When the English first settled in New England, and the French in Arcadia they found numerous tribes inhabiting this section of the country. divided into several minor tribes, each tribe located at different points, and under its own chiefs. These tribes, having no written language, their vocabulary was not only limited but as various as the tribes themselves.

Some words in use were common to several tribes, but in the main their spoken language was different and it was with difficulty that one tribe could communicate with the others, though living a short distance of each other. This fact is affirmed by Roger Williams, who devoted much time to the nomenclature of the Indians of Rhode Island.

What language they were able to speak, was confined in a measure to the common objects of nature, and to convey to each other the necessary information to supply their limited wants.

When the whites came among them, their vocabulary was extended, and in the effort to civilize and educate them, the whites undertook the task of giving them a written language. Catching the sounds, and giving the same force to their words as was given by the whites, they were able to construct a language that could be used in their education.

The orthography given by the English to the language in Massachusetts and Rhode Island was as different from that given by the French in Maine and Arcadia, as the difference in the French and English as used to-day. The sounds of the words and letters was in the one case English and in the other French, and this fact is what has caused so much dispute over the names of localities bearing the Indian name.

The Indians that inhabited Maine and Arcadia and extended across New Hampshire, and which gave the names to most of our mountains, lakes and rivers, were those who had their language written by the French Missionaries, and when we attempt to interpret these names from the English orthography, we find ourselves in error in most cases, and thereby we have failed to retain or to preserve the true meaning of those localities butbearing the names the Aborigines applied to them.

What the names thus given really meant, may not be of much interest to the present generation, and whether the true derivation has been correct, may be of but little importance, but there should be some agreement that the discussion of the question may not be longer continued. Mr. Potter in his History of Manchester devotes much space to the discussion of the derivation and meaning of the localities in this state and in Maine, which have retained something of their Indian orthography, but the mistake he made, not being familiar with the construction of the language, was in trying to apply the Massachusetts dialect to the New Hampshire Indian language when the two were as different as the nationalities speaking two tongues.

The meaning and pronunciation of Indian names can not be given correctly, unless some attention is paid to the construction and force of the language spoken by them. In order to do that, we must not forget that the orthography was given by the French, and not by the English who settled in Massachusetts.

In the work of making a written language from their vocabulary and catching the sound of their spoken words, it was found that in the construction of an alphabet the letters necessarily used, were all the English, with the exception of the letters f-q-r-v-x-y.

In the old original Abnakis the letter — r — was used, but after the enlargement of their vocabulary, when they came in contact with the whites, the harshness of the sound of that letlet and the great difficulty in pronouncing the same — they giving the same as the Chinese do at the present time — the sound of the letter — l — this letter has been entirely supplanted by — l.  Aremos, dog, old ; Alemos, modern.

The letter — o — had two sounds, the usual and the nasal sound, which nasal sound was indicated in the written word by an apostrophe after the capital and circumflex over the small letter

The fifteen consonants are sounded as in the English with the exception that b and d final being always sounded respectfully as p and t : take the word David, this word would be Tabit.  Asib, a sheep, is Azip.

G is always hard ; Ch has a softer sound than in the English.  J is sounded like ch, the word Kabij, cabbage, is pronounced as if spelled kabich.  *Ph* is not sounded as — f — for that letter is not in the language.  The Indian name for women, *phanem*, which is articulated as if it was spelled pe-ha-nem, expressed in two syllables — p'ha-nem, the apostrophe after the p shows the nasal sound.

All consonants must be sounded ; there are no exceptions.  When a letter is doubled, either a consoant or vowel, the two letters are sounded as one, the sound being prolonged.  The vowel sounds are about the same as in the English with the exception of — u — which is sounded as u, in union, except 1, when it occurs alone, 2, when it is first in a word, 3, when it is preceded by — i —.  When u is preceded by a consonant, other than g or k, it is sounded like *e*.

The plurals were formed by the termination -ak-ik-ok-k-al-il-ol-l-.  There are substantives, two kinds, animate and inanimate, and animate and inanimate adjectives and verbs, which are made to agree with the substantive.  The termination of the plural in the animate is — k — in the inanimate — l.

The plural of the adjectives is — t — for the animate and k for the inanimate.  When a noun terminates with the letter d or t, it must be changed to — j — before the annexation of the plural *ik*.

When a word ends in — w — preceded by g or k; as gw-kw-, the final w must be suppressed before the annexation of the plural — ol. The termination of two syllables, *wo-gan*, is a substantive, being suppressed, changes the expression into the Indicat. pres. 3d. per., sing., of a verb, as Kelo*wogan* — speech — by suppressing the *wogan* it would be He Speaks.

Their adjectives were not only invariable and single but variable and contracted. Their simple adjectives signified nothing when standing alone, but when prolonged by some other syllables.

Wli-good, gentle, wligo, he, she is good. Wobi, white; wobigo, he is white. Wligen, it is good; wobigen, it is white; the termination — go — was the personal pronoun, he or she, as they had no word to indicate sex; the termination — gen — was the pronoun it.

There were prefixes and suffixes that meant the same, as Mamlaw, a prefix which denoted largeness or abundance. Lake Memphremagog, derives its name from the prefix Mamlaw, abundance, and baga, a particle denoting water, and the termination of the letter k, which gives it in local term. The suffix denoting plenty is — ika — this termination to a noun as *sen*, rock, stone; senika, would mean, there are plenty of, or many rocks, it is rocky. Moniika, there is plenty of money.

The termination indicating the plural of animate nouns, when used as terminations of inanimate objects, indicated the preposition at, to, from; wajos, a mountain of middling height, with the termination ek, means at the mountain. This is the name of Mount Wachusett, in Massachusetts, and from this the state derives its name, with the prefix Massa, which means large or great — The state of the great mountain.

The word moni or mona, was derived from the whites who, when they came among them had only silver for money; the Indians hearing it called money applied that name to all silver.

Wajos, or Wachos, was one name for mountain. They had

also a name for mountain which was used in composition ; this was, aden.

From this we have the name of mount Monadnock, Mônaaden-ok ; from Mona, silver, aden, mountain with the termination, ok, which as stated before has the force of the preposition, at, At the silver mountain.

The variations of their verbs, and the transposition of words and of some of their affixes would be an interesting study, to those who have an interest in this work ; but my purpose, at this time is to give some opinion as to the orthography and etymology of some of the localities within our own state, that those who may write of them hereafter may have some authority for what they may have to say in regard to th's matter.

At the lower end of our state we find that some of the names of the several localities bear the names given from the Massachusetts Indian dialect, yet most of them are from the Abenaki who occupied this territory.

The name Abnaki was first applied to the Indians in Nova Scotia, but afterwards was applied to all the tribes who resided east of the Massachusetts. The name comes from " Wobanaki, " land or country of the East, from Woban, day break, and ki, earth, land or rather Aki, which is a term employed in composition for land, ground, place. It means also an Indian from where the daylight comes. The plural makes, wobanakiak.

Pawcatuck is from either the word for shaking river, or perhaps from pogwkategw, the shallow river.

Pawtucket, from pawtagit, who shakes himself ; which shakes itself : a figurative sense applied sometimes to falls.

Piscataqua, by the standard dictionary is said to mean great deer river. Father Aubury in his manuscript vocabulary of the language of this tribe says it comes from the word *Peskata* which means dark or gloomy.

Ammonoosuc, from O'manosek, the fishing ground, or better the small or narrow fishing river. Some pretend that it comes from pagonozik, at the walnut tree, from pagonozi walnut tree.

# INDIANS OF NEW HAMPSHIRE. 183

The absence of walnuts in that locality would go to confirm the name as from O'manosek.

Aroostook, in Maine, from Wlastegw, good river. There were two words which meant river, sibo or sipo, and tegw ; the latter was used in composition and the word *sibo* when the word river was used alone.

Awasoswi Menahan, the name of Bear Island in lake Winneplesaukee is from Awasos, bear, and menahan, island; the *wi* which terminates so many of the Indian words does not seem to have any particular signification, and is usually omitted in composition.

Connecticut, from Kwenitegw, long river ; Kwen, or Kwuni, long and *tegw*, river. The Massachusetts used the letter Q where the French used K. Qwin, is for long in the Massachusetts dialect.

Great Falls was known as Kchi Pontegok, at the great falls.

Housatonic, from awasadenik, beyond the mountain ; over the hill ; from Awasi . . . beyond, aden' mountain or hill (only in composition) and ik, one of the suffixes which gives the name in local term.

Katahdin, from Ktaden, the big or high mountain.

Kearsarge, from Kesarzet—old Abenakis—as it will be noticed that the letter r is retained—the proud or selfish. This mountain standing out proudly alone gave the name Kesarzet.

Merrimack, from Morôdemak (old Abenakis) deep or profound river.

Nashua, from Nansawi . . . between, and most likely took its name from the Indians who resided on Wachacum lake near Lancaster, Mass. They were thus called for the reason that they were located between the coast Indians and those who occupied the Connecticut river valley. Wachacum in the Massachusetts Indian dialect was sea. The original name of the Nashua river was Watagua, which meant pickerel, as the river was a great place for this fish.

Massabesic, from Mase, large, nebe, lake, water, with the

suffix, *ik*, which gives it a locality. At the great or large lake or pond.

Cohas, this brook is the Massachusetts orthography for pine tree. Coa, or Koa was pine tree, Coas, the diminutive, and means little pine tree. The full Indian name if applied to the brook would be the diminutive of the word sibo river, viz., Coas sibosis.

Uncanoonuc is a name given by the Massachusetts Indians, and is the plural of the word Kuncannowet—breasts.

Amoskeag, from Namos, a fish — ki — a place — at the fishing place. The ki, is the contraction of aki, or aukee, which when applied to a location on a river the a or au was suppressed, and the preposition, k,—at the fishing place.

Penacook, from the Massachusetts word, Penayi, crooked, and tegw, river.

Suncook, from senikok, at the rocks. From sen, a stone, with the termination ok, at. If applied to the river it would be, sentegw, stone river.

Winnepesaukee, or as sometimes spelled Winnepesaki, is from Wiwininebesaki, a lake in the vicinity of which there are other lakes, or better, lake region. It is from, Wiwin, abbreviation of wiwniwi, around, in the vicinity, nebes, a lake, and aki, land region, territory.

Winooski, Vt., from winos, onion, and ki, land. Onion land.

The White mountain region was called Wawobadenik, Wawob, white, aden, mountain, ik, at, at the White mountains.

Megantic, from namagwottik, which means, lake trout place. Namagw, means salmon trout, while Mskuamagw, was salmon.

Passumpsic, from pasômkasik, diminutive term which means, river which has a clear sandy bottom.

Saco, comes from sokwai, which means from the south side, southern, hence the name sokwaki — modern sokoki — southern country, Indians from the south.

Ossipee, from Osibi, a lake formed by the enlargement of the river.

Moosilauke is from moose, or the French orthography moz

and aki, or aukee, region or land. The letter l does not properly belong in the word, and is thrown in simply for euphony. The correct pronunciation of the word would be Moose(l)aukee. Its meaning is a place or region where there are moose, and undoubtedly applied to the whole region, and finally became applied to the mountain now bearing that name.

Coos, from the diminutive of Coa, pine tree.

Mascoma, the name of a lake in Grafton county has met with great change since the Indians gave it a name. I am informed that one of the earlier settlers said that the first white man who had heard the name from the Indians called this lake Masquane, and if that was true, which is most likely, it would be Birch-bark lake, from Maskwa, birch bark, and ne, from nepe, lake or water. Places bearing these names were localities where could be found bark or other material required in their rude condition.

Baboosuc, brook or pond in Amherst, is from Papposuc, the termination, suc, was often used by the Massachusetts Indians when applied to a person, or the final ok, *at*.

Pemigewasset, from Pamijowasik, diminutive of pamijowak, which means the swift or rapid current, Pamijowasik, the narrow and shallow swift current.

Mount Washington was called Kodaak-wajo, the hidden mountain, so called because the top was so much hidden in the clouds.

In concluding this article I append a limited

## VOCABULARY OF COMMON OBJECTS.

Awan, air; Kzelômsen, wind; Soglonbi, rain water; Nbisonbi, mineral water; Sobagw, the sea, ocean; Kchi alakws, morning or evening star; Pili kisos, new moon; Tka, cold; Pekeda, smoke; Siguana, last spring; Nibena, last summer; Pebona, last winter; Nebi, water; Pibganbi, muddy water; Kisos, the sun, moon, month; Wloda, heat; Skweda, fire, flame; Siguan spring; Niben, summer; Pebon, winter; Taguôgo, autumn, fall.

It will be noticed that the termination, a, when applied to

seasons, is equivalent to the word last, while by changing the final n to g, retaining the a, it is equivalent to the word next, as Nibega, next summer ; Peboga, next winter. The termination iwi, is the preposition in. Paboniwi, in winter ; Siguaniwi, in spring ; Nibeniwi, in summer.

The common animals found in this state, were known as Aremos, modern Alemos, a dog ; Molsom, wolf ; Wòkwses, a fox ; Tmakwa, a beaver. By the addition of the letters ia or iia, it indicated meat of the animals. Nolka, deer ; Nolkaiia, venison or deer meat ; Magô'ibo, a caribou ; Magôliboiia, caribou meat. The termination, awa, to the name of the animal was the equivalent to the word skin, Magoliboawa, caribou skin ; Akigw, a seal ; Akigwawa, seal skin.

The diminutive was formed by the termination of s, is, or sis, as Nebes, a lake ; Nebesis, a pond ; Sen, a stone ; Senis, a pebble ; Wôkwses, a fox ; Pakesso, a partridge ; Mateguas, a rabbit ; Mikowa, a squirrel ; Wôbikwsos, a mouse ; Moskuas, a muskrat ; Mosbas, a mink ; Planigw, a flying squirrel ; Kogw, a porcupine ; Saguasis, a weasel ; Segôgw, a a skunk , Awasos, a bear ; Anikwses, a striped squirrel ; Asban, raccoon ; Agaskw, a woodchuck ; Sips, a bird ; Sibsis, a little bird ; Mgeso, an eagle ; Kokokhas, an owl ; O'basas, a woodpecker ; Kwikueskas, a robin ; Mkazas, a crow ; Kchimkazas, a raven, the prefix Kchi, great, makes the raven the great crow. The crow takes its name from its color, Mkazawi, black. Ahamo, a hen, by adding the diminutive, is, it becomes Ahamois, chicken ; Nahama, turkey.

## FISHES, REPTILES, &c.

Namas, a fish ; Kabasa, a sturgeon ; Mskuamagw, a salmon ; Namagw, a salmon trout ; Kikomkwa, a sucker ; Nahomo, an eel ; Watagua, a pickerel ; Molazigan, a bass ; Skog, a serpent, a snake ; Chegual, a frog ; Maska or Mamaska, a toad ; Skoks, a worm ; Sisikwa, a rattlesnake ; Mamselabika, a spider ; Pabigw, a flea ; Alikws, an ant ; Kemô, a louse ; Mamijôla, a butterfly ; Wawilômwa, a bee, a wasp ; Wjawas, a fly ; Pegues, a mosquito.

### FOREST-TREES, &c.

Anaskemezi, an oak; Wawabibagw, a poplar; Manlakws, an ash; Maskwamozi, a birch; Kokokhôakw, a fir-tree. The fir-tree evidently derives its name from Kokokhas, an owl, and literally is the owl tree. Saskib, an elder; Môlôdagw, a cedar; Chignazakuam, a thorn-tree; Maskwazimenakuam, a wild cherry-tree; Pasaakw, a red pine; Masozial, ferns. The final *al* is the plural. Asakuam, moss; Walagaskw, bark; Awazon, (plu *al*) fuel, firewood; Mskak, black spruce; Sasôgsek, sarsaparilla; Anibi, an elm; Wajoimizi, a beech; Senomozi, a maple; Wdopi, an alder-tree; Kanozas a, willow. Kansas takes its name from Kanozas. Wigbimizi, bass-wood; Moskwaswaskw, the sweet-flag; Alnisedi, a hemlock; Msoakw, a dry tree, decayed wood; Kawasen, a wind-fall; Maskwa, (pronounced Masqua', birch-bark; Msazesso, (plu *ak*), whitespruce; Pôbnôdageso, tamarac.

Men or min was berry and was used as a termination in such as Mskikôimins, strawberry, (plu *ak*); Pessimen, currant, (plur-*al*.) Abazi, a tree, was not used in composition, but the termination akuam was tree, Azawanimen. A plum; having the final *men*, being classed under the head of berry, when applied to the tree became Azawanimenakuam, a plum-tree; Adbimen, a cherry; Adbimenakuam, a cherry-tree.

The termination of *mozi* was bush; Sgueskimen*ak*, raspberries; Sgueskimenimozi, a raspberry bush; Sata, blueberry; Satamozi, blueberry bush.

Those who in their younger days delighted in the conjugation of the familiar verb, to love, may be interested in the conjugation of the Abenaki verb, Kazalmomuk, to love. The letters N and K were used as personal pronouns, as abbreviations of the words Nia, I or me; Kia, thee or thou. In the plural N' was used for Niuna, us, we, when they did not include those to whom they spoke, and K', Kiuna, us, we, when those to whom they spoke were included; the apostrophe denoting the nasal sound.

The conjugation of the passive verb, Kazalmegwzimuk, to be

loved, Indicative Mood, Present Tense. This would stand:

    N'kezalmegwzi,      I am loved.
    'Kezalmegwzo,       He is loved.
    N'kezalmegwzibena,  We are loved.
    K'kezalmegwziba,    You are loved.
    'Kezalmegwzoak,     They are loved.

That race of peculiar people who roamed over our hills and paddled their light canoes upon the beautiful waters of the old Granite State, have nearly disappeared. The small remnant that remains have become, to a great extent, mixed by intermarriage with the white race, but their language and their names, as applied to many localities, are yet retained. Let them be cherished in everlasting rememberance of that race, which fell before the advancing columns of a cruel civilization.

# THE MANTER MILLS.

A PAPER BY WILLIAM H. HUSE, READ BEFORE THE MANCHESTER HISTORIC ASSOCIATION, MARCH 17, 1897.

Just over the Londonderry line, near the road to Derry, are the ruins of several mills, once noisy with the whir and buzz of millstone and saw, and the centers of industries of importance in former days. Now the water flows quietly by, nourishing fish and batrachian unhindered by wheel or dam, and feeding beds of glorious cardinal flowers unmolested save by some passing admirer.

The brook that turned those wheels rises in Chester, meanders through the southern part of Auburn, wanders over the line into Londonderry, and finally, fed by numerous rivulets and swamps, adds considerable to the volume of the Cohas brook, a few rods below the pumping station. Dry seasons materially reduce its size, though they seldom, if ever, completely stop the flow of water. It is known as the Little Cohas or Manter brook.

When the town of Londonderry was settled the proprietors sold the lot about the falls, where the mills alluded to afterwards stood, to Robert and Hugh Wilson, reserving the falls and some land for flowage. The papers bear the date of January 9, 1729. Nearly five years later John Douglass bought the falls and two acres of land. The original deed reads as follows:

"The proprietors of the town of Londonderry in consideration of ten bills of credit to us in hand before the delivery hereof lay out to John Douglass two acres of land situated near ye Great Falls on Cohass brook together with the right to build dam or dams, mill or mills together with the right to flow ye stream from time to time from ye 5th day of September to ye 5th day of April and so on forever, with power of attorney.

         JAMES REED
         JAMES LINDSEY
         JNO. ARCHIBALD
         JNO. WALLACE
         ALLEN ANDERSON
   Before ye Justice
         GEORGE DUNCAN.

" Ye 8th day of November, 1733."

Douglass built a house near the falls, the cellar of which can still be seen. In September, 1746, he sold his interest to one William Battey, who erected a house on the road leading to Amoskeag falls, now a part of the Derry road. This house was used as a tavern for a number of years. The cellar hole can still be seen with a large pine growing in it.

In 1747 Battey deeded one half of the sawmill that Douglass had built to James Wilson The deed reads, "one half interest in ye John Douglass sawmill, one half ye stream, one half ye dam, one half ye mill, one half ye mill saw, one half all her trackings, together with the right to use ye path that leads from ye mill to ye highway."

The deed was signed by William Battey and Robert Patterson. In 1767 Battey sold his half to John Pinkerton. In 1768 Andrew Jack acquired an interest in the property. Successive owners were John Smith and John McDuffee. McDuffee rebuilt the original mill and erected one some distance lower down the brook.

He was more than ordinarily ingenious and enterprising, for without any capital but his hands and heads he made everything about the mill except the saw and the shaft. These he could not make, and he had no money wherewith to buy, but his enterprise was not exhausted. In Deacon Pinkerton of the village, now Derry Village, he found a friend who supplied him with the necessary articles, and was renumerated in boards at $6 per thousand. Sometime, probably not much later, a grist mill was built on the opposite or left bank of the stream.

The lower mill was sold by him to James Hunter and was long known as the Hunter mill. The upper mill or mills he sold to Gilbert Pierce about 1800. Pierce operated them until 1808, when he sold them to George Manter, who came to Londonderry from Plymouth, Mass. Mr. Manter owned and used all three mills. The lower mill, which stood on the north bank, was removed about 1820. All that now remains of it is a hole in the bank and a few stones of the old dam, with one of the millstones in the bottom of the brook. Mr. Manter, with his two sons, Francis and Samuel, used the upper two mills till 1840, when the sons took entire charge. When both gristmills were in operation and the water was low, the two were used alternately. The upper one would be used first, and while the grain was being ground the water flowed down to the lower pond. When the upper pond was empty the miller went to the lower mill, where customers were usually waiting, and the water in the pond there would be utilized. Then the same arrangement would be repeated.

In winter, Francis Manter, then a young man working for his father, would usually skate from one mill to the other, often taking his rifle with him, and occasionally shooting a muskrat that ventured to show his head through an air hole.

In 1860 Francis rebuilt both mills, putting them together on the site of the grist mill on the left or southwest bank of the brook. The sawpit and remains of the rollway may still be seen on the right bank. About the time of the remodeling a box mill with machinery was added, and from this time a rushing business was done. A fall of eighteen feet gave abundant power and the mill was run day and night.

Francis Manter, the manager of the business for so many years, was a man of remarkable energy and great ability. He received his education in the district schools of the day. In the war of 1812 he took part; was connected with the militia for a long time, holding the state commission of colonel for eight years, and was appointed inspector-general, but declined on account of his private business.

In 1820 Colonel Manter married Harriet Crowninshield of Salem, Mass. By her he had three children, George W. Manter, M. D., who practiced medicine in Manchester in the sixties, Mary F., who married George W. Platts, and Harriet M., widow of James M. Platts, and who lives in this city. In 1830 he began the manufacture of shoes, being the first to begin this business on an extensive scale in this region. The shoes were sent to Boston by way of the river and the Middlesex canal and in ox teams. He also owned a cooper's shop, shipping his barrels to Cape Cod, where they were sold to fishermen. In addition to these he managed a blacksmith shop and a store, and dealt in real estate to a large extent. He always managed his own business and kept his own books. He was frequently called upon to take part in the business of the town. He died in 1889 at the age of 91.

About 1868 the gristmill was discontinued and the stones taken out. The building was leased to Thomas L. Thorpe, who put in machinery for cleansing mill waste, using both water and steam power. After a number of years the mill was again leased to John P. Lord, at one time superintendent of the print works, who put in a new set of machinery and manufactured shoddy.

After this the stones were again put in and some grinding done. Then in 1882 James H. Ryder, formerly superintendent of the Fessenden mills (now the Annis mills) of North Londonderry, leased the mill, rebuilt it, put in a turbine wheel, raised the dam two feet and filled in a large hollow southwest of the mill. Machines were put in for sawing boards and making boxes and kits. In a short time James M. Platts, son-in-law to Mr. Manter, took charge of the property, retaining Mr. Ryder as superintendent. This arrangement lasted until 1890, when

Clarence M. Platts, to whose memory and private papers I am indebted for these facts, assumed control and managed the mill for several years. Towards the latter part of this period the principal business was the making of boards for the New York market.

In the fall of 1890 there was a division of the property, and the mill privilege, right of flowage and a part of the mill were sold to Charles E. Cousins, who still owns them. The new part of the mill was removed soon after the sale, and now all but the part that covers the saw has been torn down, and little of its former appearance remains.

In connection with these mills should be mentioned a small one located on a little brook that flows into the Little Cohas some distance below, near a " great rock " that is one of the historic landmarks of the locality. It is as large as a small house, is one of the town bounds, and is mentioned under the name given above in nearly every deed of land in this vicinity. The mill was built and owned by Daniel McDuffee, brother to the John mentioned above, and in it he had a turning lathe and made wooden bowls, mortars, etc., with which the neighboring housewives were supplied. Many of these are still in existence in families that formerly lived in that vicinity. Daniel was as ingenious as his brother, and besides his other work made cradles for reaping grain and at one time was employed by the town to make bullets. This mill was known as " McDuffee's Turning Mill." It is now but a memory.

When the last of the three Manter mills was torn down, the last mill run by the Little Cohas disappeared. At some future time the power of this stream may be utilized for the production of electricity, but at present, where once half a dozen or more mills were humming, all is silent, and the water ripples idly by. Man has come and man has gone but the brook " flows on forever."

# HOME LIFE OF MAJ-GEN. JOHN STARK.

PAPER BY HENRY W. HERRICK, READ BEFORE THE MANCHESTER HISTORIC ASSOCIATION, SEPTEMBER 15, 1897.

There are three biographies of Gen. John Stark published in book form, two issued in Concord, N. H ; one in 1831, another by his son Major Caleb Stark, in 1860, and a third in Spark's American biographies, written by Edward Everett, and published by Harper & Bros. in 1854. These are carefully prepared and complete from a military point of view, as this phase of the old hero's life is of the greatest interest to the public. We think of him as a successful and patriotic fighter in two wars, and his victories lend a fascination and charm to every recital of his campaigns.

There is, however, an interesting field of research in the account of Gen. Stark's life in time of peace, while resting from the hardships of war, that has been but slightly explored, and it is this that we propose to consider. It will undoubtedly lead many readers to have an entirely new idea of the man, and may change their views as to some of his characteristics.

He is regarded by the average reader of American history as a bluff, picturesque, and somewhat hard old soldier, rough in his treatment of all subjects in public and social life, carrying his purpose with a tenacity of will that would admit of no dispute, or compromise. To a limited extent this is true. He was like the shag bark walnut tree of his native Nutfield, often rough on the surface, but within, compact, fine and enduring, with those qualities that we all admire and associate with our highest conceptions of true manhood and patriotism.

In an analysis of character of one whose life has been so long in the past, we have largely to judge of his qualities by incidents, rather than from the estimates of persons who were contemporary with him. With Stark we have from both of these sources, abundant material from which to form, without bias, a clear judgment of his domestic, social and business traits.

The influence of Gen. Stark in his capacity as citizen, was not confined even in early life to local affairs, for his enterprise and adventurous spirit was known beyond the bounds of the frontier settlements. Though his education would not be endorsed in these latter days as liberal and complete, his advantages in this direction surpassed those of most families in his vicinity. His father's early training in the University of Glascow gave him a decided prominence in the settlements, and the son manifested in his public and military life, the result of his domestic training. The official letters and friendly correspondence embodied in his biography, show a power of terse expression, and deal with the subjects in hand clearly and forcibly. When in camp, and burdened with all the cares and oversight of the innumerable questions coming for solution to a commander, he personally attended to his correspondence. Only once do we find him asking for a military secretary. Henry Parkinson acted in this capacity in the years 1775-6.

Gen. Stark united in a large degree the bluff, decisive manner of address of his ranger surroundings, and the observant, cautious dealing that intuitively stopped short of assumption and curtness. We do not find in all his history a contention with brother officers, admonition or rebuke from military superiors; neither insubordination or mutiny in his command. This is somewhat remarkable, when we recall the trying conditions in which he was often placed as commander of untrained masses of men, brought together from all parts, and organized without the most common supplies for a soldier's life. We account for this only by his great popularity with the crude militia, and his willingness to share every hardship and privation of the service, with his men.

The militia of the period were men with good judgment of the merits of their commanders, and a martinet with pretention and pomp, could have little military control of the rank and file. Stark was a man to scorn covert measures to obtain a pair of epaulets and a title ; he took only such as came to him voluntarily, as a recognition of merit, from his country. He modestly went through his entire service of the revolutionary war, with the rank of Brigadier, receiving in 1785 the complimentary title of Major-General, by brevet, and the full recognition of a commission in 1817, when his friend and comrade at Trenton, James Munroe, came to the high honor as President of the United States.

As a business man in private life, or managing in his military capacity the finances of the commands under him, there was exhibited the same skill, faithfulness and economy.

The financial account to the House of Delegates of New Hampshire for the Benningten contest, has been stated to amount for mustering, mileage, commissary stores, wages and incidental expenses to be $82,000 in the depreciated paper currency of the time, or less than $2,500 in gold. No stain or suspicion ever rested on his integrity in business, and he was too generous to indulge in niggardly over-reaching in business transactions.

In the proposed military winter expedition to Canada, in the winter following the Bennington and Saratoga victories, Stark was selected to act with Lafayette and Gen. Conway, but the project was for some reason quietly abandoned. In this matter Stark was intrusted with money and supplies in full confidence, and in his administration of the northern department, we continually find him engaged in detecting and bringing to punishment, culprits and robbers of the army's supplies.

After the battle of Bennington his methodical business habits were in evidence the day following the action. He had, previous to the engagement, promised the troops, in event of victory, the supplies they so much needed. Promiscuous looting was at once arrested by guards, the captured supplies were carefully collected and an inventory made ; after which, the whole property was sold at "vendue," the auction term of those days, and he proceeds divided equitably among the troops.

The few presents to the states, represented in the battle, were reserved, with the four cannon. The two small pieces of ordinance were transferred upon petition, in 1848, to Vermont by congress, and the two larger ones were never officially conferred by congress to any state. These guns were in use through the war of 1812, and two of them were captured at Detroit by the Canadians, and recaptured at Fort George by the Americans. The gun at New Boston is one of the larger pair, captured in the sun-set battle, from Breyman.

After the war, the interests of his farm and an extensive trade in lumber and tracts of woodland, divided his time and labors. At this period, he owned, with two partners, the present township of Dunbarton, then called Starkstown, and operated largely in pine lumber and ship timber. The facilities for getting logs and manufactured lumber to market were greatly increased by the completion of the Blodget canal in 1807, and Stark's property in timber tracts received an upward appraisal. He did not die a rich man, as we understand the term in modern phrase; he had for those times, however, a large competence, which gradually accumulated under his prudent and energetic management, and gave him power to show a generous hospitality to the numerous visitors and war veterans who came to his home.

There was a pleasant and tender side to the character of our old hero, that was manifest to his family and intimate friends, and which seemed reserved for his cherished home life. In his later years it was a pleasure for him to have at the old homestead in the autumn days, his annual "harvest-home." This was simply a festival of good-will and merry-making, in which it was his ambition and wish to have present the families of the vicinity and his old friends in adjoining towns. If a poor family, or any invalid, was from misfortune absent, he provided for conveyance or clothing. " On earth peace, good-will to men," was the sentiment of his heart, after his life's career of storm and battle. His kindness was not confined to man, however;

it extended with noticeable results to every animal and pet on his farm. His barns were filled with flocks and herds, noted for their sleek, well-fed condition. He was emphatic on this point. His favorite horse, old "Hessian," was a large, round, bay animal, cared for by his master, as if a pet child. And we are told that Hessian reciprocated the fondling, and would let his owner, or the young people of the household, play all manner of tricks about him with impunity. An extra large sleigh was provided for the big horse, and the winter rides would sometimes show a pyramid of grandchildren piled in for a happy time. This love for his farm pets extended even to his poultry. One who was an attendant of his old age said many years since, that the general's love for his poultry was equal to that of a modern chicken exhibitor at a state fair. Sitting on the sunny lawn, he would occasionally get his feathered flock about him, and with pride "show them off" to visitors. Calling the great patriarch of the flock with a handful of corn, he would feed him from the hand, and then order the bird to perch on his cane, and crow for Jim Madison, or Jim Munroe. This would bring a response from the well-trained fowl, and the political caucus was adjourned.

A vein of humor was ever present with the old veteran. He manifested it in the pet names affixed to nearly all of the children and members of his family. This characteristic was common to the Scotch Irish of those times. One little fellow would go by the name of Chippie and another was Chubbie, and others responded to Winkie, Pinkie or Chuckie. Ever Mrs. Stark (Elizabeth) was called Molly by the General, and his granddaughter, Mary Babson, was known only as Polly. These whimsical names of the household circle, and the love for pets, give us an insight into the real nature of the man. One cannot be either coarse, brutal or unloving, whose heart goes out to pets, and who finds pleasure and recreation in fondling them.

Gen. Stark possessed a taste for reading a high order of literature, and in the leisure of his declining years indulged much in this his faverite pastime. The histories of the "thirty years' war," and the biographies of Alexander and Charles XII, the Swedish King, were favorite books. The Scottish poets of the eighteenth century he much enjoyed.

In summarizing the personal qualities of the General, mention should be made of the self-command he usually exhibited in times of trial or danger. Though of a most sensitive and responsive nature, he concealed his feelings in trying ordeals, by a quiet, almost stoical facial expression. Yet, when suffering from a sense of wrong or injustice, he could at times be vehement and terribly in earnest, both by voice and action. The ignominy cast on his good name by some enemy, when his name was withdrawn from the list of honor, before Congress for promotion, aroused a tempest of wrath; and though Sullivan and Poor, in sympathy with him, sought friendly intervention, he declared that an officer who would not defend his own rights was unfit to be entrusted with the defence of the rights of his country. He proposed to give congress an opportunity to review the matter voluntarily, and at its leisure, with no petition or remonstrance from him. Gov. Everett in his biography of the old hero, has a noble and fitting illusion to this lofty and spirited position of the soldier. The sting of an invidious and undeserved slight was remembered when the time came for sending official reports of Bennington; for, observes Everett, "though he sent a report to Gen. Gates, he forwarded none to Congress, thus disdaining to make his success the instrument of a triumphant accommodation." Yet there soon came the apology and restitution from Congress, by its voluntary act, extending the thanks of that body to the general and his troops, and offering by hand of its honored president, John Hancock, its congratulations, and enclosing a brigadier's commission in the continental army. Historians have generously concealed the name of the jealous rival who would thus act toward a worthy companion in arms, but the unanimity of Congress, and the acclaim of popular sentiment, left no ground for envy to carry opposition farther, and the disagreeable incident was consigned to oblivion, except that it is referred to as illustrating the high sense of honor and spirit that prompted the action of Stark.

The General was a constant and reliable friend, knowing nothing of the fickle changes, observed in some intimacies in soldier life. His friendships included most of the commanders in the American armies, and Lafayette when in New Hampshire three years subsequent to the death of Stark, mentioned with much show of feeling, his regret and grief, that his old companion in arms had gone on before. His end was peaceful and resigned. Paralysis of half of his body came the last of April, 1822, and about two weeks of suffering and enforced abstinence from nourishment closed his noble career, May 8th, following. Lafayette survived him eleven years, and Gen. Sumter, ten years, the latter being the last surviving general of the Revolution. The simple inscription carved on the granite shaft erected in 1829 at his burial place was:

"MAJOR GENERAL JOHN STARK,

aged 93 years, 8 months, 24 days."

# STARK AS SOLDIER AND CITIZEN.

AN ADDRESS BY HENRY W. HERRICK BEFORE A UNION MEETING OF THE MANCHESTER HISTORIC ASSOCIATION AND THE NEW HAMPSHIRE HISTORICAL SOCIETY, OCTOBER 6, 1898.

President John C. French, in his address of welcome at a union meeting of the Manchester Historic Association and the New Hampshire Historical Society, said :

By request it becomes my pleasant privilege to extend cordial greetings and welcome to you and the members of the old, useful and honored New Hampshire Historical Society to the "Queen City of the Merrimack," appreciating as I do, in common with all present, that our worthy host, inspired with patriotic impulses, historic lineage and generous hospitality, invited the two societies to the former ground of the heroic Stark at this your annual field day. Without any attempt to display or extend the program, but desiring to aid in perpetuating the memories of the past relating to the heroes of the Revolution who honored our state by their valuable services, we call attention to the duty of New Hampshire to erect suitable monuments to the memory of our Revolutionary heroes. The United States senate has on two occasions voted $50,000 for an equestrian statue of General John Stark, to be located at his grave in Stark park, but the bill each time failed to be approved by the house of representatives, as is well known. The New Hampshire legislature has caused to be erected in the old town of Durham a monument to General John Sullivan, and we must submit at this time of patriotic work of historic societies, the erection of monuments be devoted to the memory of "Light Infantry Poor," and "Yorktown Scammel" and Gen. Cilley.

Manchester cannot claim many places of historic interest or ancestral homes. Passaconnaway, as a leader of the Penacooks, tradition says, had a wigwam near the Amoskeag falls near the present site of the home of ex-Governor Smyth, and annual festive field-days were held in that vicinity. Feasting and high carnival were annual occasions. Whittier, in many of his charming poems, describes most delightfully the places and scenery of New Hampshire. Among other charming verses are those describing the banquet at Amoskeag on the wedding day of the " Bride of Penacook :"

> Steaks of the brown bear fat and large,
> From the rocky slopes of the Kearsarge;
> Delicate trout from the Baboosic brook.
> And salmon speared from the Contoocook;
> Pike and perch from the Suncook taken,
> Nuts from the trees of the Black Hills shaken,
> Cranberries picked from the Squamscot bog,
> And grapes from the vines of Piscataquog.

In behalf of our worthy host we take this occasion to call attention to Gen. Stark and his surroundings, and ask Mr. Herrick to give further information, other than found in printed works, which may be interesting to the honored guests present.

Mr. Henry W. Herrick first spoke of the respect in which Gen. Stark was held by the early residents here, as shown in their naming for him the first large corporation built in this city, likewise the first street built to lead to it, the city's first military company, the Stark Guards, and one of the first fire engine companies. Since that time dozens of societies and orders have been named for him. The holding of this historic field-day in October, he said, and at such a spot, was a most appropriate thing, but was only a repetition of what Gen. Stark himself did in the last years of his life, when in October of each year he held what he called a harvest home and merry making, inviting his neighbors, and poorer people of the town, to attend.

The facts which he gave regarding General Stark's life, Mr. Herrick said, he gathered thirty or more years ago, when many adults who had known the general well were still alive.

The discipline of the French and Revolutionary wars gave Stark a brusque, bold and resolute manner of address. His was a strong, decided character, loyal to his friends and his country. To this disinterested and unselfish trait is referable the popular esteem in which he was held by his troops and the public.

He is regarded historically as of Scotch-Irish descent, but a noted member of our State Historical Society is sure that Ireland should be known as the ancestral home of the Stark family because the general's father emigrated from that country. But the family traditions of our subject give his descent as of German or Teutonic origin. The significance of the family name substantiates this view. Gen. George Stark, late of Nashua, asserted that the name was derived from the German word Starr, signifying a rough, bold, vigorous character; but a few days since I asked a German lady for the word in her language denoting what is strong and vigorous, and she said Starck. She spelled the word like ourselves except that she added the letter c before the final letter k. This genealogical matter is of some historical interest, for we find traits of both the Scotch and German as well as the Irish in the character of Stark. The general always had a fancy for the Hessians or Brunswickers in the English army. They were strong, brave and good natured, and he expressed this fancy by bringing with his troops quite a contingent of his prisoners when he returned to our state. Several of these soldiers settled in Weare and Merrimack, where their descendants are yet to be found.

Caleb Stark, the general's eldest son, died in Ohio in 1838, at the age of about 80 years. The government had ceded a tract of land in that state to him in 1828 for military services, and this tract was ultimately named Stark county. Canton, the home of President McKinley, is the most prominent of its cities, and is very near Massillon, the county seat. This Dunbarton branch of the family has been noted in the military and naval annals of the country. Four of the male descendants have been officers in our navy, the last of whom, John Ancrum Winslow, captain of the Kearsarge, received the honorable title of rear admiral, for sinking the Alabama in 1864. This branch of the family still holds the old homestead at Dunbarton, formerly Starktown, and Caleb Stark, Jr., soon after his father's death, wrote the extended memoir of his distinguished ancestor, which was published in Concord at the period of commencement of our late war of the rebellion. This includes voluminous military records of the period of Stark's public services.

If General Stark was descended from a German ancestry it

was 200 years or more that his ancestors were in Scotland before they emigrated to this country in the troublous times of George the First, for we are told by family tradition that some of the soldiers of the force raised in Germany by the Duchess of Burgundy in 1495 to resist the enthronement of Henry VII. were at the close of that unfortunate campaign settled in Scotland. Several soldiers of the name of Stark were in this army of invasion.

A trait of General Stark, not always found in a victorious commander, was his readiness to ascribe his success to the valor of other officers and soldiers. He never enlarged on his own achievements, and took a manly and noble pleasure in praising the soldierly qualities of others. This is shown in his high estimate of the qualities of Robert Rogers, his ranger captain in the French and Indian war, and also in the friendly relations he sustained with brother officers in the continental army. During the campaign at Trenton he formed an intimacy with James Monroe, then an officer in a Virginia artillery. After years had passed and Monroe was president, in 1817, one of his first acts was to secure a major-general's commission for Stark, and the same was forwarded with an autograph letter, expressing his friendship and respect.

The popular interest in the life record of Stark increased as the year's passed; for the principal traits of his character, and his life work, were so noble and genuine, that distance of time only gives us a better perspective view of them. Perhaps the victory of Bennington in its great influence in turning the fortunes of war to the defeat of Burgoyne may account in some degree for this popular interest in Stark, yet the intrinsic worth of the man bears out and sustains this attraction. Nearly a hundred different publications issued in this country and in London, giving biographical or historical narrations of Stark, constitute the biography of the old hero. These are in history, essays, biography and poems, and represent solid volumes, periodicals, pamphlets, newspapers and other forms of publication, collected by the industry and perseveronce of our esteemed bibliographer, Mr. S. C. Gould. May this collection have an honorable niche in the future collection of our young, local historic association.

# Bibliography on Major-General John Stark.

COMPILED AND CONTRIBUTED BY S. C. GOULD.

BARSTOW, GEORGE. John Stark and his military career "History of New Hampshire," Portrait of Stark. Concord, N. H., 1842.

BARTLETT, CHARLES H. Oration of Hon. Charles H. Bartlett at the dedication of the Stark Memorial Park, Manchester, N. H., June 17, 1893. Pp. 25. Manchester, N. H., 1893.

BARTLETT, SAMUEL C. Centennial oration at Bennington, Vermont, at the laying of the corner-stone of the Battle Monument, August 16, 1877. Pp. 27. Rutland, Vt., 1879.

BROWN, EUNICE KIDDER. John Stark. Memoir and exploits Two portraits and other illustrations. Portrait of Nathan P. Kidder, a great grandson of John Stark; a portrait of the author and her daughter, descendants of John Stark. In *The New Race*, Vol. II, September, 1897. Chicago, Ill.

BROWNE, GEORGE WALDO. "The Woodranger." Boyhood of Stark. Boston, 1899.

BATTLE OF BENNINGTON. In *Harper's Weekly*, Vol. XXI, August 25, 1867, p. 670, illustrated, p. 660. New York.

BLISS, CHARLES M. Birthplace of John Stark. In *Granite Monthly*, Vol. II, November, 1878. Concord, N. H.

BOLYSTON, EDWARD D. Brief Sketch of the Life and Character of General John Stark. In the *New Hampshire Magazine*, September, 1843. Frontispiece, Stark's Tomb. Manchester, N. H.

BUTLER, JAMES DAVIE, (and George Fred Houghton). Addresses on the Battle of Bennington, with memoirs of Col. Seth Warner, before Legislature of Vermont, in Montpelier, October 20, 1848. 8vo. pp. 99. Burlington, Vt., 1849.

CHAPIN, EDWIN H. Poem at the annual Celebration of the Battle of Bennington, August 16, 1837, in Bennington, Vt.

CHASE, FRANCIS. Anecdotes from the Life of General Stark. Pages 158-166 in "Gathered Sketches from the Early History of New Hampshire and Vermont." Claremont, N. H., 1856.

COLBY, FRED. MYRON. Stark Place, Dunbarton, N. H. In *Granite Monthly*, Vol. V, December, 1881. Concord, N. H.

COBURN, FRANK W. Centennial History of the Battle of Bennington; compiled from the most reliable sources, and fully illustrated with original documents and entertaining anecdotes. Col. Seth Warner's identity in the first action completely established. 1777-1877. Portrait of Stark. Plan of Bennington Heights. Pp. 72. Boston, 1877.

CROSS, ALLEN EASTMAN. John Stark. Poem at the dedication of the Statue of Stark, Concord, N. II., October 23, 1890. Published in the volume of Proceedings on the occasion. Also, in *Daily Mirror*, October 24, 1890. Manchester, N. H.

DIARY OF JOHN STARK. A manuscript volume of about sixty pages. This was in the possession of Jerome B. Stark, a great grandson, who died October 8, 1896, in Manchester, N. H. It is now in the possession of Mrs. Susan P. Abbott, a cousin of Jerome B. Stark. Manchester, N. H.

DODGE, LEVI W. Along the John Stark River, from Agriocochook to the Connecticut. In the *Granite Monthly*, Vol. V, August, 1882. Concord, N. H.

DRAKE, SAMUEL G. Memoir of General John Stark. In *N. E. Historic-Genealogical Register*, Vol. VII, p. 201. Boston, 1853.

DURNFORD'S (LIEUT.) MAP. Map of the Battle of Bennington, as furnished to Burgoyne, his commanding officer. In Jenning's "Memorials of a Century." Boston, 1869.

DUYCKINCK, E. A. & G. L. General John Stark. In "National Portrait Gallery," Vol. I, p. 166. New York, 1856.

ENGLISH, THOMAS D. The Battle of Bennington, August 16, 1777. Poem. Portrait and one illustration. In *Harper's New Monthly Magazine*, Vol. XXI, August, 1860. New York, 1860.

EVERETT, EDWARD. Memoir of John Stark. Spark's American Biography; First Series, Vol. I. Boston and London, 1834. Harper's edition, pp. 116. New York, 1854.

FASSETT, J. H.  General John Stark — Colonial Life in New Hampshire.  Chapter VII, pp. 96-119.  Boston, 1899.

FROTHINGHAM, RICHARD, JR.  History of the Siege of Boston, and the Battles of Lexington, Concord, and Bunker Hill. Services of John Stark.  16 maps and engravings.  Boston, 1849 ; second ed. 1851.

GENERAL JOHN STARK.  Biographical Sketch of John Stark. Farmer and Moore's Historical and Miscellaneous Collections.  Vol. I, pp. 92-116.  Concord, N. H., 1823.

GENERAL STARK AT BENNINGTON.  General Stark and his Gallant Command at Bennington.  In the Bennington *Weekly Banner*, July 4, 1883.  Manchester, Vt., 1883.

GENERAL JOHN STARK.  STATUE ERECTED BY THE STATE.  The Statue erected by the State of New Hampshire in honor of General John Stark.  Sketch of its Inception, Erection, and Dedication.  Oration by Hon. James W. Patterson.  Frontispiece, Statue of Stark.  4to.  Cloth; pp. 62.  Manchester, N. H., 1890.

GILMORE, GEORGE C.  Roll of New Hampshire Soldiers at the Battle of Bennington, August 16, 1777.  Compiled by George C. Gilmore.  Portrait of Maj. Gen. John Stark from the original sketch made by Miss Hannah Crowninshield, Salem, Mass., May 31, 1810.  Cloth, 4to. pp. 56.  Manchester, N. H., 1891.

GILMORE, GEORGE C.  Captain John Moore's Company of Col. John Stark's Regiment, at Bunker Hill.  Paper read before Manchester Historic Association, June 27, 1896.  In " Man. Hist. Asso. Collections," Vol. I, p. 32.  Manchester, N. H., 1897.  In *Notes and Queries*, Vol. XV, May, 1897.  Manchester, N. H.

GLAZIER, WILLIAM B.  Heroes.  Poem.  Hallowell, Me., 1853.

GOULD, S. C.  Bibliography on Gen. John Stark.  Books pamphlets, memoirs, papers, poems, etc., on John Stark · First edition. 65 titles, published in *Notes and Queries*, Vol. XV, October-November, 1897.  Second edition, 75 titles, published in Vol. XVII, May-June, 1899.  Manchester, N. H.

HALL, HILAND.  Sketch of the Battle of Bennington, prepared for and contained in the Memorial Volume of the Centennial of the Battle of Bennington, August 16, 1877.

HALLECK, FITZ GREENE.  New England Men.  A poem in Halleck's Works.  "'Or Molly Stark's a Widow tonight,'

— It was done." Also, in the *Iris and Literary Souvenir*, Vol. II, December, 1842. Manchester, N. H., 1842. (Also reprinted in many publications.)

HEADLEY, JOEL T. Washington and his Generals. Vol. I, p. 200. New York, 1857.

HEATH, CLARA B. Poem by Mrs. Clara B. Heath, read by Frank S. Sutcliffe, at the patriotic exercises, at the Stark Memorial Park, July 5, 1897. Manchester *Daily Mirror*, July 6, 1897.

HERRICK, HENRY W. Tomb of Stark. Poem in the *New Hampshire Magazine*, September, 1843. Also reprints: In "Gems for You, a Gift for All Seasons," p. 19. Compiled by Frederick A. Moore. Published by William H. Fisk. Manchester, N. H., 1850. In "Memoir and Official Correspondents of John Stark," p. 106. By Caleb Stark. Concord, N. H., 1890. In "The Poets of New Hampshire," p. 61. Compiled by Bela Chapin. Claremont, N. H., 1885. In *Granite Momthly*, Vol. III, May, 1880. Concord, N. H. In *Notes and Queries*, Vol. XII, August, 1894. Manchester, N. H.

HERRICK, HENRY W. General Stark and the Battle of Bennington. *Harper's New Monthly Magazine*, Vol. LV, September, 1877. Portrait of Stark and seven illustrations. Pp. 10. New York, 1874.

HERRICK, HENRY W. Memorials and Anecdotes of John Stark. In the *Granite Monthly*, Vol. III, April, 1880. Concord, N. H.

HERRICK, HENRY W. Stark at Bunker Hill, at Bennington, and at Home. Portrait and fifteen illustrations. Chapter in the Centennial Book of Manchester, N. H. 4to. pp. 292-310. Published by George F. Willey. Manchester, N. H., 1896.

HERRICK, HENRY W. General Stark as a business man; his public, social, and domestic life. Address before the Manchester Historic Association, September 15, 1897. Published in the Manchester *Daily Mirror*, September 16, 1897.

HERRICK, HENRY W. Address at the union meeting of Manchester Historic Asssociation and N. H. Historical society at Manchester, October 6, 1898. *Mirror*, October 8, 1898.

LEGRAND, DR. LOUIS. John Stark, the Wood-Ranger of the North. In "Men of the Time of '76," published in *Saturday Journal*, No. 182. New York, 1882.

LIFE AND MILITARY SERVICES OF JOHN STARK. Reminiscences of the French War : containing Rogers' Expeditions with the New England Rangers under his command as published in London in 1765 ; with notes and illustrations. To which is added an account of the Life and Military Services of Gen. John Stark ; with notices and anecdotes of other officers distinguished in the French and Revolutionary Wars. Cloth ; 12mo. pp. 276. Concord, N. H., 1831.

LIFE OF JOHN STARK. The Hero of the Backwoods. In *Boy's Own Paper*, Vol. VI, Nos. 6, 7 and 8. London, 1882.

LODGE, HENRY CABOT (AND THEODORE ROOSEVELT). Hero Tales of American History. General Stark at Bunker Hill and Bennington. Cloth ; pp. 335. Boston, 1895.

McHUGH (REV.) RICHARD J. The Hero of the Hills. A Tribute to John Stark. Pronounced before the New Hampshire Club, in Boston, Mass. Published in the " Poems and Prose Words of Rev. Richard J. McHugh," edited by Denis Augustine Holland. Pp. 191-201. Manchester, N. H., 1896.

NARRATIVE OF LIEUT. GLICK, a Hessian Officer, connected with the British torces at Bennington. Published in Germany.

NESMITH, GEORGE W. New Hampshire Men at Bunker Hill. In *Granite Monthly*, Vol. II, June, 1879. Concord, N. H.

NESMITH, GEORGE W. Letter of James Madison to Gen. John Stark, and his Answer. In *Granite Monthly*, Vol. IV, September, 1881. Concord, N. H.

PARKER, FRANCIS J. The Battle of Bunker Hill. Col. William Prescott the commander. A monograph. Stark and Reed's command. Boston, 1875.

PARTON, JAMES Life of John Stark. In New York *Ledger* October 3, 1891. New York.

POTTER. CHANDLER E. Biographical Sketch of General Stark. In *Farmer's Monthly Visitor*, Vol. XII, Jan., 1852. Manchester,

POTTER, CHANDLER E. Gen. John Stark and the Revolutionary War. Chapters XIX and XX in " History of Manchester, N. H," pp. 414-493. Manchester, N. H., 1856.

POTTER, CHANDLER E. Tribute to John Stark. In address before Amoskeag Veterans, Manchester, N .H., February 22, 1855. Also Tribute to Stark, in address before the Amoskeag Veterans, February 22, 1859, quoted from " Memoir of Stark," p. 99, by Caleb Stark, 1860. Manchester, N. H., 1855 and 1859.

Powers, Grant. Memoir of General Stark. In "Historical Sketches of the Discovery, Settlement and Progress of Events in Coös County and Vicinity, between 1754 and 1785." 12mo. cloth. Haverhill, N. H., 1841.

Rodman, Thomas P. The Battle of Bennington, August 16, 1777. Poem in the "Rhode Island Book." Reprinted in Memoir and Official Correspondents of John Stark, p. 104. By Caleb Stark, Concord, N. H., 1860.

Sanborn, Edwin D. Tribute to John Stark. Oration, New Hampshire at the Centennial, October 12, 1876, at Philadelphia. Pamphlet compiled by Jacob Bailey Moore. Manchester, N. H., 1876.

Sargent, Jonathan E. Baker's River—Capture of John Stark by the Indians. In *Granite Monthly*, Vol. II, December, 1878. Concord, N. H.

Smith, Mrs. Isaac W. General Stark, the Hero of Bennington. Paper before the Old Residents' Association, Manchester, N. H., September 8, 1897. In *Daily Mirror*, October 16, 1897. Manchester, N. H.

Staples, Charles J. Historic Stark Memorial Park. Patriotic address, July 5, 1897. Address and proceedings in the Manchester *Daily Mirror*, July 6, 1897.

Stark, Caleb. Memoirs and Official Correspondents of Gen. John Stark, with notices of several other Officers of the Revolution. Also a Biography of Capt. Phinehas Stevens; and of Col. Robert Rogers, with an account of his services in America during the "Seven Years' War." By Caleb Stark. Portrait of Gen. Stark. Cloth; 8vo. p. 496. Concord, N. H., 1860.

Stark, Caleb. Poem. Lines addressed to Major-General Stark at the age of 93, one of the only two surviving American Generals of the Revolutionary Army. (First published in a Boston newspaper in 1821). Reprinted in the *Farmer's Monthly Visitor*, signed "V," Vol. II, September, 30, 1840, Concord, N. H. Reprinted in *Notes and Queries*, Vol. XII, August, 1894. Manchester, N. H.

Stark, George. John Stark. In *Granite Monthly*, Vol. X, April, 1887. Concord, N. H.

Stark, George. Origin of the Stark Family of New Hampshire, and a list of Living Descendants of General John Stark. Pp. 13. Manchester, N. H., 1887.

STARK, JOHN, PORTRAIT. Portrait of General John Stark by Samuel F. B. Morse, in local Art Exhibition, Manchester, N. H. Account, with portrait, in Manchester *Daily Union*, October 14, 1897.

STATUES OF JOHN STARK AND DANIEL WEBSTER. Proceedings in Congress upon the Acceptance of the Statues of John Stark and Daniel Webster, presented by the State of New Hampshire. Addresses on General Stark by Senators J. H. Gallinger and William E. Chandler and Representatives H. M. Baker and Henry W. Blair, of Manchester, and others.

STODDARD, RICHARD A. General John Stark. In *National Monthly*, Vol. XII, p. 481.

SWETT, S. Who was the Commander at Bunker Hill? With remarks on Frothingham's History of the Battle. Stark and Reid's regiments. Boston, 1850.

THATCHER, JAMES. John Stark of New Hampshire. In a "Military Journal during the American Revolutionary War, from 1775-1783. To which is added an Appendix containing Biographical Sketches of several General Officers. 8vo. pp. 603. Boston, 1827.

THYNG, J. WARREN. General John Stark. A memoir, illustrated with portraits of General Stark and his wife "Molly," and ten others, in six and one half columns. In Manchester *Daily Union*, June 17, 1893.

TRUMBULL, HENRY. John Stark. "In Indian Wars," chapters IX and X. Boston, 1846.

WHITON, JOHN M. Periods, 1775-1784, 1784-1805, from the commencement of the Revolutionary contest in 1775 to the commencement of Gov. Langdon's Administration in 1805. In "Sketches of the History of New Hampshire," pp. 125-175, chapters IX and X. Concord, N. H., 1834.

WITHERELL, J. Letter of Judge Witherell to General John Stark, dated Detroit, Mich., 26th May, 1811. In *Farmer's Monthly Visitor*, Vol. XIII, August, 1853 (p. 247) Manchester, N. H., 1853.

WORCESTER, SAMUEL T. New Hampshire Soldiers at the Battle of Bunker Hill. Paper before the New Hampshire Historical Society, June 14, 1882. Vol. I, pp. 353-364. Concord, N. H., 1888.

(75 titles.)

# PROCLAMATION MONEY.

A PAPER BY HON. JOHN G. CRAWFORD, READ BEFORE THE MAN-
CHESTER HISTORIC ASSOCIATION, JUNE 16, 1897.

During the Colonial Period of America there is found often mention of bills and obligations being ordered paid in what was then known as *Proclamation Money*, and the question has been asked, "What was Proclamation Money?"

On December the 25th, 1704, the Council of the Province of New Hampshire held at Portsmouth, at which was present John Hinker, Robert Elliott, Samuel Penhallow and John Plaisted, members of the council, took action as follows, viz.:

"Pursuant to his Excellency's Letter of the 18th. instant, setting forth her Majesties Command to proclaim the Proclamation about the coyne (coin) in a most solemn manner –

"Ordered, that the Justices and sheriffs attend the publication of said Proclamation this present day at Portsmouth and also at New Castle some day this week as the weather will permit; and accordingly the said Proclamation was proclaimed at Portsmouth, the Justices, Secretary and Sheriff attending the same in a serious and solemn manner."

This proclamation was put forth to promulgate the proclamation of the queen fixing the relative value of the foreign coins then in circulation within the several provinces in America. Acts of Parliament were promulgated by a proclamation of the Sovereign of the Nation, and these proclamations were proclaimed by the Council of the Colonies on command of the several governors.

On January 20, 1708-9, the council at Portsmouth passed the following order:

"His Excellency's letter dated Boston 10th. January current, relating to two Acts of Parliament to be proclaimed with the usual solemnity, to wit:

"An Act for ascertaining the rates of Foreign Coins in her Majisty's plantations in America, which was ordered to be proclaimed as usual in such cases."

This act above referred to passed Parliament 1708, was proclaimed in New Hampshire, January, 20, 1708-9, and as follows:

### AN ACT OF PARLIAMENT.

An act for ascertaining the Rates for Foreign Coins in Her Majesty's Plantations in *America*.

Whereas for remedying the inconveniences which had arisen from the different rates at which the same species of foreign silver coins did pass in her Majisty's several colonies and plantations in America, her most excellent Majesty has tho't fit by her royal proclamation, bearing date the eighteenth day of June, one thousand seven hundred and four, and in the third year of her reign, to settle and ascertain the currency of the foreign coins in her said colonies and plantations, in the manner and words following.

We having had under our consideration the different rates at which the same species of foreign coins do pass in our several colonies and plantations in *America*, and the inconveniences thereof, by the direct practice of drawing the money from one plantation to another; to the great prejudice of the trade of our subjects: and being sensible, that the same cannot be otherwise remedied, than by reducing of all foreign coins to the same current rate within all our dominions in America; and the principle officers of our mint having laid before us a table of the value of the several foreign coins which usually pass in payments in our said plantations, according to their weight; and the essays made of them in our mint, thereby showing the just proportion which each coin ought to have to the other; which is as follows; viz: *Sevill* pieces of eight, old plate, seventeen penny-weight twelve grains, *four shillings* and *six pence;* Sevill pieces of eight, new plate, fourteen penny-weight twelve grains, *four shillings* and *six pence*; Sevill pieces of eight, new plate, fourteen penny-weight, *three shillings seven pence one farthing*;

Mexico pieces of eight, seventeen peny-weight twelve grains, *four shillings* and *six pence*; Pillar pieces of eight, seventene peny-weight twelve grains, *four shillings* and *six pence three farthings*; Peru pieces of eight, old plate, seventeen peny-weight twelve grains, *four shillings* and *five pence,* or thereabout; Cros dollars, eighteen peny-weight, *four shillings* and *four pence three farthings*; Ducatoons of *Flanders,* twenty peny-weight and twenty one grains, *five shillings* and *six pence*;

Ecu's of *France,* or silver *Lewis,* seventeen peny weight twelve grains, *four shillings* and *sixpence*; Crufadoes of Portugal, eleven peny weight four grains, *two shillings* and *ten pence one farthing*; Three Gilder pieces of *Holland,* twenty peny weight and seven grains, *five shillings* and *two pence one farthing*; Old Rix Dollars of the empire, eight peny weight and ten grains, *four shillings* and *six pence*: The halves, quarters and other parts in proportion to their denominations. and light pieces in proportion to their weight: We have therefore thought fit for remedying the said inconveniences, by the advice of our council, to publish and declare, that from and after the first day of January next ensuing the date thereof, no Sevill, Pillar, or Mexico piece of eight, though of full weight of seventeen peny weight and a half shall be accounted, received, taken or paid within any of our said colonies or plantations, as well those under proprietors and charters as under our immediate commission and government, at above the rate of six shillings per piece current money, for the discharge of any contract or bargains to be made after the said first day of January next, the halfs, quarters, and other lesser pieces of the same coins to be accounted, received, taken or paid in same proportion :And the currency of all pieces of Peru dollars, and other foreign pieces of silver coins, whether of the same or baser alloy, shall after the said first day of January next stand regulated, according to their weight and fineness, according and in proportion to the rate before limited and set for the pieces of Sevill, Pillar, and Mexico; for that no foreign silver coin of any sort be permitted to exceed the same proportion upon any account whatsoever. And we do hereby require and command all our governors, lieutenant-governors, magistrates, officers, and all other good subjects within our said colonies and plantations, to observe and obey our directions herein, as they tender our displeasure.

And whereas notwithstanding the said proclamation, the same indirect practices as are therein mentioned, are still carried on within some of the said colonies or plantations, and the money thereby drawn from one plantation to another, in prejudice of the trade of her Majesty's subjects: Wherefore for the better enforcing the due execution of her Majesty's *said proclamation* throughout all the said colonies and plantations; and for the more effectual remedying the said inconveniences thereby intended to be remedied;

*Be it Enacted* by the Queen's most excellent majesty, by and with the advice and consent of the Lords spiritual and temporal, and Commons in this present parliament assembled, and by the authority of the same, That if any person within any of the said colonies or plantations, as well those under proprietors and charters, as under her Majesty's immediate commission and government, shall after the first day of May, which shall be in the year of our Lord, one thousand seven hundred and nine, for the discharge of any contracts or bargains to be thereafter made, account, receive, take or pay any of the several species of silver coins mentioned in the before-recited proclamation, at a greater or higher rate than at which the same is hereby regulated, settled and allowed, to be accounted, received, taken or paid, every such person so accounting, receiving, taking or paying the same contrary to the directions therein contained, shall suffer six months imprisonment, without bail or mainprize: Any law, custom or usage in any of the said colonies or plantations to the contrary hereof in any wise understanding.

And shall likewise forfeit the sum of *ten pounds* for every such offence; one moiety thereof to her Majesty, her heirs and successors; the other moiety to such person or persons as shall sue for the same: to be recovered with full costs of suit, by action of debt, bill plaint or information, in any of her Majesty's courts of justice of the charter or proprietary governments where such offence shall be committed.

Provided, nevertheless, and it is hereby declared, That nothing in the before-recited proclamation, or in this act contained, shall extend, or be construed to compel any person to receive any of the said species of foreign silver coins, at the respective rates in the said *proclamation* mentioned.

*Provided also*, and it is hereby further declared, That nothing in this act contained, shall extend or be construed to restrain her Majesty from regulating, and settling the several rates of the said species of foreign silver coins within any of the said colonies or plantations, in such other manner, and according to such other rates and proportions as her Majesty by her *royal* proclamation for that purpose to be issued, shall from time to time judge proper and necessary; or from giving her royal assent to any law hereafter to be made in any of the said colonies or plantations, for the settling and ascertaining the current rates of such coins within the said colonies or plantations but that such further regulations may be made, and such assent given, in as full and ample manner, to all intents and purposes as the same might have been done in case this act had not been made, and no otherwise: Any thing herein before contained to the contrary hereof in any wise notwithstanding.

The colonies provided for the coinage of subsidiary coins, the copper or other metal being provided by the colonies and the same were coined at the mint in London, these coins were also put into circulation by the proclamation of the King.

Proclamation Money, was the coins used in the colonies, other than the coins of the Realm, the value of which was fixed by Parliament, and proclaimed by the Proclamation of the King, or Sovereign of England. These coins being issued and used on a different basis than the ones of the Realm, and not being legal tender for the payments of debts, except to a limited extent, and being more convenient to the colonists, in the discharge of their obligations, provisions were therefore made for these payments in *Proclamation Money.*

This money was declared and made lawful money by Proclamation, and to distinguish it from the English coinage was called and known as *Proclamation Money.*

# MANCHESTER FIRE DEPARTMENT.

A PAPER BY FRED W. LAMB, READ BEFORE THE MANCHESTER HISTORIC ASSOCIATION, SEPTEMBER 21, 1898.

### EARLY FIRE APPARATUS.

The *Scientific American* a few years ago gave an engraving of an enormous syringe carried upon trucks. The water was poured or ladled in through a funnel at the top. It would contain a barrel of water and by turning a crank the piston was forced forward which projected the water with considerable force. The cut and description were taken from "Besson's Theatre des Instruments," and the apparatus was said to date from 1568. This is the earliest mention of a practical fire engine which I have been able to find.

In 1615 a hand fire engine appeared in Germany. It was merely a pump, without hose of any sort. About 1700 Van der Heide of Amsterdam invented flexible hose, both for suction and as a substitute for the fixed inflexible gooseneck or pump nozzle with which the old engines were equipped. It was not until nearly a century later, however, that this invention was made available.

Shortly after 1700, Richard Newsham, of England, built the first fire engine that became of practical utility. Water was carried to the engine by hand and pumped by hand through hose or a gooseneck, as the case might be. In 1731 the city of New York purchased two of Newsham's engines. These imported engines were worked exclusively by treadles and the water was brought in buckets and poured into the tanks from whence it was pumped through a gooseneck. In 1808 Sellers

& Pennock of Philadelphia made the first riveted hose and soon came the hose reel. India rubber hose came from England in 1827 and canvas hose came later.

About this time "old handtubs," so called, began to be built by various manufacturers and improvements in hand fire engines became numerous. The most prominent manufacturers in this country were the Agnew, Button, Howard & Davis, Jeffers, Thayer, Roberts, and last but not least the famous Hunneman Company.

### DAYS OF THE OLD HANDTUB DEPARTMENT.

From Potter's "History of Manchester," I glean the following account of the beginning of the Manchester Fire Department:

"At a town meeting called by the selectmen the 26th of October, 1839, on motion of Mr. Bell it was voted that an act, entitled an act, defining the powers and duties of firewards, and other persons in certain cases, passed December 16th, 1828, and an act entitled an act, in addition to an act, defining the powers and duties of firewards and other persons in certain cases, passed December 16th, 1828, passed July 3d, 1830, be adopted and in force in the town of Manchester.

"Provided, however, that such inhabitants of said town of Manchester as live remote from the compact part of said town, that is to say, more than one mile from the corner of Amherst and Elm streets, shall be exempted from the operation of the (10) tenth section of said first-mentioned act.

"Voted that the inhabitants of the New Village have the privilege of nominating firewards. Chose accordingly, John H. Maynard, George W. Tilden, Amory Warren. William P. Farmer, Isaac N. Ford, Hiram Brown, Timothy J. Carter, David A. Bunton, James Wallace, Henry S. Whitney, Mace Moulton, firewards.

"Voted on motion of Mr. Bell that the selectmen and firewards be authorized to borrow not exceeding $1000 to purchase engines and apparatus for extinguishing fires, provided the same can be obtained on reasonable terms and extended credit."

The Board of Firewards organized with Amory Warren as chairman forthwith and agreeable to the vote above purchased a Hunneman tub and apparatus for the same at a cost of $631.25. This was the first step towards our present efficient fire department.

Prior to this there had been an engine in the Stark yard, but it was owned by that corporation and this one now purchased, "Merrimack, No. 1," was the first engine owned by the town. As early as 1818 there was a fire engine in Piscataquog, now a part of the city, then a part of Bedford. This engine was obtained through the influence of Isaac Riddle and the company was incorporated as the Piscataquog Village Fire Engine Company in 1820, approved December 13th, 1820. The incorporators were Isaac Riddle, Jr., Jonathan Palmer and Mace Moulton. Col. George C. Gilmore belonged to a handtub company at one time, joining October 20, 1843, which was located in Goffstown under the name of Amoskeag Fire Engine Company, No. 1. This company was also incorporated, the incorporators being Mayo Pond, Charles Morgan and John T. Morgan. The incorporation was approved July 3d, 1827. The company consisted of eighteen men.

The late Col. John S. Kidder belonged in 1829 to this Piscataquog Village Handtub Company, which was handled by eighteen men, John Parker being foreman. The little red engine house stood about where West Hancock street intersects South Main street.

In a recent interview in the *Mirror* with George Elliot and Charles K. Walker they tell quite a number of interesting incidents in connection with this engine. Mr. Elliot served as a torch boy in one of the old-time companies and recalls that the old machine was not fitted with suction hose but had a tank, which being kept full of water by the bucket brigade, provided water to be thrown by the pump through the hose.

Mr. Walker says that the old engine house was never locked and was roughly finished inside. For seats there was a row of benches made of boards supported on uprights, and extending around the four sides of the room. Moody Quimby was clerk of the company and its members were volunteers, and at that time each man was supposed to be provided with a fire-bucket, and on an alarm of fire all turned out and, hustling the old handtub to the nearest water in the vicinity of the fire, all would pitch in and by passing the buckets along a line would fill and keep the tank full of water, so that the engine could be of use. When quite a small boy, Mr. Walker remembers that this engine was in use when the "Island Mill," on the Amoskeag, just below where the P. C. Cheney Company's Paper Mills now are, was burned. This fire occurred in May, 1840. Shortly after the old "Goffe" place near Bowman's Brook was burned and this engine was used there.

Later this old machine was used up, and in his school days at the old academy, then located where the South Main Street Church now stands, Mr. Walker remembers that the boys used to go down and haul this old handtub out of the engine house up to the Milford Street watering trough, and filling the tank, would amuse themselves throwing water over each other.

This old machine had a record of throwing water over the old church spire that towered 110 feet in the air. The late Col. George W. Riddle finally secured the old machine and for years kept it in his barn as a relic of former days. The old leather fire buckets then with the machine were also taken charge of by Mr. Riddle and years after were distributed by him among friends as relics of days when they ran with the machine.

At the second annual meeting of the Board of Firewards held March 30, 1840, Mace Moulton was chosen chairman, and T. J. Carter, clerk. The same rules and regulations as governed the former board were adopted and the following one added: That in selecting fire engine men, the firewards will give a preference to such persons as are able bodied, laboring men, likely to be permanent residents in the place and that they will not give a warrant to the members of any engine company unless it shall be one of the regulations of the company, that the members shall meet once each month, from March to November, and exercise their engine and see that such engine is in complete order for use."

The following committee was then chosen to take charge of organizing companies: Joseph M. Rowell, No. 1, Merrimack; James Wallace, No. 2, Manchester; and T. J. Carter, No. 3,

Bennington Company. Another committee was also chosen to make " respectful application " to the Amoskeag Company for a donation of a suitable plot of land for the erection of an engine house for the engine recently purchased.

At a meeting of the board April 18th a constitution was adopted to be presented to the several companies that might be formed, and soon after or at the same meeting eighteen names were submitted as members of Engine Company, No. 1. These were accepted, but the board thought the number too small and added twenty-two more to the list.

On the 28th of the same month Walter French was chosen chief engineer of the department. It was at that time and for several years after only an honorary office with no salary. At the same time Mace Moulton, Isaac C. Flanders, J. T. P. Hunt and T. J. Carter were chosen to form lines at fires, James Wallace and Joseph M. Rowell to procure water, and Foster Towne, W. P. Farmer and Dustin Marshall to remove goods, etc. An engine house for the new engine was built the same year on Vine Street " not to exceed $100 in cost," and which, according to the records, was accomplished at a cost of $90. A new hose carriage was also procured the same year.

At the organization of the board for the year 1841, George Porter was chosen chairman, and Walker Flanders, first engineer ; Isaac C. Flanders, second ; and George Hall, third. The Machine Shop Engine Company, No. 2, was formed in the early part of this year and the list of members, as reported, adopted by the Board of Firewards. The officers of the company were : A. Brigham, foreman ; O. W. Ainsworth, assistant foreman ; Edward Griffin, hose master ; S. G. Patterson, assistant ; J. H. Knowlton, clerk. The Stark Mills Engine Co., No. 3, was soon after formed with George Perry, foreman ; David Ricker, assistant ; Orlando Bagley, hose master; and Horace Gordon, assistant.

At a meeting of the board held April 30th, 1841, it was voted "the firewards deem it very necessary that a hook and ladder company should be formed to act in concert with the other fire companies in Manchester, and that a request should be made to the selectmen for funds to procure the necessary apparatus."

That this request was complied with is evident from the fact that the board accepted the names of and organized a hook and ladder company with W. Boyd, foreman; A. B. Morrill, assistant, and seventeen others as members of the company. They also accepted a list of ten names for Hose No. 1.

The first muster of any account occurred on the 2d of August, 1841. The companies met on Concord Square to operate their engines and apparatus. In 1842 John A. Burnham was chairman of the board and also chief engineer. In 1843 the late Moody Currier was chief with J. B. Congdon as director of Engine No. 1, Ira Bliss of No. 2, R. G. Smith of No. 3, W. L. Lane of Hose and Ladder, No. 3, and Ezekiel Blake of Hook and Ladder, No. 1.

In 1844 John S. Kidder was chief, Edward McQueston director of No. 1, D. W. Grimes of No. 2, Gilman Riddle of No. 3, S. P. Greeley, Hook and Ladder, No. 1, and E. C. Foster of Hose and Ladder, No. 3. In August of this year the old Town House was burned. Potter says, speaking of this fire: "On Monday the 12th day of August, 1844, the new Town House was destroyed by fire. Smoke was discovered issuing from the bell deck about half past ten o'clock A. M., and in a few moments was forcing itself through every crevice and cranny of the roof. Shortly after the flames burst out of the northwest corner of the roof and in an hour the whole structure was a heap of smoking ruins. The fire took in the armory of the Stark Guards from a lighted piece of paper carelessly thrown upon the floor. This doubtless, through some grains of powder scattered upon the floor, communicated to shavings beneath, between the floor and Hall. Here it was confined and had been burning sometime before the smoke and flame found vent. Upon breaking out at the northwest corner of the building, the fire seemed to spread at once all over it. Taking in the attic and being thus underway no effort could save any part of the building. Most of the goods in the stores and cellars were removed as also the contents of the Postoffice, but the printing office of Mr. J. C. Emerson in the third story, and the effects of the Stark Guards and Granite Fusileers in their armories in the attic, were almost entirely destroyed. The loss to individuals and the town was about $30,000, of which $11,000 was covered by insurance. At the time of the fire Mr. Charles Chase of this city was standing on the street in front of the Riddle Building. He was one of the first to respond to the alarm and went into the building and up into the armory of the Stark Guards before the fire which was burning below, between the floors, had reached the armory.

"A town meeting was called immediately to be held on the 30th day of August, to take into consideration the rebuilding of the Town House and other matters for the protection of the town against fire." At this meeting it was "Voted to build the Town House as good or better than the old one and put a clock and bell on the same." They also appointed a committee to take charge of the building of the Town House. "Another committee was raised consisting of Messrs. Samuel D. Bell, John A. Burnham, Walter French, Ezekiel Blake, E. A. Straw, Isaac C. Flanders and Moody Currier to examine the different sources from which water might be obtained for the purpose of extinguishing fires; the selectmen were also directed to purchase two fire engines with the necessary apparatus and authorized them to borrow a sum of money not exceeding $20,000 to meet the expenses of the Town House, bell, clock, and engines. The meeting adjourned to September 17th then to hear the committee on the subject of water. In accordance with the above vote two engines were purchased immediately, Massabesic, No. 4, being made by Thayer at a cost of $855.50, and Torrent, No. 5, being made by the Hunneman Company at a cost of $780. Companies were formed for the two new machines with William Shepherd as foreman of No. 4 and I. C. Frye as foreman of No. 5. The report of the committee on water made on the 17th of September, stated that a full supply of water could not be obtained short of bringing the water of Massabesic Lake into the town by an aqueduct. Upon this report being made the meeting dissolved. A new meeting was organized and the following votes were passed:

"Voted that the Board of Firewards be authorized to construct a new reservoir on Pine Street, near the culvert, and a reservoir on Lowell Street, near the School House, to complete the reservoirs now commenced on Union Street, to deepen and improve the reservoir in Concord Square and to make necessary arrangements to render the Pond which is expected to be made by the Amoskeag Manufacturing Company, on Merrimack Street, useful in case of fire.

"Voted that the sum of $1000 be appropriated for the foregoing purposes and that the selectmen be authorized to hire the sum on the credit of and to give notes in the name of the town.

"Voted that the Firewards be authorized to procure if possible the land necessary for a reservoir on Union Street, of such height that the water may be distributed thence to other reserviors in the Village, and make report at the town meeting to be held in November next, with an estimate of the expense necessary for that purpose.

"Voted that the selectmen be authorized to establish such a watch as they may deem necessary for the protection of the town against fire. "Voted that the selectmen be authorized to build two or more engine houses for the use of the town. "Voted that the selectmen be authorized to procure by purchase or otherwise at such place as the Firewards shall direct, lots of land for the erection of engine houses.

"Voted that the selectmen be authorized to borrow on the credit of the town, $1000 for the purpose of procuring lands and erecting engine houses thereon. "Voted that the selectmen prohibit as far as possible the digging in the streets to the injury of the reservoirs now built or that may be built at any time hereafter."

"In accordance with these votes the various reservoirs were enlarged, new ones were built, the ponds on Concord and Merrimack squares were made available as reservoirs and the pond upon Hanover Square was so fitted up as to afford an abundant supply of water at all times to most of the reservoirs below Pine Street. Also a night watch was established. Lots were purchased and engine houses were built upon them, one on Chestnut Street for Massabesic, No. 4, and one on Pine Street for Torrent, No. 5.

In December the Board of Firewards was re-organized with Daniel Clark, chairman, and I. C. Flanders, assistant.

The Department was again re-organized in the early part of 1845, a board of engineers taking the place of the old Firewards. This board consisted of Daniel Clark, chief, and William Shepherd, R. G. Smith, W. C. Clarke, Walter French, David Gillis and J. G. Cilley, assistants. There was a little trouble among the members of No. 5 at this time and the company was disbanded and a new one formed. At a meeting of the board on October 29, 1845, notice was given of the disbandment of No. 4, and the apparatus was placed in charge of Mr. French until a new company could be formed. At the annual town meeting, March 10, 1845, it was voted to pay the firemen 10 cents an hour for actual service at fires.

In 1846 O. W. Bagley was recommended by the board as chief and they also recommended that twelve assistants be appointed. But I find by the city report for 1846 that W. C. Clarke was chief in that year. This year the companies were ordered out for inspection on Concord Square and they held quite a muster. Complaint was made by No. 4 Company that their apparatus was in bad condition and unless something was done they should disband. As a consequence a new engine was purchased for this company at a cost of $887 and the old machine was sold. The old hook and ladder truck was also sold this year and a new one purchased.

In 1847 W. C. Clarke was chief. In 1848 W. C. Clarke was again chief. In this year the "Old Mill" and "Bell Mill," so called, were burned on March 28th. These mills occupied the site of the P. C. Cheney Company's Paper Mills. They were completely destroyed.

In 1849 Isaac C. Flanders was chief. After the city was incorporated in 1846 the appointment of the chief engineer was placed in the hands of the mayor.

In 1850 W. L. Lane was chief. In this year old Merrimack, No. 1, was repaired in Boston and returned to the city as good as new. Right here it might prove interesting to narrate a little incident which occurred to the old Merrimack after she was moved across the river which is quite amusing. It happened at the fire at Dan Palmer's and was the first run the boys were called out on. It was about half a mile away and the boys got there in good time, and put their suction hose into a cistern but could not get a drop of water. The suction was taken up and examined and again put in with no better result. It was taken up again and unscrewed and behold the trouble! A large turnip was taken out. The suction hose was then put in again and worked all right.

On the 16th of March, 1850, a destructive fire broke out in No 1 Stark Mill, which destroyed the upper story of the north wing (the second mill built) and did considerable damage to the machinery in that wing and also the rest of the building. The loss was $30,000.

In 1851 Jacob F. James was appointed chief engineer. During this year the engineers were provided with speaking trumpets.

Daniel Clark was chief in 1852. Fire on July 5th burned Baldwin & Company's Steam mill where Varney's Brass Foundry now is, and several adjoining buildings.

In 1853 John H. Maynard was appointed chief, and J. A. Stearns, John B. Clarke, R. D. Mooers, Charles S. Brown, C. Duxbury, W. B. Webster, J. Q. A. Sargent, Harry Leeds, and J. L. Kelley, assistant. On September 22, about 5 o'clock in the morning, the main building of the Manchester Print Works was discovered to be on fire and in less than an hour was in ruins. The fire caught in the dry room, near the center of the building, and having been subject to a high temperature for years, ceiling and timbers had become of the most combustible nature. By the greatest exertions the counting, engraving, and store rooms were saved and the Madder Dye House and Boiler House. Loss was estimated at $125,000, and fully insured.

In 1854 John H. Maynard was again chief and his salary was $50. This year there was some trouble again with No. 5, resulting in the disbandment of the old company and a new one being formed. Assistant chiefs were the same in 1854 as in 1853.

In 1855 Jacob F. James was appointed chief. This was a very important year in the history of the Manchester Fire Department. Engine No. 7 and hose carriage was purchased this year and cost $1250. This machine went by the name of Pis-

## MANCHESTER FIRE DEPARTMENT.

cataquog, No. 7, or A. C. Wallace, No. 7. It might be well here to give a list of the engines in the department at this time, each of which was a Hunneman:

Merrimack, No. 1, located on Vine Street, where the central station now is; Niagara, No. 2, located on Canal Street in the building still standing, used by the Amoskeag Company as a remnant store; Stark, No. 3, located in the Stark Corporation yard; Massabesic, No. 4, located on Chestnut, between Lowell and Concord Streets; Torrent, No. 5, on Manchester Street, where the battery building now stands; Manchester, No. 6, in the Manchester Mills yard; A. C. Wallace, No. 7, in Squog, on South Main Street.

Besides these there was the Excelsior Hook and Ladder, No. 1, located on Manchester Street, where the battery now is, and the Hose and Hydrant Company. Each handtub, with the exception of the Niagara, had fifty members, while the latter had a working force of sixty men. The handtubs in the corporation yards were owned by the corporations and were loaned to the city in case of fire. The Hose and Hydrant Company disbanded in 1859 and from it grew the present Pennacook Hose Company

July 5th, 1855, one half of the largest Manchester Mill was destroyed by fire. I give a condensed description of this fire and the one on the street at the same time from the *Daily American Extra* of July 16th, 1855:

"The first fire took in the south end of No. 1 mill on the Manchester Corporation at 20 minutes before 1 o'clock. It took in the carding room. The watchman was passing through the room with a lantern in his hand and the bottom dropped off and rolled into a pile of roving which immediately took fire. He attempted to extinguish it before giving an alarm and the alarm was not given until the flames had reached the ceiling. The water from one of the hydrants was soon brought to bear upon the fire and it was somewhat checked, but three other hose were put on, which so reduced the head that the fire gained again. The water was drawn out of the canal at the time to permit the workmen to put in the 'connection' with No. 5, Amoskeag Mill. The engine companies were promptly on the ground and played manfully but it was found impossible to arrest the progress of the fire and it was not checked until about 4 o'clock. The loss was estimated to be $271,353.

"The fire department was all at the Manchester Mills and some one on top of the burning mill told the crowd that there was a 'fire on the street,' and soon the bell confirmed the fact. It was about 3 A. M. When first discovered it was in a small building between Manchester and Hanover Streets, opposite Brown & Colley's Paint Shop in the rear of Elm. The flames immediately communicated to adjoining buildings, spreading until they reached Manchester Street on the one side, Hanover on the other, with Elm on the west end, and extending east as far as the Rundlett Block on Manchester Street and the McCrillis Shop on Hanover Street. The Barnes & Putney Block and Postoffice building at the corner of Elm and Hanover Streets alone being saved.

"The buildings burned were, with the exception of L. Raymond's and J. N. Brown's, of wood, and so quick were the flames in accomplishing their work, that at sunrise the ruin was completed. The loss on the south side of Manchester Street was very slight. The Franklin House was injured to the amount of about $200, a part of the roof being burned badly and the paint somewhat charred. Had the Franklin House burned nothing could have prevented it seems, the whole square bounded by Chestnut, Merrimack, Elm and Manchester Streets, from a fate as fearful as that now in ashes.

### LIST OF THOSE DESTROYED ON ELM STREET.

"J. A. Perry, apothecary; Lyman Raymond, grocer; Raymond & Thomas, buildings; J. B. Hoitt, millinery; D. Clark, D. J. Clark, J. G. Cilley, Putney's Block; F. H. Ellsworth, millinery; William A. Putney & Company, dry goods; William H. Elliot, jeweler; Pressey & Jones, millinery; M. Currier, buildings; A. Branch, harness maker; Raymond & Walker, shoe dealers; H. Batchelder, hosiery; Mrs. Wright, boarding house; C. A. Putney, millinery; Straw & Tewksbury, jewelers; J. W. Mitchell, millinery; C. M. Putney, confectionery.

### REAR OF ELM STREET.

"Brown & Colley, paint shop; J. M. and G. A. Barnes, buildings; Neal & Holbrook, carpenters.

### MANCHESTER STREET.

"S. James' stable, some eight or ten horses.

### HANOVER STREET.

"Postoffice building, city bank, some six or seven houses. About thirty families have been driven from their dwellings. The loss at the first on the street was estimated to be $40,000."

The fire on the street covered a territory of about two acres in extent. The origin of fire was thought to have been incendiary.

In 1856 John H. Maynard was again appointed chief. On February 5th Patten's Block was burned, destroying the City Library, three newspaper offices, etc. Loss about $75,000.

In 1857 Peter S. Brown was chief. It was in September of this year that the Torrents had their memorable victory at the muster at Worcester, Mass., when out of fifty-four companies, they took the first prize of $300. A few days before the muster Mr. Orrin E. Kimball, the foreman of the hose, went down to the Stark Mills and procured a quantity of heavy duck which he tore up into narrow strips. With these strips he double wound four hundred feet of hose which was to be used in the contest at Worcester. The procession was three miles long. At 1 o'clock in the afternoon three guns were fired as a signal for the trial to commence. The pole to be played at was 180 feet high and the companies were required to play through four hundred feet of hose and through hoops attached to the pole. Fifteen minutes was the amount of time allowed for arranging hose and play. The Manchester boys were not looked upon as winners and their machine never looked in a worse condition, all the paint having been worn off. Then their hose being wound with the stripes of duck gave them the name among the other companies of the Rag Hose Company.

"You aint a going to work that machine, are you?" inquired a member of Yale, No. 1, of South Reading, Mass., of Mr. Kimball. The latter gentleman said it was all the boys had and they were going to try it. "Why," said the South Reading man, "you can't get water through four hundred feet of hose with that machine."

The Torrents were the sixteenth on the list and not only did they reach the top of the pole but twenty-one feet higher. When the judges made their report it said: "First prize, $300, Torrent, 5, Manchester, N. H., 180 feet." On the morning after the great day in Worcester the Torrents gave an exhibition of fine playing on the common. The Rag Hose was none too good for the Worcester people then. On their way home they halted in Nashua and were banqueted and received with

speeches and a general good time. The mayor and aldermen
of Manchester voted in the afternoon to meet the boys at the
depot and at 7 o'clock they were there, together with engine
companies Massabesic, Merrimack, Manchester and Piscataquog
Miss Ann Melissa Stevens stepped forward from the crowd as
the Torrents came off from the cars and handed the foreman,
Mr. B. C. Kendall, an elegant bouquet. They were then escorted through the principal streets and were given a collation
in the City Guards armory, after which they were escorted to
Smyth's hall, where rousing speeches were made by Hon. Jacob
F. James, Col. John B. Clarke, Peter S. Brown, Eben French,
George W. Morrison, David Cross, Capt. J. N. Bruce, and others. The young ladies presented them with an elegant banner
inscribed, " We go where duty calls."

This year Baldwin's Steam Mill in Janesville was burned and
a man named Horr was killed by falling walls.

In 1858 Peter S. Brown was again appointed chief.

In 1859 J. T. P. Hunt was chief. One of the three largest old
time musters ever held and the last one of importance was held
in this city September 15, 1859. There were fifty-two engines
participating in the muster in this city. I condense a description of the muster and the riot which preceded it from an account
written by Frank M. Frisselle for the *Mirror* some years ago

" All day long on the 14th the fire companies were arriving
on all the incoming trains. The majority occupied temporary
camps on the common. There were fully two thousand red
shirted firemen in the city. The gambling fraternity which then
existed in this city in too great a number for the city's credit
was reënforced by large numbers from Boston. Elm street was
their principal hunting ground, while others made the old
American House their headquarters. Two rooms in E. P.
Offut's building. together with his auction rooms at 29 and 31
Elm Street, were let to gambling hall proprietors for this occasion and here in this auction room began the trouble which
resulted in the worst riot this city ever witnessed. At a little
before 11 o'clock a dispute arose between an out-of-town fireman and the proprietor relative to some change which the latter paid the former and which the former claimed was counterfeit or else not so much as it should have been. The proprietor

and his confederates added more fuel to the flames by charging the fireman with stealing $32 from them which resulted in a row in which the gamblers used firearms, fortunately with no serious effects. The firemen victims were run or thrown out by the gamblers, who outnumbered them. The firemen then in the city were at once acquainted with the situation of affairs and as if by magic commenced to assemble on Elm Street, and proceeded to clean out the den where the trouble had taken place. Their approach was a warning to the proprietors who made good their escape through a rear entrance. This place was sacked in a few minutes and the infuriated firemen turned their attention to the other gambling resorts and started on a crusade to clean them all out, which during the ensuing four hours they succeeded in doing. The police force consisted of thirty men, I. W. Farmer, marshal, who were powerless to check the mob, although they were quieted by an address from Marshal Farmer, who advised them to retire, assuring them that justice would be done those who offended any of their number This caused a temporary lull, but only for a few minutes, when the clearing out work was again in progress. The Elm House beneath which the Revere saloon was located was assaulted, but when assured by one of the proprietors, Samuel B. Perkins, that they were on the wrong scent they left with only slight damage being done to the lower stories. The American House was sacked from top to bottom and greatly damaged. The resort of William Martin on Elm Street, the old museum building and numerous other places were raided and the city freed for a time of the gamblers who infested it. There were over three hundred gallons of liquors also destroyed. Mayor Harrington appeared on the scene about 2 o'clock and addressed the rioters, promising them that justice would be done the gamblers, which checked and soon terminated the riotous proceedings, but not until the firemen had accomplished their purpose and done what the city was unable to do, driven the blacklegs out, for which they were afterwards given due credit.

"September 16th was a most excellent muster day. At 9 o'clock the procession formed and paraded the principal streets. The line reached the common at 11.30 and dispersed for dinner. The playing commenced at 12.40 and finished at 6. The rules of playing were for each company to draft its own water and through four hundred feet of hose play a perpendicular stream up a pole which was spaced off into feet and numbered with figures sufficiently large to be seen by the judges, who were stationed in the belfry of the old church opposite Merrimack common. Ten minutes were allowed for each company.

"The judges were Hon. Jacob F. James, Col. Bradbury P. Cilley, Israel Dow, Isaac C. Flanders, and Col. Thomas P. Pierce. The prizes were six in number, $400, $200, $150, $100, $50, and a patent hose washer. The Manchester companies did not compete. The winners were as follows:

First prize, 170 feet, Alert, 1, Winchendon, Mass.
Second prize, 166 feet, Yale, 1, Wakefield, Mass.
Third prize, 156 feet, Cataract, 2, Clinton, Mass.
Fourth prize, 154 feet, Jacob Wesbter, 2, Woburn, Mass.
Fifth prize, 152 feet, Gaspee, 9, Providence, R. I.
Sixth prize, 151 feet, Tremont, 12, Boston, Mass.

A trial of two Amoskeag steam fire engines, the Amoskeag, No. 1, and the Machegonne were among the most interesting features of the day."

The day following the muster the Manchester companies took their turn under the same rules with the following result:

Merrimack, 1, 150 feet, broke plunger; Niagara, 2, 160 feet; Stark, 3, 148 feet; Massabesic, 4, 158 feet; Torrent, 5, 151 feet; Manchester, 6, 185 feet; A. C. Wallace, 7, 140 feet.

The Manchester handtubs went out of service gradually as steam engines were purchased. The first steam fire engine purchased by this city was the Amoskeag, No 1, purchased in 1859. The Manchester handtubs went to the following places:

Merrimack, No. 1, to Bennington, N. H.
Niagara, No. 2, to Hooksett, N. H.
Stark, No. 3, to Franklin, N. H.
Massabesic, No, 4, to Groton, Mass
Torrent, No. 5, to East Rochester, N. H.
Manchester, No. 6, to Bradford, N. H.

The Manchester Veteran Firemen's Association was formed in 1890 and now has 232 members, and is in a flourishing condition. They purchased the old Torrent, No. 5, from East Rochester, N. H., for $400 and it has lately been repaired and is almost as good as new.

In the preparation of this paper I am greatly indebted to Orrin E. Kimball, James R. Carr, George C. Gilmore, Chief Thomas W. Lane, Frank M. Frisselle for imformation and I have freely quoted from Potter's history, "Fire Service of Manchester," and newspaper extras and interviews in both the *Union* and the *Mirror.*

# COL. JOHN GOFFE.

A SKETCH BY HIS GREAT GRANDSON, GORDON WOODBURY, ESQ.,
READ BEFORE THE MANCHESTER HISTORIC ASSOCIATION,
MARCH 15, AND JUNE 21, 1899.

It is not easy to gain a correct idea of any man, his life, his character and his place in history without a knowledge of the times and circumstances in which he lived. The subject of our sketch was a man distinctly the product of the most stirring period of English history and without some appreciation of the historical events which must have been to him the familiar topics of family discussion and tradition we cannot understand the mold in which his youthful impressions were formed, nor know in the true sense the quality of which he was composed.

The circumstances and surroundings in which he lived must also be borne in mind, and by an effort of the imagination we must picture the locality of his home, not as it appears now at all, but as it was when he lived there.

This is no easy task. He has been dead 119 years. It is 200 years since he was born. The place where he lived would now be to him as strange and unnatural as the planet Mars would be to us.

The mode of our lives would be as strange and impossible to him as the lives of people in another world. A railroad, a steam boat, a factory, a spring carriage, a telephone or telegraph instrument, a trolley car, even an ordinary lucifer match, he not only never saw but never heard of.

The clothes we wear, the food we eat, the things we read of were never even dreamed of by him or his contemporaries.

Col. John Goffe, as we shall call him, was the son of John

Goffe and Hannah Parrish. He was born in Boston in 1701, and was baptized in the Second or North church on March 23 of that year. The then minister of this church was the celebrated Dr. Increase Mather, who was at the time President of Harvard college. The colonel's grandfather was also named John Goffe and he appears to have come to this country in 1662 or '63. In 1676 he was a member of the old North church, in which, as I have said, his grandson was baptized in 1701. We shall remember that it was in the belfry of this church that the lantern was hung as a signal to Paul Revere of the intended surprise by the British in their march to Lexington and Concord at the outbreak of the Revolution. There has always been some question among Colonel Goffe's descendants as to the exact relationship between John Goffe, the emigrant who came to Boston in 1662 or '63, and from whom Colonel Goffe was descended, and William Goffe, the regicide. There seems to be an adherent probability that some relationship existed for there is a noticeable similarity between the names of William Goffe, the regicide's brothers and sisters, and those of John Goffe, the emigrant's sons and descendants to several generations. The names Stephen and William and John appear with great regularity and persistency. There is also the tradition among Colonel Goffe's descendants to the same effect. His great granddaughter used always to maintain her descent from Goffe, the regicide. This Goffe, the regicide, was a man of some note in his time. He was the son of Stephen Goffe, rector of Stanmore in Sussex, and two of his brothers were named Stephen and John respectively. Stephen was a Roman Catholic priest and confessor of Henrietta Maria, queen of Charles I, and John was a Presbyterian minister. In early youth William was apprenticed to one Vaughan, a salter in London, and a zealous Presbyterian. But when his time as an apprentice was nearly out "he betook himself to be a soldier," as his biographer says, "for the righteous cause and instead of setting up his trade went out as a quartermaster of foot and continued in the wars until he forgot what he had fought for. At length through several millitary grades he became a colonel, a frequent prayer maker, preacher and presser for righteousness and freedom, which in outward show was expressed very zealously, and therefore in high esteem in the parliamentary army. In 1648 he was one of the judges of King Charles I, sat in judgment when he was brought before the high court of justice, stood up as consenting when sentence was passed upon him for his decollation and afterwards set his hand and seal to the warrant for his execution. Afterwards he was the man with Col. William White who brought musqueteers and turned the Anabaptistical members that were left behind of the little or barebones parliament out of the house A. D. 1654. Complying thus kindly with the design and interest of the said General Cromwell he was by him when made Protector, constituted major-general of Hampshire, Sussex and Berks, a place of great profit, and afterwards was of one if not of two parliaments; did advance his interest greatly, and was in so great esteem and favor in Oliver's court, that he was judged the only fit man to have Major Gen. John Lambert's place and command as Major-General of the army of foot and by some to have the protectorship settled on him in future time. He being thus made so considerable a person was taken out of the house to be a lord and to have a negative voice in the other house and the rather for this reason that he never in all his life (so he says) fought against any such thing as a single person, or a negative voice, but to pull down Charles and set up Oliver, etc., in which he obtained his end.

"In 1660, a little before the restoration of King Charles II, he betook himself to his heels to save his neck without any regard had to his majesty's proclamation, wandering about, fearing every one that he met should slay him and was living at Louisanna in 1664, when John L'Isle, another of that number, was there, by certain generous royalists dispatched. He afterwards lived several years in vagabondship but when he died or where his carcass was lodged is as yet unknown to me.". Governor Hutchinson in his History of Massachusetts says: "In the ship, Captain Pierce, which arrived at Boston from London, the 27th of July, 1660, there came passengers Colonel Whalley and Colonel Goffe, two of the late king's judges. Colonel Goffe brought testimonials from Mr. John Row and M. Seth Wood, two ministers of a church in Westminster. Col. Whalley had been a member of Mr. Thomas Goodwin's church.

"Goffe kept a journal or diary, from the day he left Westminster, May 4, until the year 1667; which together with several other papers belonging to him, I have in my possession, almost the whole in characters, or short hand, not difficult to decypher. The story of these persons has never yet been published to the world. It has never been known in New England. Their papers, after their death, were collected, and have remained near an hundred years in a library in Boston. It must give some entertainment to the curious. They left London before the King was proclaimed. It does not appear that they were among the most obnoxious of the judges; but as it was expected vengeance would be taken of some of them, and a great many had fled, they did not think it safe to remain. They did not attempt to conceal their persons or characters when they arrived at Boston, but immediately went to the governor, Mr. Endicott, who received them very courteously. They were invited by the principal persons of the town; and among others they take notice of Colonel Crown's coming to see them He was a noted Royalist. Although they did not disguise themselves, yet they chose to reside at Cambridge, a village about four miles distant from the town, where they went the first day they arrived. They went publicly to meetings on the Lord's day, and to occasional lectures, fasts, and thanksgivings, and were admitted to the sacrament, and attended private meetings for devotion, visited many of the principal towns, and were frequently at Boston; and once when insulted there, the person who insulted them was bound to his good behaviour. They appeared grave, serious and devout; and the rank they had sustained commanded respect. Whalley had been one of Cromwell's lieutenant-generals, and Goffe a major-general. It is not strange that they should meet with this favorable reception, nor was this reception any contempt of the authority in England. They were known to have been two of the king's judges; but Charles the second was not proclaimed, when the ship that brought them left London. They had the news of it in the Channel. The report afterwards, by way of Barbadoes, was that all the judges would be pardoned but seven. The act of indemnity was not brought over until the last of November. When it appeared that they were not excepted, some of the principal persons in the government were alarmed; pity and compassion prevailed with others. They had assurances from some that belonged to the general court, that they would stand by them, but were advised by others to think of removing. The twenty-second of February, 1661, the governor summoned a court of assistants, to consult about removing them, but the court did not agree to it.

"Finding it unsafe to remain any longer, they left Cambridge, the 26th following, and arrived at New Haven the seventh of March, 1664. One Captain Breedan, who had seen them at Boston, gave information thereof upon his arrival in England. A few days after their removal, a hue and cry as they term it in their diary, was brought by the way of Barbadoes; and thereupon a warrant to secure them issued, the eighth of March, from the governor and assistants, which was sent to Springfield, and other towns in the western part of the colony; but they were beyond the reach of it."

The governor adds in a long marginal note, "they were well treated at New Haven by the ministers, and some of the magistrates, and for some days seemed to apprehend themselves out of danger. But the news of the king's proclamation being brought to New Haven, they were obliged to abscond. The twenty-seventh of March they removed to Milford, and appeared there in the day time, and made themselves known; but at night returned privately to New Haven, and lay concealed in Mr. Davenport, the minister's house, until the thirtieth of April. About this time news came to Boston, that ten of the judges were executed, and the governor received a royal mandate, dated, March 5, 1660, to cause Whalley and Goffe to be secured. This greatly alarmed the country, and there is no doubt that the court now were in earnest in their endeavors to apprehend them; and to avoid all suspicion, they gave commission and instruction to two young merchants from England, Thomas Kellond and Thomas Kirk, zealous royalists, to go through the colonies, as far as Manhados, in search of them. They had friends who informed them what was doing, and they removed from Mr. Davenport's to the house of one Jones, where they had hid until on the thirteenth of April, into the woods, where they met Jones and two of his companions, Sperry and Burril, who first conducted them to a place called Hatchet Harbor, where they lay two nights, until a cave or hole in the side of a hill was prepared to conceal them. This hill they called Providence Hill: and there they continued from the fifteen of May to the eleventh of June, sometimes in the cave, and in very tempestuous weather, in a house near to it. During this time the messengers went through New Haven to the Dutch settlement, from whence they returned to Boston by water. They made diligent search, and had full proof that the regicides had been seen at Mr. Davenport's and offered great rewards to English and Indians who should give information, that they might be taken; but by the fidelity of their three friends they remained undiscovered. Mr. Davenport was threatened with being called to an account, for concealing and comforting traitors, and might well be alarmed. They had engaged to surrender, rather than the country or any particular person should suffer on their account; and upon intimation of Mr.      resolved to go to New Haven and deliver themselves to the authorities there. The miseries they had suffered, Davenport's danger, they generously and were still exposed to, and the little chance they had of finally escaping, in a country where every stranger is immediately known to be such, would not have been sufficient to have induced them. They let the deputy governor, Mr. Leete, know where they were; but he took no measures to secure them; and the next day some persons came to them to advise them not to surrender. Having publicly shown themselves at New Haven, they had cleared Mr. Davenport from the suspicion of still concealing them, and the twenty-fourth of June went into the woods again to their cave. They continued there, sometimes venturing to a house near the cave, until the ninteenth of August—when the search for them being pretty well over they ventured to the house of one Tompkins, near Milford meeting house, where they remained two years, without so much as going into the orchard. After that they took a little more liberty, and made themselves known to several persons in whom they could confide, and each of them frequently prayed, and also exercised, as they termed it, or preached at private meetings in their chambers. In 1664, the commissioners from King Charles arrived in Boston. Upon the news of it, they retired to their cave, where they tarried eight or ten days. Soon after some Indians in their hunting, discovered the cave with the bed; and the report being spread abroad, it was not safe to remain near it. On the thirteenth of October, 1664, they removed to Hadley, nearly one hundred miles distance, traveling only by night; where Mr. Russell, the minister of the place, had previously agreed to receive them. Here they remained concealed fifteen or sixteen years, very few persons in the colony being privy to it. The last account of Goffe, is from a letter, dated Ebenezer, the name they gave their several places of abode, April 2, 1679. Whalley had been dead some time before. The tradition at Hadley is, that two persons unknown were buried in the minister's cellar. The minister was no sufferer by his boarders. They received more or less remittances every year for many years together, from their wives in England Those few persons who knew where they were, made them frequent presents. Richard Saltonstall, esq., who was in the secret, when he left the country, and went to England in 1672, made them a present of fifty pounds at his departure ; and they took notice of donations from several other friends. They were in constant terror, though they had reason to hope, after some years, that the enquiry for them was over. They read with pleasure the news of their being killed, with other judges, in Switzerland. Their diary for six or seven years, contains very little occurrence in the town, church, and particular families in the neighborhood. They had indeed, for five years of their lives, been among the principal actors in the great affairs of the nation : Goffe especially, who turned the little Parliament out of the house, and who was attached to Oliver and to Richard to the last ; but they were both of low birth and education. They had very constant and exact intelligence of every thing that passed in England, and were unwilling to give up all hope of deliverance. Their greatest expectations were from the fulfillment of the prophecies. They had no doubt, that the execution of the judges was the slaying of the witnesses.

They were much disappointed, when the year 1666 had passed without any remarkable event, but flattered themselves that the Christian era might be erroneous. Their lives were miserable and constant burdens. They complain of being banished from all human society. A letter from Goffe's wife, who was Whalley's daughter, I think worth preserving. After the second year, Goffe writes by the name of Walter Goldsmith and she of Francis Goldsmith, and the correspondence is carried on as between a mother and son. There is too much religion in their letters for the tastes of the present day ; but the distresses of two persons, under their peculiar circumstances, who appeared to have lived very happily together, are very strongly described.

Whilst they were at Hadley, Feb. 10, 1664-5, Dixwell, another of the judges, came to them ; but from whence, or in what part of America he first landed, is not known. The first mention of him in their journal, is by the name of Colonel Dixwell ; but ever after they call him Mr. Davids. He continued at Hadley some years, and then removed to New Haven. He was generally supposed to be one of those who were obnoxious in England ; but he never discovered who he was, until he was on his death bed. I have one of his letters, signed James Davids, dated March 23, 1683. He married at New Haven, and left several children. After his death, his son, who before had been called Davids, took the name of Dixwell, came to Boston, and lived in good repute; was a ruling elder of one of the churches there, and died in 1725, of small-pox by inoculation. Some of his grand-children are now living. Colonel Dixwell was buried in New Haven. His gravestone still remains with this inscription: ' J. D. Esq., deceased March 18th in the 82d year of his age, 1688.'

It cannot be denied, that many of the principal persons in the colony greatly esteemed these persons for their professions of piety, and their grave deportment, who did not approve of their political conduct. Mr. Mitchel, the minister of Cambridge, who showed them great friendship upon their first arrival, says in a manuscript which he wrote in his own vindication :

"'Since I have had opportunity, by reading and discourse, to look a little into that action for which these men suffer, I could never see that it was justifiable.'

" After they were declared traitors, they certainly would have been sent to England, if they could have been taken. It was generally thought they had left the country; and even the consequence of their escape were dreaded, lest when they were taken, those who had harbored them should suffer for it. Mr. Endicott, the governor, writes to the Earl of Manchester, that he supposes they went towards the Dutch of Manhados, and took shipping for Holland; and Mr. Bradstreet, then governor, in December, 1684, writes to Edward Randolph, 'that after their being at New Haven, he could never hear what became of them.' Randolph, who was sent to search into the secrets of the government, could obtain no more knowledge of them than that they had been in the country, and respect had been shown them by some magistrates. I am loth to admit an ancedote handed down through Governor Leverett's family. I find Goffe takes notice in his journal of Leverett's being at Hadley.

" The town of Hadley was alarmed by the Indians in 1675, in the time of public worship, and the people were in the utmost confusion. Suddenly, a grave elderly person appeared in the midst of them. In his mien and dress he differed from the rest of the people. He not only encouraged them to defend themselves, but put himself at their head, rallied, instructed, and led them on to encounter the enemy, who by this time were repulsed. As suddenly the deliverer of Hadley disappeared.

The people were left in consternation, utterly unable to account for this strange phenomenon. It is not probable they were ever able to explain it. If Goffe had been then discovered, it must have come to the knowledge of those persons, who declared by their letters that they never knew what became of him."

Governor Hutchinson's house in Boston was burned at the time of the Stamp act riots, and with it, all the papers, letters and manuscripts of Goffe, including his diary, so that the priceless memorials of the man are lost forever.

"General Whalley died about the year 1678, and General Goffe the year following."

Potter's History of Manchester has this to say :

"It has been claimed that John Goffe of Londonderry was a grandson of General Goffe, but this is altogether improbable. The connection, if any, must have been collateral. True, General Goffe had one or more sons, but there is no evidence showing that a son of his was ever in this country. Unerring circumstances show to the contrary.

"The retreat of the father was well known to his family, certainly to his wife, and as the utmost pains had been taken to apprehend him on the part of the royalists, it is not at all probable that his son would have been permitted to come to the country, openly bearing his father's name, and almost in daily contact with those who would have been glad to have destroyed the regicide, lest the presence of the son should have led to the apprehension of the father. And it is not at all probable that either of his children came to his country; on the contrary, it is evident from a letter, written by General Goffe to his wife, in 1674, that his son was then in England. Now John Goffe, of Londonderry, came to this country in 1662 or 1663 and was a member of Dr. Increase Mather's church in 1676. These facts show that he could not have been a son of General Goffe. Yet he may have been a nephew, and the fact, that his immediate descendants continue the family names of Stephen, John and William, would seem to indicate that he might have been a descendant of Rev. Stephen Goffe, of Stanmore, who had those names in his family.

"John Goffe came to Londonderry as an agent for the Scotch-Irish emigrants. He was a man of some considerable business capacity, and performed his stipulated duties to the satisfaction of his employers, as is shown by the fact that he had a special grant in the charter for his 'good service in promoting the settlement of the said town.' The closing stipulation of the charter reads thus:

| | | |
|---|---|---|
| To | Mr. McGregore, | 250 acres. |
| To | Mr. McKeen, | 250 acres. |
| To | Mr. David Cargill, | 100 acres. |
| To | Mr. James Gregg, | 150 acres. |
| To | Mr. Goffe, | 100 acres. |

for good services, and to the last two mentioned, namely Gregg and Goffe, a mill stream within the said town for their good services in promoting the settlement of said town."

Mr. Goffe was the first town, or rather proprietor's clerk. He was chosen in 1719 and served in that capacity until March, 1723, having been chosen town clerk at the organization of the town under the charter of 1722. Soon after the organization some difficulty ensued betwixt him and a portion of the proprietors, in relation to his acts while agent and clerk. It was alleged that his son John Goffe, Jr.'s name was introduced improperly among the grantees and that a "transcript of land" was improperly recorded in his own favor. The subject of the alleged improper record was referred to a committee, March 5, 1731, with directions to commence a suit at law against him, but it does not appear that the committee had any action upon the subject, or that a suit was commenced against him. This fact would seem to show that upon investigation, there was no cause of action. The difficulty however in relation to the insertion of his son's name in the schedule attached to the charter, continued, and the town refused to lay out any land to John Goffe, Jr. Upon this he brought a suit against the town. This action was brought some time prior to May 18, 1731, as on that day a warrant was posted calling a town meeting to act upon the subject. This was the first notice of the matter on record. The town defended the suit stoutly, but after six years of litigation Mr. Goffe obtained a judgment against the town, and in 1738 they adjusted the matter with him by laying him out a home lot of sixty acres, and paying his costs, amounting to twenty-six pounds and eight shillings. The result, coupled with the fact that the committee to prosecute the father, never took any action in the matter, shows pretty conclusively that the whole charge against John Goffe, Sr., had no foundation in substance. Yet his enemies made the most of the matter and succeeded in keeping him out of any public employment.

Mr. Goffe's farm in Londonderry proved to be next to worthless, as upon making a clearing, his position was such, that it was subject to frosts, and he could not succeed in raising Indian corn, to him a Massachusetts man, an indispensible product. Upon this, his son, John Goffe, Jr., invited him to move to the Cohas Brook, and live with him, where he had plenty of good land for corn and other purposes. He accepted the invitation, taking the principal charge of the farm of his son, who from his connection with public affairs, had little time to devote to farming. This was probably in 1722, as before suggested. He resided with his son until his death, Aug. 9, 1748, at the age of 69 years.

John Goffe, 2d., called John Goffe, Esq., the oldest son of Emigrant John Goffe, and father of the subject of this sketch, was born Sept. 18, 1679, married Hannah Parrish in 1700, and moved to Londonderry, N. H., the same year. His wife was the daughter of Robert Parrish, who had a garrison house in the southern part of Nashua, N. H. He, Parrish, his wife and one of his daughters, were killed by the Indians in an attack on their home made somewhere about the year 1691. Their two youngest children, girls, hid under a hogshead in the cellar and were saved. One of these girls, Hannah, was afterwards married to John Goffe, Esquire, as above stated.

He was town clerk of Londonderry, and as we have seen, a man of some consequence in the settlement. His name is found in the list of military officers of the Province, who took the oaths of allegiance, supremacy and abjuration on the accession of George II, and in 1729 he was a member of the provincial assembly. His family of children were all brought up to a life of industry and frugality. They were not of the same race as the rest of the settlers, among whom they lived, but were of English antecedents.

On Oct. 16, 1722, at the age of 21 years, Colonel Goffe, the subject of our sketch, was married to Hannah Griggs of Roxbury, Mass. Their children were ten in number: Hannah, born Jan. 16, 1723, married, first, Thomas Chandler; second, Capt. John Bradford; Esther, born Feb. 15, 1725, married James Walker of Bedford; John, born Feb. 17, 1727, married Jemima Holden; Mary, born June 12, 1730, died young and unmarried; Ebenezer, born Feb. 7, 1732; Margaret, born Nov. 26, 1734, married Maj. John Moore; Sarah, born March 26, 1737, married the Rev. John Rand; Elizabeth, born Aug. 17, 1739, married —————— ———; Rebecca, born Dec. 15, 1724, married Samuel Moore (brother to Margaret's husband); Mary, born Dec. 20, 1744, married Nathaniel Martin.

In 1724, the locality where Colonel Goffe lived and where we now are, was the remote frontier. It was situated on a great waterway near Amoskeag Falls, then the famous fishing place well known to the Indians, not only of the locality, but also to members of distant tribes who resorted here to obtain a supply of fish for winter. There was a white settlement at Nutfield, or Londonderry, and another at Dunstable, now Nashua, or near Nashua, but other than these two places the whole country westward to Lake George and Albany and northward to Montreal and Quebec, was a vast unbroken forest, whose paths were known only to the trappers and scouts as savage as the Indians they lived among. Cohas brook is the outlet of Massabesic lake and on its southern bank near where the stream empties into the Merrimack river, at what we now call Goffe's Falls, stood the home of the young frontiersman and his wife. Until recently the foundations of his house could be seen near that of Nathaniel Moore. Near him lived his brother-in law, Benjamin Kidder and Edward Lingfield, and these three were the only white men who lived within the limits of what we now call Manchester.

At that time, 1724, although there was nominal peace between King George I of England and the Regent Orleans who ruled in France during the minority of the young king, Louis XV, yet there was always in existence a more or less acute condition of hostility between the French settlers in Canada and the English settlers in New York and New England. Their main and real cause of discord arose over the boundaries of their separate provinces, but in spite of nominal peace with the French there was always present in the minds of the English a well grounded fear of attack from the Indian allies of the French incited by the French provincial government. On the remote frontier these incursions were of almost yearly occurrence and so, while at times it could not be truly said that the French and English were at war with one another, it was also true that the English frontier settler lived in daily and hourly dread of Indian war parties whose deeds of horribly cruelty and barbarity it is difficult now to even read about. In the year 1724 two men, Nathan Cross and Thomas Blanchard, crossed from nether Dunstable to the north side of the Nashua river, and were engaged in making turpentine. While at their work a party of Indians seized them, stove their casks of turpentine and hurried them towards Canada as prisoners. Feeling sure they would be followed by the friends of their captives they lay in ambush all one day to receive them. When night came and Cross and Blanchard did not return to their sleeping place, a sawmill on Salmon brook, their friends at once imagined the reason and the alarm was given through the neighborhood. A party of ten men started at once. When they reached the place where the workmen had been captured they found the barrels cut open and the turpentine slowly spreading over the ground.

They inferred that the Indians were not far off and decided on instant pursuit. Their route was up the west bank of the Merrimack. At the brook near Thornton's Ferry they were waylaid by the savages and the larger part of them instantly killed. A few fled but were overtaken and destroyed, with one exception. He, Farwell by name, managed to escape and returned to Dunstable with the news of this second disaster. The greatest excitement prevailed. Three men of approved skill and courage were selected to organize an expedition and the general assembly of Massachusetts was petitioned for aid in the undertaking. In answer the Legislature gave permission to raise a company " to range, and to keep out in the woods in order to kill and destroy their enemy Indians," and voted a bounty of £100 per scalp.

With such encouragement the borderers soon raised a company and chose John Lovewell as their leader. In it was included our hero, John Goffe, afterwards known as Colonel Goffe, but then a young man of but 23. With him were two of his brothers-in-law, Benjamin Kidder and Edward Lingfield. Their home was on the opposite side of the Merrimack river about five miles north of the ambush in which the year before the Indians had destroyed so many of their neighbors. They were but recently married and must leave wife and babies at home while they hunted the savage to his lair and grappled him to the death. But they were not men to hesitate, and joined the expedition at once. Eighty-seven men were mustered at Dunstable on the 29th of January, 1725. The destination was the main village of the Pequakets, the remnant of the once powerful confederation of the Pennacooks, whose home was in a section of country north and east of Lake Winnepesaukee. Their main village was in a bend of the Saco river near what is now Fryeburg, Me. About midnight on the 20th of February they found a party of Indians. They were asleep round a large fire and by the side of a frozen pond. Determining to make sure work Lovewell placed his men in convenient position and at the signal they fired. In a few moments all were destroyed and some attempt against the New Hampshire frontier prevented.

For as Penhallow in his " Indian Wars" says : " Their arms were so new and good that most of them were sold for seven pounds apiece and each of them had two blankets with a great many mocassins which were supposed to be for the supply of captives they expected to have taken." The party returned to Boston and received the bounty out of the public treasury.

Such was their delight at their success that they resolved to try again and this time to attack Paugus, the great war chief of the Pequakets, in his home. Paugus had frequently been to Dunstable and was personally known to most of the hunters of the valley of the Merrimack, as a bold and wily chieftain, who at the head of his warriors had taken part in many of the attacks on the frontiers. The second expedition started April 16, 1725. Young Goffe and his brothers-in-law were again among the numbers, this time consisting of 47 men. At Ossipee lake, Benjamin Kidder fell sick and building a small fort and leaving him with the doctor and eight others, the remainder pushed on. On the 8th of May, about 10 o'clock in the morning, while at prayers they heard a gun across a pond near where they then were. Soon they saw the Indain who had fired it. Shortly after they fell in with the main body of the Indians, Paugus among them, and the famous "Lovewell's fight" ensued. It will not be necessary for our present purposes to describe it. Suffice it now to say that it resulted in the death of Paugus, the utter defeat and destruction of the Indians, and is, perhaps, the most famous of all the many bush fights of this frontier. Soon afterwards, in 1726, a treaty was made by the Province of Massachusetts with the Eastern Indians, and for a long time its provisions were faithfully observed. Indian depredations in this neighborhood ceased and young Goffe seems to have taken up his ordinary routine of life on a farm in the wilderness. His main occupation seems to have been hunting, for in some deeds he is spoken of as "Hunter John Goffe." This would bring him into frequent contact with Indians and give him a knowledge of their language and manners, and customs, besides making him—as he was— an excellent marksman. His family increased and he began to accumulate property. Numerous deeds to him of land in Derryfield, Starktown or Dunbarton, Goffstown and Bedford, are extant, and among other things, he became the owner of Uncanoonuc mountain. Such land was at that time and in such a neighborhood practically the only form in which wealth existed, we must conclude that John Goffe, Junior, as he was then known, in distinction from his father, John Goffe, Esquire, was a man of property. His house had been already formed into a garrison for the convenience of safety of his family and neighbors, and near it he had erected a mill for grinding corn, the power for which was supplied by the Cohas brook and is the same power which now turns the Devonshire mills at Goffe's Falls. His nearest neighbors were the Scotch-Irish settlers at Londonderry. They were a class of colonists distinct from the English Puritans, who had originally settled at and near Boston and between the two little sympathy existed. The English regarded them as little better than Papists, would neither marry with them nor live among them on any terms of peace, denied them a location for their settlement and regarded the Presbyterian form of worship and church government to which the Scotch-Irish were devotedly attached, as a pestilential heresy. They classed them with Quakers, Baptists and Unitarians, and denied them all welcome to the more protected settlements of the colony. Accordingly the Scotch-Irish sought the remote wilderness for their homes and choosing the district of Nutfield as it was called they made their homes there. They were a hardy race. For the sake of their religion they and their fathers had endured the horrors of the siege of Derry in Ireland and now they had come here to this new country prepared to hew out a home in the forest and to live their lives and bring up their families in their own way. Goffe was of English descent and so was his wife. It may well be supposed therefore that he shared to some extent in the prejudices of his English connections against the Scotch-Irish. There had been the suit also between the town of Derry and himself regarding his right to a hundred acre lot which has been above referred to and so when the province of Massachusetts opened the town of Bedford or Narragansett, No. 5, for settlement, he bought land there and interested himself in its development and growth.

His land in Bedford was also on a brook—he seems to have had an eye to water power—and soon after he built a dam and erected a saw mill and grist mill there. His farm lay on the River road, as we now call it, or as it was then known—the road from Souhegan falls to Amoskeag.

Land titles in this neighborhood were in those days in a chaotic condition. Massachusetts claimed titles and granted townships in Londonderry, Derryfield and at Amoskeag. The province of New Hampshire did the same thing in the same place. The Masonian Proprietors had a good title to all the territory included in these provincial grants and back of them were the grants from various Indian chieftains. No man therefore could feel absolutely sure of undoubted ownership in his farm. Goffe claimed his land at Cohas brook by right of grant from the township of Londonderry. But his title was disputed by a collateral relative named Elizabeth Rand, as appears by her petition, to the Masonian Proprietors as follows:

(Petition of Elizabeth Rand, 1749.)
(Masonian Papers, Vol. 6, P. 121.)
Province of
New Hampshire
Portsmouth 12th April 1749.
The memorial and Petition of Elizth Rand of Harry's Town Widow of Robert Rand Deceas'd Humbly Sheweth
To the Honourable Theodr Atkinson Esqr & and the other Gentn Purchasers & Proprietors of Capt John Tufton Mason his Right in Lands in the Province of New Hampshire—
That the General Court of the Prove of the Massachusetts Bay held at Boston April ye 10th 1734 upon Consideration of the Eminent Services done by Thomas Goffe Esqr Great Uncle to the Said Robert Rand, in Advancing the Settlement of their Late Colony, Did Grant unto the Said Robert One Thousand Acres of Land in Said Harry's Town, which one Thousd Acres is Commonly known by the name of Rands Farm & Scituate on the Eastward side of Merimack. About fourteen years past one Ephrm Bushell built a Frame of a Dwelling House upon the premises, but upon Information of the title of Said Rand to the Land, he quitted. Said Rand paying him for his frame, which afterwards he finished and Dwelt therein with his Family

about eighteen months.—And one Mr Duncan of London Derry about the Same time, enclosed about Three Acres & Cleared & broke up about half an Acre near Sd House which Improvement he Surrender'd to Said Robert, and John Goffe Esqr Improved between 4 & 5 Acres of Said Farm on the Westerly Side of Cohas Brook just by Merimack River & built a Log House thereon, who held possession of the Same. So that the Said Robert by the Assistance of his Brother Doctr Wm Rand Sued Sd Goffe for Sd Land who promised to Go off the premises if Said Robert would Drop his Action against him therefor, who Removed himself and Family, but placed his Father thereon & one Robert Walker & James Walker had Enclosed near One hundred Acres of Said Farm, and Improved about Eight Acres by planting which parcell of Land is Lying Contiguous to the Improvement of John Goffe aforesaid westerly & by the River Merimack Southerly—About 12 years since, the Said Robert Rand Demanding of the Said Robert & James Walker this Land, the Said James Walker being under age. Said Robert Walker, his Brother Engaged for him Vizt. that they would quit their Said Possession and Improvement upon Condition Sd Robert Rand would pay them for their Improvement in Said farm which the Said Robt Rand Agreed to And Accordingly it was Referr'd to Men mutually Chosen by the Said parties to Judge what the Said Robert Rand Shou'd pay to the Sd Robert & James Walker For their Said Improvement, & that according to the Report of the Said Referees, the Said Robt Rand paid the Said Robt & James Walker money for their Sd Improvemt & Sd Robt Walker quitted Said Improvement to the Said Robert Rand, thereupon applied to Coll l Blanchard for Advice for Further proceeding (who is well acquainted with the Affairs Relating to Said Farm) and Afterwards James Walker agreed to quit upon Consideration of Reaping Two Thirds of the Crop then on the ground—and that one Smith Fenced and Improved about 4 Acres of Said Farm Joining upon Said Walkers Improvements, and by the River Merimack who Gave the Said Robert Rand Six Bushels Corn for his Improved & quitted.—

And that Your Petitioner has a Daughter a Widow with Four Small Children who lives on a part of Said Farm Containing about Forty Acres joining upon the Land Improved by the Robt & Js Walker—Tho' the Said Robert promised her his Sd Daughter 100 Acres of Sd Farm, and also promised your Petitioner on his Death bed One hundred Acres more of Said Farm—And that your petitioner (upon the Removal of the Sd Rt & Js Walker) Settled with the Said Robt Rand her husband, upon the Said one hund d Acres and Dwelt there for about five or six years when he Died & was buried—And when the Southern boundary Line between the Provinces of the Massachusetts bay & New Hampshire. the whole of Said Grant from the General Court of the Massacusetts Bay, fell within, by which Acident your Memorialist Aprehends the Greatest part of Said 1000 Acres falls allso within Londonderry Charter Bounds, and the Said John Goffe Esqr who only improved about 4 or 5 Acres, has Since Enclosed and Improved a Large Farm out of your petitioners Grant and Since the Commencement of the warr, your petitioner Improved part of the Said 100 Acres for Two years & Continued in the peaceable possession thereof till about a fortnight past your petitioner Removed to Said place to Dwell there and after being there Eight Days John Goffe Esqr aforesaid hath Enc'osed the whole 100 Acres your petitioner is possessed of and am fearful with an Evil Intention of Circumven ing & Defrauding your petitioner of that part of the 1000 Acre Grant, more Especially as he did in a formall manner before 8 or 9 witnesses warn your petitioner to move out of Said premises Claiming the Same as his property for that he had a Conveyance therefor from you the proprietors of masons Right &cr—Wherefore your petitioner humbly prays that as the Said Robert Rand Deceas'd my Late Husband was at the time of the Grant of the General Court of the Massachusetts Bay of the thousand acres of Land : in Good Circumstances having full & Constant Employment at his trade of Sail making which Employment he quitted to settle and Improve this Land So Granted to him as aforesaid but by Reason of the molestation of Persons who were Trespassers on Said Tract. The Running of the Dividing Line between Sd Provinces, so as that the Grant aforesd Conveyed no Real Title to the Premises. And the Grant to London Derry Proprietors Comprehending the Greatest part of Said 1000 Acres, And the Attempts of Sundry persons to Get into Possession of and to Obtain Grants from your honours the proprietors of what parts of the 1000 Acres of Good Land aforesaid is not within any Township or that Some Persons have without Leave or Licence made Some Improvements in, And more Especially John Goffe Esqr his Attempts or Aims of Supplanting yr petitioner of that small piece of Ground that was Enclosed as aforesaid by which means the Substance of the Sd Robert was Diminished before his Death & under went much Fatigue & Difficulty by Reason of his Endeavoring to settle & Improve the Premises before his

Decease, & Since your Petitioner is Exceedingly Reduced by means aforesaid, having no Means or place of Living but on the premises which affords at Best a very small subsistance, being thus Reduced to Such Needy Circumstances I humbly pray you would take into Consideration my Deplorable state & of that of my Widow Daughter and her Fatherless Children and Grant us what Relief and favour in the premises you shall think meet—And Your Petitioner Shall Ever pray &cr—

The Mark of Elizath E Rand—

She claimed title through her husband who received the grant from the province of Ma-sachusetts. Goffe, however, replied that at a suit at law in Massachusetts had in 1735, between him and Dr. William Rand, the husband aforesaid, he, Goffe, recovered judgment against Rand and had been in possession ever since. The Masonian Proprietors recognized Goffe's title as paramount, but granted to Elizabeth Rand, the widow, sixty acres, and to Elizabeth Secomb, her daughter, forty acres of the tract. The entire parcel was 1000 acres.

Province of
New Hampshire
    Portsmouth November ye 5th 1748—

To the Gentlemen Purchasers & Proprietors of Capt John Tufton Mason Esqur his Right in Lands within Said Province—

I the Subscriber in behalf of James Walker and myselfe represent that ye tract of land included within ye above Plan was claimed by Doctor William Ran by virtue of a grant from ye Province of ye Massa Bay about which a Suit at law was had in ye Prove of ye Massa Bay between ye said Ran and ye Subscriber for ye Property of Said Tract—against whom ye Subscriber Recover'd a Judgement upon ye Premises against said Rann in or about ye year 1735—and as Said Tract is within your Right we pray your favour that as ye Said Walker and myselfe are in ye Possession & improvement of ye said Tract, namely of about two thirds thereof—that you would grant our Possession & improvement to us and the other third thereof reserve to your own Use & Disposall your Compliance herein will very much oblige said walker in whose behalf I am and also your most Hum: Servt     JOHN GOFFE

I insert a letter of Col. Blanchard to the Proprietors bearing on the subject.

(Joseph Blanchard to Proprietors, 1748.)
(Masonian Papers, Vol. 6, p. 23.)

Gentlemen

at the Importunity of Capt Goffe Relating his Expected Grant at Cohas the East Side Merrimack river. Who Complains that One Dunkin Unfairly, tryes to Defeat his good Intention of Setting up a mill under pretence that he had possession there I have this nere thirty Years bin knowing of those Lands, and know that that Stream has never properly bin in possession of any but Capt Goffe, there was, a number in a frenzy both of Derry & of the Massachusetts People Without any Order each of them Separately Lotted all the Lands on the River and Rediculously dugg holes in the turffe and planted some Corn on Most of the Lotts and in Severall places fell Some trees in Course, Where a fence might be Built but all a Sham from first to Last, Some persons did one or two Years plant a Small bit of the Land South of Cohass, and When Capt Goffe Entered there no house had bin Built nor Since no person Improving, in that time it was Lay'd out to One Robert Rand, by the Massachusetts I at his request often treated with all then In possession or making pretence. I never heard for ten Years or more the Least Intimation of Claim of this Dunkin Goffe in fact has kept Settlement there, and maintained Something of a Bridge And be very Serviceable to a great many people in keeping boats and Canoes to help people both Over that And the Great River Merrimack without ever being one Quarter paid to all these things I am knowing. And many Other facts in his favor might be Intimated & provided no Regard be had to Rand. Capt Goffe for that trate by the Small River and the Conveniencys of Both Sides to the Great River, for about half a mile is the Only man that can Honestly pretend Any Couler to a grant from this Society—Those Are the true facts, the Relating them Excuse me In, And Accept the very Hume Service of your most Obedt

J Blanchard

Londondonderry 29th of Novr 1748
To the Honl Proprs of Masons Grant
P S Gentn We are in Expectation yt Capt Goffe will this Journey finish his township I have Quieted with his help Severall proprs who perhaps Would have Wrangled As much As any, but now be Stanch frinds to the Affair I Hope Honest Capt

Colburn Will be Remembered in Starks town And be Equally Helpful as Capt. Goffe has bin and if any Hindrance Happens to Starks tis pitty but Goffes town now Getts through that people may See tis more than a fiction Yrs

ut Supra J B

When Goffe moved to Bedford is not exactly known. The petition of Mrs. Rand, above referred to, states that he moved himself and his family from Cohas brook farm, but left his father there behind him.

In Feb. 2, 1739, he and others presented to the Governor and council a " petition touching the Parrishes in Londonderry as it is entit'ed." So it would seem as if he was then resident there. But in 1744 his name is found in a list of the inhabitants of Souhegan East, as Bedford was then called, and on April 11, 1748, an order was made by the Governor and council directing Capt. John Goffe to hold the first town meeting in Bedford and to give fifteen days' notice thereof to the inhabitants of the town.

We know that in 1748 John Goffe, Esquire, the colonel's father, died, for he is buried in Bedford, and so while the exact date of the first change in the colonel's residence cannot be fixed, there seems no reasonable doubt that somewhere about 1740 he had moved his home from one side of the river to the other and had established himself on the farm which since that day has descended practically intact to his lineal descendant, the present owner. Later he removed again to Derryfield and seems to have retained his residence here until old age. It is not known whether he died in Derryfield or in Bedford, but he is buried in the latter place between his father and his son and with his wife by his side.

In 1744 war broke out between England and France. What its causes were we need not here elaborate. They were far enough removed from the interests of the frontiersmen, who were the most active participants in it and whose exploits we now take pride in recalling. Here the war was known as King George's war. At once the dread of Indian attacks on the frontiers awoke. War parties from Canada appeared. The settlers were again in hourly fear of their lives, and being so far from the seat of Government must protect themselves as best they could.

At Boston the Louisburg expedition was set on foot and resulted most successfully. Here Governor Shirley organized what was known as the "Canada expedition," but it came to nothing. In 1744 a regiment was raised and John Goffe became the captain of the Eighth company under Joseph Blanchard as colonel. In the summer of 1745, two men from Bedford, James McQuade and John Burns, went to Pennacook—now Concord—to purchase corn for their families. They were waylaid by Indians and one of them, McQuade, killed. Burns escaped. In October, of the same year, the Indians appeared Howe near Great Meadows—now Walpole—and took Nehemiah prisoner and killed David Rugg. These outrages and others not here necessary to detail roused the Government. Orders were issued to Colonel Blanchard to take the field and he detached Captain Goffe to scour the woods for the enemy.

As the men selected for such work were those only who had some reputation for sagacity and courage, it seems a fair inference that their leader must have possessed these qualities to a marked degree. Preparations were made in December of 1745 and in January following a "scout" of twenty men started up the Merrimack on snow shoes. While on this expedition Goffe wrote the following letter to Governor Wentworth:

5 May, 1746.

May it please your Excellency—I got to Pennycook on Saturday early in the morning, and notwithstanding I sent the Monday after I left the Bank yet my bread was not baked; but there was about 250 pound weight which supplied 20 men, which I sent to Canterbury as soon as I got them—and I kept the baker and several soldiers to baking all Sabbath day, and prop ised to march on Monday, as soon as possible; but about midnight two men came down from Contookook and brought the unhappy news of two men being killed; and the two men that came down told me that they saw the two men lie in their blood and one man more that was missing. And hearing I was here, desired me to assist in making search, so that I am with all expedition going up the Contookook and will do what I can to see the enemy. I shall take all possible care for the protection of the frontier and destruction of the enemy. The Indians are all about our frontier. I think there was never more need of soldiers than now. It is enough to make one's blood cold in one's veins to see our fellow creatures killed and taken upon every quarter, and if we cannot catch them here I hope the general court will give encouragement to go and give them the same play at home. The white man that is killed is one, Thomas Cook, and the other is Mr. Stevens, the minister's negro. These are found and one Jones, a soldier, is not found. They have but few soldiers in the fort, and have not as yet sought much for him. I am going with all possible expedition and am

Your Excellency's most humble and most dutiful subject and servant, JOHN GOFFE.

Pennycook about 2 o'clock in the morning, May 5, 1746.

The attack on Contoocook was made on Monday, the 4th of May, 1746. The Indians made one prisoner, Elisha Jones, and with him they made directly for Canada. Goffe and his company followed in pursuit but without success. They were gone about two weeks returning about the 20th of May. Reporting to his superior officer, Goffe, with thirteen others, set out at once again and was gone ten days on another "scout," as these expeditions were called, but without success. The Indians and their prisoners escaped to Canada.

He seems to have been on similar service prior to this time also, for the assembly of the province voted to him and his associates in varying numbers from year to year, their pay for scouting and guarding the frontiers from the Merrimack river westward to the Connecticut in the years 1744, '45 and '46. In 1747 he petitions the Governor and council for men to guard the towns of Hollis and Souhegan East (Bedford) and his petition was granted. In April, 1747, Hopkinton was attacked by Indians and Samuel Burbank, his sons, Caleb and Jonathan, and David Woodwell, his wife and three children were murdered. Soon after two men were killed near Keene and one carried away prisoner. Goffe was ordered to Hopkinton with fifty men at once, but arrived too late to prevent the massacre. The raising of fifty men was not the work of a day in those times, but that number of fighting men could more easily be raised at Amoskeag than at any other section of the province. The attack on Hopkinton took place April 27. The company of fifty men was raised and Captain Goffe was twenty miles on his way at their head on the 3d of May, following, all in the space of six days. Attacks by the Indians were frequent through the whole of 1747 and garrisons to protect the inhabitants were established at Dunstable (now Nashua), Monson (now Milford), Souhegan (now Bedford), Derryfield, Suncook, Pennacook, Contoocook and Canterbury. The garrisons at Miford, Bedford and Derryfield were under command of Captain Goffe as appears by his muster roll of men under the command of Captain John Goffe employed in scouting and guarding the Souhegan, Monson and Stark garrisons, anno 1748. He seems also to have had a double command at this time, for there is extant a muster roll of his men of names different from those of this last muster employed in scouting and guarding the frontier, anno 1748, and it is doubtless owing to his vigilance and activity that this immediate frontier suffered no more than it did during this war. The attacks on the settlements along the Connecticut river and near Rochester and Somersworth were both more frequent and more bloody than here. But in 1748 peace was declared between France and England and the Provinces had relief from these forays of the savage allies of the most Christian king.

With the close of the war Goffe returned to his farm. We have seen that he had been appointed by the Governor to summon his fellow-townsmen in their first town meeting and in 1750 he presented for them a petition for their incorporation as a town. This was granted.

He seems to have resumed his practices as a hunter for numerous stories are extant of his adventures at this time in hunting catamounts and bears in Bedford and elsewhere in the neighborhood. One of them seems worth repeating. Goffe was once returning from a hunting excursion up the Piscataquog valley when he discovered a catamount upon his track. He immediately cut a part of a quarter of a buck he was bringing home and throw it in his track in hopes that his hunger satiated, the animal would leave his track. He could see the catamount threw the deer's leg into the air as if in play and soon after he lost sight of him. Tired and jaded he camped on a small brook that empties into the Piscataquog from the north below Goffstown Center. Here he slept till sunrise, when upon waking up and looking upon a tree nearly over him he saw his companion of the day before viewing the group in the camp. Without moving from his position he jostled his dog near him asleep, which jumped up and commenced barking. The catamount upon this leaped upon an adjacent tree but soon returned to its first position lashing itself into a rage. Upon this Goffe raised his gun and fired; the catamount fell near to the camp and was soon skinned and carried home. Since then the scene has been and is now called Catamount brook.

Although a treaty of peace between England and France had been signed in 1748, the settlers on this border were not, in consequence, relieved from fear of Indian attacks. It was the settled policy of the French government to assert for themseves a more extended dominion westward and southward from Quebec and Montreal and to shut up the English to a narrow strip of Atlantic seaboard.

To this end they began the construction of a chain of forts from the great lakes to New Orleaus and to this end also their Indian allies were continually urged on expeditions against the English frontier after scalps. So that although peace had been officially declared in 1748 war between the French Indians and the English settlers hardly ceased at all. Their attacks did not concentrate here, however, to any great extent. The streams were the highways in those days and the easiest and speediest road from the French capital Quebec to the main

English settlements was up the St. Lawrence from Quebec to the river St. Francis, which is the outlet of Lake Champlain. Then up Lake Champlain to Lake George. At the head of the latter the distance to Albany is short and the road easy. And at Albany the French believed a more effective attack by organized force or English power could be made than any where else. Accordingly forts were built at various intervals from the St. Francis river southward. The principal ones, however, were that at Crown Point, a jutting promontory in Lake Champlain, and that at Ticonderoga, the narrow strait at the foot of Lake George, where its waters descend into Lake Champlain. At these two points the French erected at enormous expense extensive works calculated to receive in garrison any where from 10,000 to 15,000 men, and from here as bases, the intention was to move to the head of Lake George and so to Albany in force. Thes preparations of course alarmed and excited the colonial governor.

A treaty between New York, Massachusetts, Connecticut and South Carolina was concluded with the six nations of Indians, as the Iroquois of the Mohawk valley were called. A conference of colonial delegates met at Albany and to them was submitted by Benjamin Franklin a plan of union of all the colonies, but it was rejected.

The purpose of their meeting was to plan for mutual defence against the Indians but they accomplished little if anything. At last in 1755 the petty attacks from Indian scalping parties had become so frequent and so unendurable that war was formally declared between the two countries. It is not desirable here to enter into any extended account of the French and Indian war as the ensuing conflict is called in history. This is merely a hasty summary of the important occurrences in the life of a New Hampshire borderer whose place in the great drama to be enacted on Lake George and Ticonderoga was but small. Since the close of the former war he had been busy mainly at home although we find that in 1753 he was making a survey and plan of Winnepiseogee pond and vicinity as he calls it. But the mutterings of coming war grew louder and in May of the next year the Indians were on the war path again and Goffe was mustered in once more. At first as a lieutenant in one of the companies of Col. Joseph Blanchard's regiment posted on Merrimack river. The next year he was ranked as major of the same regiment. There is extant a letter of Captain Goffe showing the harassing and wearisome nature of the Indians' attack to which the settlers were subjected. The alacrity and frequency with which the colonial legislature responded to the demands for men and money made on them by the crown can be traced to the deep determination of the colonists to end these Indian attacks at any cost.

Contoocook, Sept. 1, 1754.

Sir: I arrived at Pennicook at 12 o'clock on Thursday, where I met the troops who came down to guard 10 or 12 horses to mill and I took their places and they went home and I got safe to the fort at Contoocook with all those that went to mill and have given the people I believe good satisfaction since I have been here considering the few men I have. Those that went to Hillsborough not being yet come, but expect them tomorrow. We have done considerable in guarding the people whose hay was cut before the mischief was done has lain ever since till we came and a great deal more hay and grain we must guard them to get or they will lose it and shall do what we can for them as soldiers, for they are here more concerned than ever I knew them any time last war, and durst not go anywhere without a guard. I have not been to Stevens town (Salisbury, N. H.) yet and it's tho't dangerous to attempt without any more men. There is nobody there but I am informed that there is a good deal of good corn there which is a pity that should be lost, but four or five or the inhabitants will go back to stay and then not without 20 men at least as soldiers with them. The Indians are certain y about, they are traced and guns heard every day almost in the woods. I went with my scout to a number of the inhabitants.

I heard up to the westward when I was four miles out of town 2 guns very plain. Upon Saturday last we made a considerable scout and went near to Hopkinton, marched down Contoocook river and so to the fort. We saw fair moguson tracks in several places, some new and some older. I pray you would send me express what I should do about going to Stevenstown if I have no more men. If I go I must take them all with me and I don't see but Contoocook must lose or sell or kill most of their cattle for they have got but very little hay since the mischief was gone and have a great deal to get. All their pease almost in the field unhooked and loosing every day, and abundance of them there is. Mr. Lovejoy's garrison are all moved off but three familys and he told me that he would not stay any longer without he had some souldiers—and if he had several familys would come to them which if that fort weaks up they can grind none to Contoocook, and must be forced to go to Eastman's mill on Turkey river (12 or 14 miles, a dangerous road), and it will be much more dangerous to go to Pennicook. Please to take their things into consideration and send me what I shall do. I am ready to obey if you will command.

The scout must go up to Stevenstown to take care of their effects and stay a night or two and I believe if I was ordered to go once in a week or ten ten days up there it might possibly have this effect to daunt the enemy or find 'em or fight 'em. If you think it best to go and live at Stevenstown, I am ready to do it and heartily willing but they have no provision but salt. I must buy an ox and drive up and kill there which will be costly, and to carry meal so far will be bad luggage. Pray your advice by the bearer, but if I go there pray your interest for Contoocook and Lovejoy's mill and Eastman's mill that there may be an addition of soldiers, etc. J. GOFFE.

P. S. The most of Contoocook people desire me to acquaint you that they are destitute of any military officers and by that means nobody will watch or ward but such as see cause and by that means some are oblidged to do duty and some none at all and they think it is owing to their living at so great a distance from Colo. Smith to whose regiment they belong that they have none and desired me to acquaint you that it is their desire to be annexed to your regiment as they joyn upon it and think they shall be taken better care of if they were and pray your interest to get it done and pray also that if they can't be in your Regiment you would recommend Mr. Steven Gerrish for their chief officer, and I assure you that there is necessity that some thing be done in that respect soon. I am, etc. J. G.

I have my full comp'nt of men and I think one more, pray your advice in that ——— as I was sealing up this, Rec'd yrs relating to No. 4. Shall follow your directions. J. G.

I came down with a guard with two teams to Lovejoy's mill

and to relieve my soldiers from Hillsborough who, it seems, did not care to come alone.  J. G

(Eastman's mill was on Turkey river, near where St. Paul's school is located.)

The British government determined to render effective aid to the colonists and in 1755 General Braddock was sent over with two regiments of regulars to operate against the French. He was utterly defeated at Fort Du Quesne and was killed. We will not extend the details here. And the expedition was sent under General Shirley to Lake Ontario, but it accomplished nothing. A third under General Sir William Johnson was more successful. In June his forces met at Albany to the number of 6000 men. General Lyman of Massachusetts commanded the New England contingent and under him was Colonel Blanchard of Dunstable (Nashua) with 500 men, Of these, three companies were raised in Derryfield, one commanded by John Goffe, one by John Moore, his son in law, and the third by the afterwards celebrated Robert Rogers. Their duty was mainly that of scouting or ranging as it was called and here we may quote from Parkman's description of them. "These rangers wore a sort of woodland uniform which varied in the different companies, and were armed with smooth bore guns loaded with buckshot, bullets or sometimes both. The best of them were commonly employed on Lake George and nothing can surpass the adventurous hardihood of their lives. Summer and winter, day and night, were alike to them. Embarked in whaleboats or birch canoes they glided under the silent moon or in the languid glare of a breathless autumn day when islands floated in dreamy haze and the hot air was thick with odors of the pine, or in the bright October, when the jay screamed from the woods, squirrels gathered their winter hoard and co gregated blackbirds chattered farewell to their summer haunts; when gay mountains basked in light, maples dropped leaves of rustling gold, sumach glowed like rubies under the dark green of the unchanging spruce, and mossed rocks, with all their painted plumage lay double in the watery mirror; that festal evening of the year when jocund nature disrobes herself, to wake again refreshed in the joy of her undying spring Or, in the tomb-like silence of the winter forest with breath frozen on his beard the Ranger strode on snow shoes over the spotless drifts ; and like Duver's Knight, a ghastly death stalked ever at his side."

Colonel Blanchard's regiment had its rendezvous at Stewartstown, now Salisbury. Thence they marched to Charlestown, or No. 4 as it was called, on the Connecticut river, and thence to Albany. They were posted at Fort Edward on the road from Albany to the head of Lake George. General Johnson was at the lake making preparations for an advance to Crown Point when word came of the approach of a French force against Fort Edward, behind him.

This force was under command of Baron Dieskau, a veteran of the European wars and a good soldier But his troops were mainly composed of French colonists and half breeds with a large contingent of Indians. As they approached the fort they became panic-struck and refused to attack it. They were willing, however, to attack Johnson at Lake George, and having no alternative Dieskau turned back for the purpose. Johnson, hearing of his approach, sent a force to meet him, under Colonel Williams, from whom Williams college was afterwards named. They were ambusded by the French and Indians about four miles from Johnson's camp, and retreated to their main camp on the shore of Lake George where Johnson had commenced a rough breastwork afterwards known as Fort William Henry.

Here Dieskau attacked him, but was beaten off after an all-day fight. At its close the English and their Indian allies leaped the breastworks and drove the French in utmost confussion. Colonel Blanchard, at Fort Edward, hearing the firing, marched his men in its direction. They fell in with the retreating French and though much inferior in numbers, dispersed them utterly. All their baggage and many prisoners were taken. Upon the approach of winter Johnson's army was disbanded with the of exception of small garrisons at Fort Edward and another at William Henry. Goffe and Moore and their companies returned home, but Rogers and his company remained. Their exploits through the winter are a history in themselves.

The next spring another expedition was organized against Crown Point, by General Shirley and a regiment was raised here for the service. It was commanded by Colonel Meserve. Goffe was its major and his son went as an ensign. The regiment was put in charge of Fort Edward, and from it were enlisted an independent command of Rangers under the orders of Robert Rogers. Whether Goffe was among these or not is not known. The year 1756 was one of inactivity in military affairs and according to the custom of the times, the soldiers were withdrawn into winter quarters by October, and active hostilities were at an end. This, however, did not apply to the Rangers. They continued upon scouting duty all winter as well as all summer. The fortification at the head of Lake George which Gen. William Johnson had completed in 1755, and which was known by the name of Fort William Henry, was a constant source of chagrin and irritation to the French ; and Montcalm, their commander-in-chief, determined to destroy it. So as early as March of 1757, he made his first attack upon it, but it was defended by the Rangers so stoutly that he was obliged to withdraw, though his force numbered some 1500 men. With the opening of summer of 1757, the English commander in-chief, the Earl of Loudon, prepared for an attack on Louisburg. Troops were called for from the colonies and New Hampshire raised 1000 men. They were placed again under command of Colonel Meserve and John Goffe of Derryfield was commissioned lieutenant colonel. The regiment was divided. One battalion, under command of Meserve, joined the expedition against Louisburg. The other, under Goffe, marched from Charlestown to join General Webb at Albany, and was placed by him with other contingents, at Fort William Henry, under command of Colonel Monroe.

The French hearing of the intended attack on Louisburg,

determined on a counter attack in force on Fort William Henry. An army of 8000 men started from Ticonderoga at the end of June and guided by their Indian allies, concentrated at the head of Lake George for the attack. General Webb, though commanding a force adequate to cope with the French, withdrew to Fort Edward and Albany, leaving Colonel Munroe with but 2000 men to resist an army of 8000. Among the garrison was the battalion of 200 men from the New Hampshire regiment, commanded by Goffe. Besides these there was a ranger company commanded by Richard Rogers, brother to the famous Robert Rogers. The story of the siege and capture of Fort William Henry is a moving one. I shall not here go into it in detail. Enough to say that after repeated calls for aid and reenforcements from Webb which were refused, after their ammunition had been completely exhausted so that cannon and muskets lay useless on the ramparts, after an intercepted letter from Webb had been sent into the fortress by Montcalm, the French commander-in-chief, advising Munroe to capitulate upon the best terms obtainable, then and then only was the place surrendered. But even then Munroe would yield only upon terms, and these were, that the garrison should march out with the honors of war, with their arms, baggage and a field piece and that they should be protected from the outrages of the savages. On these terms they yielded and the evacuation began.

The stipulation of protection from Indian outrage upon helpless captives and upon the women and children in the fort was the more necessary because only the year before such an agreement had been made at the surrender of Oswego, and yet in gross violation of it twenty English prisoners had been delivered by Montcalm into the hands of the savages for torture. But at William Henry, before the English had left the fort, the Indians, in search of plunder, had broken into the spirit room, stove the rums casks and were drinking themselves to frenzy. The evacuation began. The garrison with the women in the center marched out. The New Hampshire contingent was in the rear. They had gone but a short distance when by a preconcerted signal the savages rushed upon them all, sounding the war whoop and brandishing their tomahawks. No guard had been furnished by Montcalm. There was not a single ound of powder among the surrendered garrison and only the regular troops had bayonets. They were in advance and were not molested. But the provincials and the women were attack by the savages with the utmost ferocity. They were killed in scores, and those who were taken prisoners were reserved for torture worse than death itself. The exact number of the slaughtered can not be ascertained, but it is estimated at from 500 to 1500.

The whole transaction sent a shudder of horror through the country and remains till now an indelible stain on the honor of its responsible author, the Marquis of Montcalm.

Of the 200 New Hampshire soldiers 80 were killed or made prisoners' and among them Benjamin Kidder, whom we may recall was Colonel Goffe's brother-in law and who lived with him at Cohas brook, and John Moore, his son-in-law. Kidder was carried to Quebec, thence sent to France as a prisoner and died in prison at Rochelle, France. Moore, likewise taken prisoner to Quebec, was carried to Brest in France and served in the galleys, thence he escaped to England, sailed to Boston, was impressed there for the royal navy and after being two years at sea, at last reached home. The losses of Colonel Goffe were stated by him at £178 15s., and this sum was reimbursed to him by the New Hampshire Legislature the next year. From his experience in such occurrences we can gain an idea of how he and others like him must have regarded a Frenchman, and how they enjoyed apparently to the utmost the continuous war against them in which they were engaged.

The expedition against Louisburg ended in complete failure, and so the year 1757 ended with the English hopes at their lowest. But in the next year, 1758, William Pitt, Earl of Chatham, was at the head of the English foreign office and a different temper was diffused through all the public service. Louisburg capitulated in July. An army of 15,000 men was assembled at Albany for the recapture of William Henry and the reduction of Ticonderoga; 6000 were regulars and the remainder, provincial levies. Besides the companies of Rangers which had been enlisted almost exclusively from the former New Hampshire regiments and which numbered now some 500 men under various subordinates but all under Robert Rogers as their chief, the province furnished a regiment of 800 men under Colonel Hart of Portsmouth, and John Goffe of Derryfield was commissioned again as lieutenant-colonel.

His son was a lieutenant in one of the companies. Fort William Henry had been burned and abandoned by the French after its capture. Nothing was left but its charred ruins when the English arrived in the spring of 1758. They moved down Lake George toward Ticonderoga with bands and artillery in more than a thousand boats and rafts, and the sight must have been both imposing and grand. The nominal head of the expedition was General Abercrombie and second in command was Lord Howe. He was killed in a skirmish as the expedition approached Ticonderoga and with his death all the courage, enthusiasm and promise of success departed. After an obstinate attack the English were beaten off, and here might be noted a singular instance of the dogged resistance which the British commanders so often exhibited to ideas and suggestions from the colonial commanders, their subordinates. John Stark was with the expedition, knew the fort and knew how it might be captured. He suggested to his commanding general the use of his artillery and declared the place could be battered down in an hour. But General Abercrombie, had the report of his superior engineer officer that this could not be done and ordered an assault. The result was defeat. And again the next year, 1759, the campaign against Ticonderoga was undertaken, and again New Hampshire sent her regiment. Again John Goffe of Derryfield was its lieutenant-colonel, but this time the commander-in-chief was General Amherst, a very different man from any of his predecessors. During the winter of 1758 and '59, he was actively engaged in preparations at Albany and the Rangers were kept on duty scouting and skirmishing against the enemy all winter long. The first of May, 1759, the army was organized for the field; the 21st of July 11,000 men embarked on Lake George for Ticonderoga, the New Hampshire regiment among them. On the 26th, after many skirmishes and a galling fire on the fort kept up night and day, the French blew up the magazine and abandoned the place. They retreated to Crown Point. Amherst followed them. On the 1st of August the French abandoned that place also and withdrew to the fort of Lake Champlain, where it emptied into the Richelieu River and the River St. Lawrence. After following them there, but being unable to make any impression, Amherst withdrew into winter quarters at Crown Point.

The principal service in the campaign had been rendered by the Rangers and they were recruited almost entirely from men at Amoskeag and Derryfield. While Amherst had been busy at Ticonderoga and Crown Point, General Prideaux had reduced Niagara and in 'September came the news that Wolfe had captured Quebec. Little was left of French power on this continent, but such as there was, centered now at Montreal. The English only waited for the opening of spring to invest the place. General Murray was in command of his majesty's forces and the colonies were called upon to furnish levies. New Hampshire furnished a regiment and this time John Goffe was commissioned its full colonel. A singular order published by him is preserved: "Collo. Goffe recommends it to the officers to examine the state of the men's shirts, shoes and stockings and further acquaint them that they are to be answerable that the men shirt twice every week at least, that such as have hair that will admit of it must have it constantly tied, they must be obliged to comb their hair and wash their hands every morning and as it is observed a number of the men accustom themselves to wear woolen night caps in the day time, he allows them hats. They are ordered for the future not to be seen in the day time with anything besides their hats on their heads, as ye above mentioned custom of wearing night caps must be detrimental to their health and cleanliness, the men's hats to be all cocked, or cut uniformly as Collo. Goffe pleases to direct." The regiment was marched up Souhegan river, through Amherst, Milford, Wilton, over the Pack Monadnock to Peterborough up the Contoocook and down the Ashuelot to Keene. Thence up the Connecticut river to Charlestown, thence across Vermont to Crown Point, where it joined the main army. Thence down Lake Champlain and the Sorel river to Montreal, where they arrived on August 8, 1760. September 8, Montreal capitulated and French power in Canada was at an end.

The war was over but not the actual employments of the man in public affairs. In fact all his life long he was busy in one way or another in the public service of the community in which he lived.

He seemed to have been a man of means also. In 1758 he was a member of the committee to build the Londonderry meeting house and was the largest individual contributor to the work. In 1761 the town of Goffstown was granted by the Masonian Proprietors and was incorporated by the Governor and council, receiving its name from John Goffe, in appreciation of his public services. In 1766 he was the largest tax payer in Derryfield. In 1761, 2, 3, 5, 6, 7, '70, 1, 2, 3, 4 he represented Amherst and Bedford in the Provincial Legislature In 1771 he was appointed judge of probate of Hillsborough county, and continued in the office until 1776 and took the oaths of allegiance and obligation. In 1764 the town of Piermont was granted to him outright, and in 1765 the town of Jefferson was granted to him and 63 others by the name of Dartmouth. The customary dispute over the location of the meeting house, which seems to have absorbed a large part of the energies of our ancestors, began in due time in Derryfield. In New Ipswich things went so far that the inhabitants petitioned the Governor to locate their meeting house for them, and in accordance with their wish, Colonel Goffe, John Hall and James Underwood did so. The French war interrupted the dispute in Derryfield. But at its termination the quarrel began again. John Goffe was eagerly interested to have the meeting house located near the river; John Hall to have it somewhere else.

The Governor and council were finally petitioned to amend the action of the regular town meeting, which had decided the question, and to appoint another for the purpose. The petition was granted and leave was given to bring in a bill for vacating the action of the town. The bill passed. In accordance with it the inhabitants were warned to hold another meeting which they did. The Goffe party was entirely defeated and the meeting house was located in the place the Hall party had chosen. Hall was the committee to build it, and in order to do so found it necessary to borrow some money to finish the job. This the town refused to refund. He sued the town for it. Goffe and William McClintock were chosen agents to defend. But the suit was settled after the town had been thoroughly stirred up over it and all the bad blood possible engendered by it.

At the outbreak of the Revolution Colonel Goffe was a man 74 years old and not fit for service in the field. His son was at Bunker Hill and at Bennington, but the colonel was too old for military service. Command of his regiment was given to his son-in-law, John Moore, and the old man could only forward the cause by precept and example. He signed the association test in Bedford and in 1776 represented Derryfield and Goffstown in the Provincial assembly. In 1777 he was again in the legislature and sat on a military board of inquiry into the conduct of Col. Nathan Hale at the battle of Trenton. In 1778 he was a member of the committee of safety of his town, Bedford. A letter written by him to his son indicates the feelings of the man.

Portsmouth, Sept. 24, 1777.

Sir:—Colonel Bellows goes off today to head as many volunteer as will push off to reinforce General Gates. Our army is now in possession of Ticonderoga. In order to cut off Bur-

goyne's retreat, who was on the 17th of this month within four miles of Stillwater, with his main body as we are assured by General Stark's letter of that date, pressing the State to exert every nerve and to march at least half the militia of this State, and now is the time to cut off the whole army. And if we do but all go without hesitation, I verily believe it will put an end to the war. And if you could go yourself for a fortnight or three weeks, I believe it would encourage many. Every man will have to pay as the last militia had. But it must be done without loss of time. And if your brother-in law, Samuel Moor, would be forward in this affair, it would be to his everlasting honor. Pray show yourselves friends to the country this once. I am your loving father, JOHN GOFFE.
To Major John G ffe.

Pray let Captain Moor read this after you have read it.

Colonel Goffe was a religious man. The place where he lived was the remote frontier and a savage wilderness. Until a meeting house had been built and a place provided he was accustomed to conduct public worship in his own house on the Sabbath. People from Bedford, Goffstown, Merrimack and Litchfield resorted here, and Colonel Goffe preached the discourse. His grandson, the Rev. Joseph Goffe, thus speaks of him: "My grandfather was a man of some eminence in his day as a military man, and commanded a regiment when Canada was surrendered to the British and Colonial arms. Besides his military commission, he held a variety of civil offices in the State, such as judge of probate, justice of the peace, often a member of the state Legislature and was an intimate friend of Governor Wentworth and Colonel Atkinson and other public men of that day. But what is infinitely more for his honor, he was a man of distinguished piety and did much for the promotion of religion in the new settlement around him. I can remember him well. He was rather above the middle stature, not corpulent, but of a commanding presence and aspect."

Colonel Goffe was a man of marked character and for sixty years was identified with all the stirring scenes of the most exciting period of our country's history. From Lovewell's fight in

1725, through the Indian and French wars and the war of the Revolution, he was almost constantly in the public service, and how well he acted his part has been related in the preceding pages. Through all the military grades, from private service in the field, he sustained the offices up to colonel, and in all of them in actual character of an energetic and courageous soldier, receiving on all occasions the hearty commendations of his superior officers. In civil life he was equally distinguished for energy of character. He was a close friend of Governor Wentworth and Theodore Atkinson. One of his grandsons was named Theodore Atkinson Goffe, but when the time came for choice between the Patriot party and the Tories, his decision was made on the instant. When Colonel Goffe told the Governor of his mistake in endeavoring to control the Legislature against the will of the Revolutionists, Governor Wentworth lost his temper and abused the old man roundly. In spite of his years, the colonel seized his former friend, tried to throw him out of the window, but friends interferred and ended the scene.

He was an experienced Indian fighter when John Stark was born, as was most natural in view of the fact that he was twenty seven years his senior. He was the military instructor of the Rogers, the Todds, the Havens and Starks, and the account they gave of themselves in the French and Indian war, and the Revolution did ample credit to their teacher. He died Oct. 20, 1781, leaving a large family of daughters and one son surviving, and is sleeping in Bedford old burying ground by the side of his wife and among the friends and neighbors who knew him and respected him in life. We in turn cannot read the story of his deeds without a feeling that here was a man, strong, simple, silent, a power for good, a terror to evil doers in his day and generation, and a trusted leader among the honest, faithful men and women who cleared this wilderness an hundred and fifty years ago.

> "While we their children gather as our own
> The harvest that the dead have sown."

# MANCHESTER FIRE DEPARTMENT.

(SECOND PAPER.)

READ BY FRED W. LAMB BEFORE THE MANCHESTER HISTORIC ASSOCIATION, SEPTEMBER 20, 1899.

### EARLY STEAM FIRE ENGINES.

In 1829 the first steam fire engine was built, foreshadowing the complete overthrow and disuse of the system of hand engines, except for small towns. The model, however, was not very practical and few steam fire engines were built until about 1852. Meanwhile various attempts of a similar nature had been made in America. Capt. John Ericsson built a steam fire engine in New York in 1839-40. It would throw 10,824 pounds of water a minute, 166 feet in the air, through a $2\frac{1}{8}$ inch nozzle, drawing four lengths of hose. A stationary boiler from which hot water could be transferred to the engine boiler was kept in the engine house. The machine proved cumbrous, heavy and expensive and was discarded. The prize gold medal, offered for the best plan of a steam fire engine by the Mechanics' Institute of New York, was awarded to Ericsson for this engine.

In 1852 A. B. Latta and Abel Shawk of Cincinnati built a steam fire engine that could throw a stream of water 170 feet, and afterwards Latta built another capable of throwing four streams 200 feet, or six streams 175 feet, through a $\frac{7}{8}$ inch nozzle. This engine weighed ten tons and went by the name of "Uncle Joe Ross," and required four horses for transportation. Its excessive weight was its most detrimental feature, as it was with its two successors, the "Citizens' Gift," of Cincinnati, and the "Miles Greenwood," of Boston. Its boiler finally exploded when out on trial, Dec. 6, 1855, killing its engineer. The firebox not being properly stayed was the cause.

In reply to the question as to what are the merits of steam over hand engines, asked by a committee from another city, Chief Greenwood of Cincinnati replied, "First, it never gets drunk; second, it never throws brickbats, and the only drawback connected with it is that it cannot vote." There is on record a report made by the Chief of the New York Fire Department, before the introduction of the steam fire engine, that "steam fire engines would do more damage with water than could possibly be done by fire." The "Latta" engines are now known by the name of their successor, the "Ahrens." Among the various steam fire engines manufacturerd may be mentioned the "Silsby" and "American," of Seneca Falls, N. Y., and Cincinnati, Ohio; the "La France" of Elmira, N. Y.; "Button," and last but not least the famous "Amoskeag" built by the Manchester Locomotive Works, who purchased the business from the Amoskeag Manufacturing Co.

In 1857 N. S. Bean was working as a locomotive machinist in the machine shop at Lawrence, Mass. There were a number of old fashioned hand tubs there and Mr. Bean belonged to one of its companies. Mr. Bean had for some time pondered over a better means of fire fighting and had wondered if steam could not be used advantageously to that end. He communicated his ideas to Thomas Scott, a fellow mechanic of considerable ingenuity, and together they managed to construct in the winter of 1857 and 1858, the first steam fire engine ever built in New England, which they named the "Lawrence." This machine was sent to Boston, where it was tested on Boston common, together with machines from Cleveland, Cincinnati and Philadelphia. The Bean machine was superior in its boiler and pump, but in the general arrangement, the Philadelphia machine was the better. Boston finally purchased the Bean machine for $3,500.

Neither Mr. Bean nor his companion had ever seen any early

engine of this kind and they worked on their own ideas. In 1859 he returned to this city and built the "Machigonne" and "Amoskeag, No. 1," and then entered upon the manufacture of the Amoskeag Steam Fire Engine for the Amoskeag Manufacturing Co. This engine, now built by the Manchester Locomotive Works, is unexcelled by any manufactured and has been sold and is in use all over the world.

### DAYS OF THE STEAM FIRE ENGINE.

In 1859 on a petition of N. S. Bean and others for organization as a steam fire engine company, the city purchased the Amoskeag, No. 1, a first-class rotary pump, at a cost of $2000 from the Amoskeag Manufacturing Co., and it was delivered to the city in August, 1859, and continued in service until October, 1876, when it was replaced by a first-class double plunger engine, made by the same company. This engine has taken part in several musters and took first money at the trial at Providence, R. I. The company was organized July 6, 1859, with the following officers: S. G. Langley, foreman; J. C. Ricker, assistant foreman; N. S. Bean, engineer; H. W. Ritner, assistant engineer; J. S. Batcheldor, assistant engineer; David B. Varney, clerk.

At a meeting July 11, 1859, Charles Dunbar was elected a member of this company. May 1, 1860, John R. Bruce and Arthur N. Hall were elected torch boys. In this year Hand Engine Co., No. 6, disbanded. This year, J. T. P. Hunt was chief, with Phinehas Adams, Samuel Parsons, Eben French, Benjamin F. Martin, A. C. Heath, Daniel W. Fling, John Moulton, Samuel G. Langley and Alpheus Branch, assistants.

In 1860 Albe C. Heath was chief, with D. W. Fling, A. Branch, Israel Dow, C. H. G. Foss, J. C. Young, B. S. Flanders, assistants. In April Fire King Steam Fire Engine, No. 2, a first size double plunger, round tank engine, was delivered to the city by the Amoskeag Manufacturing Co., and in June the E. W. Harrington, No. 3, a second size single U-tank engine was delivered. In April three hand engines, Nos. 1, 2 and 3, the two later owned by the Amoskeag and Stark corporations, were discharged from service Steamer Fire King was placed in No. 1's house. In July A. C. Wallace, No. 7, was discharged and no record has ever been found of what became of it. Steamer E. W. Harrington was placed in its house. The first of October Massabesic, No. 4, was discharged and the machine was sold to Groton, Mass., for $450. This year horses were introduced into the department for the first time.

On the 1st of April, 1861, Torrent, No. 5, on Manchester street, was discharged from service and the machine was sold to the town of Rochester, N. H., for $500. A. C. Heath was chief this year.

In 1862 Daniel W. Fling was chief, with Charles H. G. Foss, Israel Dow, E. W. Harrington, N. S. Bean, assistants. This year old Merrimack, No. 1, was sold for $425, and a hose carriage was purchased at a cost of $535. May 19 a fire broke out on Manchester street, about half way between Elm and Chestnut streets, which burned across to Hanover street, destroying a number of tenement houses and causing a loss of $15,000.

In 1863 Albe C. Heath was chief, with Ezra Huntington, Israel Dow, Moses O. Pearsons, Daniel W. Fling, N. S. Bean and Freeman Higgins, assistants.

In 1864 A. C. Heath was again chief. As the city hall bell was rung for all purposes it was almost impossible to distinguish an alarm of fire. A bell was accordingly purchased of H. N. Hooper & Co., at a cost of $853.65 and weighing 1026 pounds and it was placed on the Vine Street Fire Station. They divided the city into five districts and rung the number of the district and did not ring this bell for any other purpose.

In 1865 N. S. Bean was chief, with Ezra Huntington, M. O Pearsons, B. C. Kendall, D. W. Fling, Israel Dow and Freeman Higgins, assistants. A hook and ladder truck was purchased this year at a cost of $1175, from C. E. Hartshorn. Dec. 20 fire broke out in the State Reform school building on the River road about two miles from city hall. One steamer reached there after some delay and finally the steamer from Piscataquog, but the greater part of the building was consumed. The inmates were quartered in the old Stark mansion and in 1866 it was also destroyed by fire. This year the Amoskeag Co. built the Dr. Dean, a second size, single, harp tank engine for the Manchester Print Works.

In 1866 N. S. Bean was again chief, with Ezra Huntington, Freeman Higgins, B. C. Kendall, D. W. Fling and Israel Dow, assistants.

In 1867 Israel Dow was chief, with E. P. Richardson, B. C. Kendall, Elijah Chandler, G. H. Kimball, assistants. In November of this year the city purchased of the Amoskeag Manufacturing Co., N. S. Bean, No. 4, a second size, double plunger, straight frame engine.

In 1868 Israel Dow was again chief, with B. C. Kendall, E. P. Richardson, Elijah Chandler and Wilberforce Ireland, assistants.

In 1869 E. P. Richardson was chief, with B. C. Kendall, Elijah Chandler, Wilberforce Ireland, George Holbrook and Andrew C. Wallace, assistants. August 29, this year, a fire which started in the carding room of the stocking mill on Mechanics' Row, occupied by John Brugger, caused a damage of $15,000.

In 1870 E. P. Richardson was again chief, with B. C. Kendall, Elijah Chandler, Wilberforce Ireland and Andrew C. Wallace, assistants On July 8, at 2 30 o'clock in the morning, the largest fire which this city ever experienced started in a building in the rear of Merchants' Exchange and rapidly gained ground. From an article in the Manchester *Mirror* and another from the Manchester *Union* I condense the following description of this fire:

"It is not definitely known just where the blaze originated. Some facts go to show that it took in the room occupied by Drake and Carpenter, spice and coffee dealers. The testimony shows that it must have caught in the engine room and sought egress through the coffee room. In close proximity and connected with it was the brick building in which was located the steam printing works of the *Mirror* and the presses upon which the *Daily Union* was printed. This was soon on fire and the presses destroyed.

"From this point the fire spread in all directions, the wind blowing a gale all the time. North was the wooden building occupied by paint and carpenter shops. The fire then moved east, taking the wooden buildings in its course, until it reached Masonic Temple, which was a large three story block. Still further east it took Johnson's block, Brown & Colley's block, and all the tenements east to Chestnut street. On Manchester street was James' stable, Bartlett's block, Harrington and Johnson's block and the First Baptist church at the corner of Manchester and Chestnut streets.

"On the south side of this street was the Farmers & Mechanics Hotel, otherwise known as the old 'American House,' the scene of the famous firemen's riot of 1859, and many shops and tenement houses between Elm back street and Chestnut street. The Post Office on Hanover street next to Elm back street was in great peril, and was several times on fire, as was also Merchants' Exchange, then the largest block in the city. The whole area burned over was from five to six acres. The amount of property destroyed was not far from $250,000 on which there was about $125,000 insurance. About 200 families were thrown out of homes."

The water which came from the pond in Hanover square failed at a critical time. The old First Congregational church suffered, its surface being somewhat scorched and the old trees which stood in front of it being ruined. The engine from the Manchester Print Works and the Amoskeag corporation rendered valuable aid. There not being any fire alarm telegraph it was a long time before the engine in Piscataquog could be obtained.

Among the old residents who well remembers the big fire is David O. Furnald, who was in the photograph business in Merchants' Exchange. In speaking of the fire, he said he considered that Col. A. C. Wallace and himself were the men who saved the central and southern portions of the Exchange.

"In the middle of the roof," said Mr. Furnald, "was a conduit to carry away the water. By scraping the dirt on the roof into this hole we stopped it up and made a pond out of the water played upon the roof by the engines. Then we took brooms and wetting them in the water, extinguished the fire as fast as it burned along the coping. In this way we kept the southern end of the Exchange from going.

"I saw the flames breaking out of a window about midway of the block and called the attention of Col. Wallace, who was a member of the board of engineers, to it. He procured a few men and sought the room, which appeared to be on fire. When the door was opened the whole interior of the room was found to be in a blaze. Soon the fire here was drowned out and this portion of the building was practically saved.

"The fire was so hot that efforts to check its progress were well-nigh fruitless. All hope of saving the First Congregational church was given up. Fortunately, however, a shower came up and the wind changed, blowing the flames back over the burning district and the Hanover street church was saved."

J. J. Abbott, who was in the paint business in the rear of the place where the Big Six is now located, and who was burned out, well remembers the fire. He says it was discovered by a man coming out of the notorious Waverly Rooms, a gambling resort in Masonic Temple. "It was almost incredible," said he, "how rapidly the flames spread. The water supply was contained in reservoirs in the streets; supplied by springs, and the ponds in Hanover and Merrimack commons. These reservoirs were called fire plugs. One of these fire plugs was located at city hall, and another at the corner of Hanover and Pine streets. These were supplied by the pond in Hanover square. Owing to the fact that the man whose duty it was to open the gate in the pond failed to do so there was a scarcity of water and so the progress of the fire was unimpeded.

"The wooden buildings at the corner of Chestnut and Manchester streets are survivors of the conflagration. The First Baptist church on the northwest corner of Manchester and Chestnut streets was about the last building to go. It was a magnificent sight when the steeple blazed up. The Head Guards were on duty to protect property in the burned stores, but in spite of this many of the storekeepers lost some of their goods. The Amoskeag Steam fire engine was disabled through the destruction of one of its flues and so could not render very efficient service. A relic of this fire may still be seen in the scars upon the big trees in the yard of the Buck property on Hanover street just above the old post office block." A list of those who suffered losses will give some idea of the extent of the conflagration and also of the business men on the street at that time.

"Among them were Drake and Carpenter, coffee dealers; M W. Gove, bonnet bleachery; Independent Order of Good Templars; James' stable; James M. Clough, grocer; Colley and Brown, landlords; Colley and Blackmer, painters; W. B. Johnson and Sons, dry goods; First Baptist church; W. S. Hill, machinist, Masonic Temple; Scott and Jewell, grocers; Waite Bros., dry goods; G. W. Hunkins, landlord; Thomas Sullivan, house and barn; Abbott and Kelley, painters; Mrs. Theodore French, landlady; Barton and Co., dry goods; Charles S. Fisher, city sexton; J. Q. A. Sargent, gas pipe fitter; N. S. Clark, dry goods; Dr. Jones; John Custalow, barber; A. Bunton, engraver; Capt. John N. Bruce, painter; City bank; Amoskeag bank; P. B. Putney, confectionery; the Misses Howard, milliners; Joseph Mitchell, hotel; E. W. Bartlett, landlord; Thomas Smith, landlord; Fearing store; Jackson's store; Shepard and Piper; Merrill and Aldrich, joiners; G. S. Holmes, hosiery and fancy goods; E. O. Abbott, confectionery; W. E. Moore, printer; Neal and Holbrook, carpenters; John Connelly, house; Stephen James, landlord; Sheridan Guards' armory; Misses Shattuck and Fairfield, milliners; Moore and Knowlton, lodging house; New Hampshire Fire Insurance Co.; S. C. Richardson, shoe maker; Miss E. M. Taggart, confectionery; the *Union* and the *Mirror*."

In 1871 B. C. Kendall was chief, with Wilberforce Ireland, A. C. Wallace, Elijah Chandler and W. T. Evans, assistants. This year the salary of chief was raised from $50 to $100 and the salary of the assistant chiefs from $25 to $50.

In 1872 B. C. Kendall was again chief, with Wilberforce Ireland, A. C. Wallace, W. T. Evans and A. H. Lowell, assistants. Two new hose carriages were purchased this year and placed, one at Goffe's Falls and the other at Amoskeag. A new hook and ladder truck was also purchased this year. The Gamewell system of fire alarm telegraph was put into service in this city at a cost of $12,042.24 for 29 boxes this year. The old bell tower in the rear of Parson and Ricker block, at Prospect street, was erected to place the Vine street engine house bell on for the fire alarm telegraph. In the old days the city hall bell was rung and the firemen had to find the fire if they could, says Capt. Joseph E. Merrill of the Penacooks. Once the city hall bell was rung for a fire on Amherst street and somehow the firemen got the idea that it was for a fire in Piscataquog and across the river raced the men.

In 1873 B. C. Kendall was again chief, with Wilberforce Ireland, A. C. Wallace, A. H. Lowell and Freeman Higgins, assistants. The year the salary of the chief was raised from $100 to $115, and that of the assistants from $50 to $65 per year.

In 1874 B. C. Kendall was again chief, with Wilberforce Ireland, A. H. Lowell and Freeman Higgins, assistants. This year the waterworks were substantially completed and the city was furnished with a perfect hydrant service. This year the Amoskeag Manufacturing Co. built the T. Jefferson Coolidge, a first size, double plunger, straight frame, steam fire engine, which is still connected with their private fire department and is housed in the mill yard, in the lower canal building, just opposite No. 5 mill.

In 1875 A. H. Lowell was chief, with Wilberforce Ireland, B. C. Kendall, Freeman Higgins and A. C. Wallace, assistants. The Penacook Hose Co., No, 1, was organized April 7, 1858. The company ran as a hand hose company from the time of its organization until April of this year, when it was furnished with a horse hose carriage and was reduced to twelve men. This year the Massabesic Hose Co, No. 2, was organized and located on Maple street. On June 2 of this year the Granite Flour mill was destroyed by fire causing a loss of $25,000.

In 1876 James F. Pherson was chief, with John Patterson, Patrick Sullivan, Daniel H. Young and George H. Dudley, assistants. Amoskeag, No. 1, was replaced this year by a first size, double plunger, crane neck frame engine.

In 1877 A. H. Lowell was chief, with Thomas W. Lane, A. C. Wallace, B. C. Kendall and Sam C. Lowell, assistants.

In 1878 A. H. Lowell was again chief, with A. C. Wallace, Thomas W. Lane, B. C. Kendall and Sam C. Lowell, assistants.

FIREMAN'S MUSTER ON MERRIMACK COMMON, SEPT. 15, 1859. (SEE PAGE 230.)

In 1879 Thomas W. Lane was chief, with A. C. Wallace, B. C. Kendall, Sam C. Lowell and Orrin E. Kimball, assistants. Thomas W. Lane has been elected continuously ever since.

In 1880, 1881 and 1882 the assistant chiefs were the same as in 1879. At an alarm of fire on Dec. 11, for a fire on Milford street in Piscataquog, the Penacook Hose met with an accident at the canal bridge, in responding to the alarm. The driver, A. B. Cushing, was severely injured. He was not to blame for the accident. A new one horse hose carriage was built to take the place of the injured one. The N. S. Bean steamer also collided with the bridge, damaging the steamer to the extent of $257.75.

In 1881 the salary of the chief was raised from $115 to $300, and that of assistants from $65 to $100 per year.

On June 26, 1882, at a fire in the Museum building, several persons were severely injured by jumping from the third and fourth story windows to the pavement below.

In 1883 the assistants chiefs were Orrin E. Kimball, James F. Pherson, B. C. Kendall, Frank Hutchinson, resigned, and A. C. Wallace elected to fill the vacancy. A new hose carriage was purchased this year and placed in service with a company of 12 men on July 1. It was known as Merrimack Hose, No. 4.

In 1884 the assistants chiefs were Fred S. Bean, Orrin E. Kimball, James F. Pherson and Ruel G. Manning.

In 1885 the assistant chiefs were Fred S. Bean, Orrin E. Kimball, James F. Pherson and Horatio Fradd. A new hook and ladder truck was purchased this year. The old Fire King was exchanged this year for a new steamer.

On August 7 fire was discovered by Capt. George E. Glines and Officer Goodwin at 10 40 p. m. in the Webster block on Elm street, occupied by a large number of tenants upstairs and the Amoskeag Ice Co., William Raynor's bottling works, the Boston laundry, A. S. Heath, proprietor, and Perkins' cafe on the ground floor. Captain Glines and Joseph Blanchard entered the building and warned all the persons they could find out of the building. Joseph Blanchard warned 15 or 20 persons. The Amoskeag and N. S. Bean steamers were soon pouring great quantities of water upon the burning building, but the more water that was thrown on the fire, the more it seemed to gain. Another alarm was rung in, bringing all the apparatus it was possible to spare from other sections of the city, and soon the firemen began to get control. At one time there were ten streams playing upon the fire. The entire front of the building was swept away on the top floors and the loss was estimated at $15,000. Eight lives were lost by suffocation. They were Mary Ann O'Brien and child, and Philomine Campeau, Justine Parent, Olivine Campeau, Prospire Campeau, Elize Parent and Leonard Parent. The last six were crowded into a clothes closet and were suffocated. Capt. Orrin E. Kimball had charge of the fire in the absence of Chief Lane. One of the funny incidents of the fire was that of a lady at one of the third story windows of the block who was trying to keep cool by the vigorous use of a fan. She was observed to engage in the packing up of her effects for a few moments and would then seat herself at the window and fan away. These movements were continued until the woman could hold the fort no longer, her escape being made by means of a ladder.

In 1886 the assistant chiefs were Fred S. Bean, Orrin E. Kimball, resigned, James F. Pherson, Ruel G. Manning, elected to fill vacancy, and Horatio Fradd. This year a brick engine house was erected on North Main street, 'Squog, and the Fire King steamer, No. 2, was placed in this house and the company was organized Jan. 1. On the first of April, a new Babcock chemical engine of two sixty gallon tanks, was purchased at a cost of $2250 and placed in commission. It has demonstrated its availability in extinguishing numberless small fires.

In 1887 and 1888 the assistant chiefs were Fred S. Bean, James F. Pherson, Orrin A. Manning and Eugene S. Whitney. This year the call members' pay was increased from $75 to $100. The salary of the chief was raised from $300 to $1000, and that of the assistants from $100 to $125 per year. In responding to an alarm Nov. 23d steamer No. 4 overturned in rounding the corner of Concord and Vine streets, which damaged the engine considerably and injured the driver, Frank J. Dustin, slightly. No blame was attacked to him. Merrimack Hose, No. 4, in responding to an alarm from box 32, on Dec. 31, owing to the icy conditions of the streets, overturned at the corner of Lake avenue and Maple street. The apparatus was damaged very little, but the clerk of the company, W. P. Emerson, who was on the reel, was injured in the knee quite severely. At a fire on the 30th of November, Mrs. Margaret Fahey was struck by the horse of hose No. 4, at the laying of a line of hose, and was killed. No blame was attached to the driver, as the evening was dark, and she was evidently crowded out into the street by the throng on the sidewalk and was not seen by him until struck by the horse. In August the city purchased of the Manchester Locomotive Works, Merrimack, No. 3, a second size, double plunger, craned-neck frame engine. On May 21 Mrs. Ellen Knight was filling a kerosene lamp at 24 Spruce street when the lamp exploded, burning her so severely that she died in a few hours.

In 1888, on Feb. 8, the Merrimack Hose, No 4, was changed to Merrimack Steam Fire Engine Co., No 3. The city had built a substantial brick engine house on Lake avenue for its reception at a cost of $11,005.23. In March, the city purchased of the Manchester Locomotive Works, General Stark, No. 5, a third size, double plunger, crane-necked frame engine at a cost of $3,657; and a hose carriage at a cost of $1000, and the company was organized April 5 in the new brick engine house on Webster street, which was built in 1887 at a cost of $4.285.16. On Jan. 29 fire broke out in the house of Col. Benjamin C. Dean, owned by the Manchester Print Works, and occupied by him as their agent. The fire was caused by a defective chimney, and obtained considerable headway in the partitions before being discovered. The total damage was $13,892. fully covered by insurance.

In 1889 the assistant chiefs were Fred S. Bean, Clarence D.

Palmer, Ruel G. Manning and Eugene S. Whitney. On Friday, Nov. 8, at 10.56 a. m., at a fire in Bedford on the River road just across the city line, the house and barns belonging to S. W. Dunbar were destroyed. Two children perished in the flames. On Thursday, Dec. 26, at 6.44 a. m., fire was discovered in the cottage house at No. 1 Wilson road owned by Annie S. Head and occupied by Charles A. Savory. The fire originated in a closet, probably from matches, and was first discovered by outside parties. Before all the inmates could be aroused, Mrs. Savory was found suffocated and two children nearly so, though they subsequently recovered. The house and contents suffered little damage.

In 1890 Fred S. Bean, Clarence D. Palmer resigned, and Clarence R. Merrill elected to fill the vacancy, Ruel G. Manning and Eugene S. Whitney were the assistant chiefs, and all held their positions till 1898. On Wednesday, May 14, at 9.15 p. m., fire broke out in the Elliot hospital building. It originated in the kitchen or pantry adjoining, from some cause not definitely known, but as Chief Lane thinks probably from the explosion of a kerosene lamp. Mrs. Daniel Harriman, who occupied a room directly over the kitchen, was suffocated in the early stages of the fire, and it was impossible to rescue her body until the flames were almost extinguished. The building and contents were damaged to the extent of $2,600.

In 1891 the salary of the chief was raised from $1,000 to $1,125. In 1892 the salary of the chief was raised from $1,125 to $1,300. On Sunday, Feb. 7, at 2.51 a. m., fire broke out in John B. Varick's immense hardware store at 809-813 Elm street. Two alarms were immediately pulled in. The fire spread into some of the adjoining buildings before it could be extinguished. The enormous amount of water which had to be used to subdue the flames damaged the stocks of a great many stores in the square. The total damage footed up to $100,377. Insurance paid amounted to $80,432.50.

A list of those damaged follows: Mrs. Georgietta Chamberlin and John B. Varick, owners of Varick's building; Mitchell and Truesdale, owners of Mitchell and Truesdale's block ; A. & W. S. Heath, b( ots and shoes ; George Benoir, boarding house ; Straw block, owned by Mrs. Hannah F. Straw; Manchester One Price Clothing Co. ; William H. Mara, custom clothing; John C eworth, owner of Granite block ; J. F. Dignam and Co., drugs ; R. E. McKean, custom clothing ; R. G. Sullivan, cigars ; Catholic Total Abstinence society hall and Weston and Hill Co., dry goods. The Amoskeag Manufacturing Co. loaned the city the use of T. Jefferson Coolidge steamer. Several causes are assigned for the origin of the fire but Chief Lane's opinion is, that it was caused by electric wires. On Feb. 18 fire broke out in the new building of the Benedictine college in Bedford, which was nearly completed. It was totally destroyed. On Wednesday, June 15, Mrs. Margerita Eismann had a kerosene lamp explode in her hand and was so severely burned that she died from her injuries in a few hours. On Sunday, July 24, fire was discovered in what was known as the East Manchester Laundry on Belmont street. It was caused by the explosion of a can of gasoline. The flames spread so rapidly as to prevent the removal of any of the contents of the building. The occupants, except Mrs. Nancy Sargeant, escaped. She was so overcome by the smoke and heat that as a ladder was raised to her assistance, she fell back into the flames. The total damage was $3,850.

In 1893 the city purchased of the Manchester Locomotive Works the N. S. Bean, No 4, a first size, double plunger, crane-necked frame engine at a cost of $4,200, and the old N. S. Bean, No. 4, was transferred to McGregorville and placed in the new engine house; which was built at a cost of $13,219.57, under the name of Walter M. Fulton, No. 6. A new ladder truck was also purchased this year for this company. On Monday, Dec. 4, fire was discovered at 10.39 p. m. in the John Robbie Co.'s dry goods store in Ferren's building. The total damage was $43,490.75. The insurance paid amounted to $35,069 98. The city also purchased this year a Babcock Aerial truck at a cost of $3,500, and it was turned over to Hook and Ladder

Co., No. 1, for their use. At this place it might be well to give a short sketch of the Hook and Ladder Co., No. 1, which I will quote from " Fire Service of Manchester:"

"The Hook and Ladder Co., No. 1, or as it is now known, Aerial Truck Co., No. 1, was first organized in 1844 as a volunteer company, serving without pay until 1852, at which time it was reorganized with forty five men. The members were paid a salary of $5 per year, 20 cents for each alarm, and 40 cents an hour for actual service. The carriage at the time of the reorganization consisted of four heavy wheels, attached by strong timbers, with arms on each side to prevent the hooks and ladders from falling off. This organization existed until 1856 at which time the salary of the members was fixed at $10 per year with no extra pay for alarms or by the hour. In July, 1861, the pay was again raised, this time to $25 a year and the number of men reduced to thirty. Jan. 1, 1862, the number of men was further reduced to twenty-five. In 1866 a new carriage was purchased. This carriage was in use until 1872, the number of men having in 1870, been increased to thirty. In 1872, a new carriage was received by the city and turned over to the company. In December, 1877, the company was reduced to twenty five members, at which time important changes were made in the carriage and a pair of horses supplied for fire service. In July, 1885, a new carriage of modern make and durability was procured for the company's use. It was built by Galen M. Bowditch of Boston, Mass. In July, 1888, the company was reduced to twenty members. Jan. 27, 1894, the Aerial Truck went into commission and the company was reduced to fifteen men."

One Tuesday, Oct. 2, 1894, at 1.18 a. m., fire broke out in a four-story brick block, 37 to 43 Manchester street. The fire started from some unknown cause in an arched partition over Conner's saloon, and extended to the tenement upstairs. In the early part of the fire an explosion of hot air or gas occurred, burning Driver Walter Blenus of the Penacook hose so severely that he has been unable to do any work since, and Hoseman Patten and Ladderman Edgar, who were burned quite seriously about the face and hands.

In 1895 the city purchased a new ladder truck. On Monday,

July 1, at 9.38 a. m., fire was discovered in a back entry of a two story tenement block at 83 Orange street, owned and occupied by Mrs. Sarah E. Fisk. The fire originated from a leaky gasoline stove, doing little damage to the building but burning Mrs. Fisk so that she died in the afternoon.

In 1896 the salary of the assistant chiefs was raised to $175 and the salary of the call members was raised from $100 to $150 per year. Thomas E. Gorman, lieutenant of Engine and Ladder Co., No. 6, was thrown from the truck at Clapp's Corner while responding to an alarm, and instantly killed.

In 1897 on Feb. 13, at 4.33 a. m., fire was discovered in the two-story wooden dwelling at 168 Milford street, owned and occupied by Mrs. Amanda Sargeant. The cause is unknown. It was first discovered by neighbors. Mrs. Sargeant, the only occupant, perished in the flames. The damage was $2250, with no insurance. On Monday, March 15, at 6.48 p. m., the explosion of a kerosene lamp at 112 Central street caused the death of Miss Emma Garceau. On Thursday, July 8, at 5.33 p. m., Mrs. Galvin of 259 Pine street was lighting fire with kerosene when the oil can ignited, burning Mrs. Galvin so seriously that she died from her injuries.

In 1898 the assistant chiefs were Fred S. Bean, Eugene S. Whitney, Clarence R. Merrill and Frank M. Frisselle. On Thursday, May 12, at a fire in the boarding house, No. 1161 Elm street, kept by J. Miner Sargeant, Mr. John Concannon, one of the roomers, was so overcome by smoke as to be unable to get out of the building, and lost his life. On Saturday, Dec. 24, Mrs. Margaret Griffin, living at No. 416 Laurel street, was so severely burned by dropping a lighted lamp, that she died shortly afterwards from injuries received.

In 1899 the assistant chiefs were Eugene S. Whitney, Clarence R. Merrill, Frank M. Frisselle and John Montplaisir. On March 3, in the evening, fire was discovered in the Trefethen-Stearns house at the corner of Hanover and Wilson streets, and before it could be distinguished practically gutted the house. In the early stages of the fire, a hot air explosion took place which blew several firemen out of the door of the building, severely burning and injuring them.

On Thursday, April 6, in the evening, fire was discovered in the residence of John C. McKeon at 289 East Spruce street. Mr. McKeon was alone at the time, and it is supposed that he had a shock and in falling from his chair, knocked over the light and so set fire to the room. He died soon after from injuries which he received. The damage to the building was slight.

On Sunday, May 14, in the morning, a threatening fire was discovered in the Kennard building. It started in the basement of the clothing store occupied by a man named Custin, and swept up the main stairway and walks, doing considerable damage, until it reached between the third and fourth floors, where it was finally extinguished with a loss of about $10,000.

On July 6 a fire started in a woodyard on Spruce street. A high wind blowing at the time, it spread rapidly and practically all of the fire apparatus of the city was called out, including the steamer from the Manchester Locomotive Works, the Abe Lincoln. It burned out four houses, and caught on not less than thirty different roofs before it could be extinguished. Damage was estimated at $10,000.

On Oct. 12 an old fashioned "firemen's muster" was held by the united efforts of the Manchester Board of Trade and the Manchester Veteran Firemen's association with twenty-three "handtubs" participating. The prizes were won as follows:

First prize, $400, Goffstown Handtub Co., 206 ft 6¾ in
Second prize, $200, Neptune, Newburyport, Mass., 205 ft 10½ in
Third prize, $125, Eagle, Lynn, Mass., 202 ft 1 in
Fourth prize, $100, Conqueror, So. Weymouth, Mass., 194 ft 4¾ in

The affair was a great success and had perfect weather for a muster. The playout was held on Merrimack common, (the site of the famous '59 muster), after a lengthy parade about the town. Playing was commenced about 1.30 p. m. and finished about 5 p. m., ten minutes being allowed for playing time. The Goffstown Tub, the D. A. Taggart, winner of the first prize, was made by the Hunneman company. The prize of $50 for the best appearing company on parade was awarded to the Neptunes of Newburyport, Mass., and the prize of $50 for the company coming the longest distance was awarded to the Conquerors of South Weymouth, Mass.

On Nov. 15, at a fire in the Nason Hall block on Pine street, at 3.50 p. m., a man by the name of John Morrison was burned severely and died at the hospital a few hours later

At the present time there are in the department 160 men, consisting of 33 permanent men and 127 call members. There are now 724 hydrants and 65 boxes in the fire alarm telegraph. A storage battery system has taken the place of the old jar battery at the central station. A steam fire gong has been added and attached to the boiler at the gas works. Today Chief Thomas W. Lane stands at the head of one of the finest, if not the very finest, fire department of the world. In the prepartion of this paper I have been greatly assisted by Chief Engineer Thomas W. Lane, Assistant Engineer Frank M. Frisselle and Col. George C. Gilmore.

# JOSEPH HENRY STICKNEY.

A PAPER BY HENRY W. HERRICK READ BEFORE THE MANCHESTER HISTORIC ASSOCIATION, JUNE 22, 1898.

Joseph Henry Stickney was born in West Brookfield, Mass., August 6, 1811, and died at his residence in Baltimore, May 3, 1893. He began his mercantile career in Baltimore, where he afterwards continuously resided, in 1834, more than sixty years ago. He was seventh in descent from William Stickney, one of the earliest settlers who came from Lincolnshire, in England, to the Plymouth colony. He was educated at Hopkins academy, Hadley, Mass., and when a youth served an apprenticeship to the hardware business in Boston. Owing to the preponderance of English manufacturers at that time there was much hesitancy on the part of hardware dealers about establishing the sale of American hardware as a distinct branch of business. Mr. Stickney formed a partnership in November, 1834, with N. E. Noyes to conduct an American hardware business in Baltimore. The manufacturers were scattered throughout the northern states and were difficult of access, as private conveyances were in general use. Baltimore being farther from the factories than many other cities, many agencies were required. Mr. Stickney's firm represented more than one hundred and thirty manufacturers, and made sales in two-thirds of the United States, largely developing the hardware trade.

About 1840, at the age of 29, Mr. Stickney turned his attention to the production and sale of iron and Cumberland coal.

He was agent for several companies, in which he was part owner. His firm held agencies for two-thirds of the blast furnaces in Maryland and for many bar, plate and sheet iron mills in Maryland, Virginia and Pennsylvania. The firm also engaged in the importing of iron, and represented different steel and iron manufacturers in England and Scotland. In 1852 and 1853 Mr. Stickney went to Europe in the interest of his business. He was president of the Avalon Nail company from its organization until he sold his interest, a short time before the works were swept away by the flood of 1868. He was president for many years and principal owner and founder of the Stickney Iron company, whose works are on the north side of the Patapsco river, in Lower Canton. He was also a director in the Merchants' bank, the Merchants' Mutual Insurance company and other institutions. In 1876 he withdrew from business and lived a retired but not inactive life.

Mr. Stickney was much impressed with the advantages of the township system in the eastern, middle and western states, and distributed a pamphlet in Maryland explaining the system. Many publications were also distributed at his expense on colonial and Congregational church history. Pilgrim hall, at Plymouth, Mass., which contains the relics of the Mayflower, was remodeled and made fireproof at his expense, at a cost of about $25,000. He was vice president of the New England Pilgrim's society, having declined the honor of an election as president to succeed ex Gov. Long, now secretary of the navy. When John Hopkins university was temporarily embarassed in 1889 Mr. Stickney contributed to the emergency fund, subscribing $5000. He also contributed largely for church work and helped to build several churches. To this city he gave a monment to his ancestor, Judge Blodget. He also built a monument to the memory of William and Elizabeth Stickney, his emigrant ancestors, at Rowley, Mass.

The gifts from his estate, which was estimated at over a million, were munificent. Seventy-six bequests appear in his will, including one of $150,000 to the Congregational Home Mission society, and one of about $200,000 to the Church Building society, which by the methods of loans will thus be able to help in the erection of several hundred new churches in the West every year.

Mr. Stickney was descended from the best of New England Pilgrim stock and on the paternal side was related to Major-General John Stark, whose daughter Mary married B. F. Stickney, a near ancestor. The Stark farm adjoins the estate of Samuel Blodget at Amoskeag Falls; and in adjusting the material and financial interests of Judge Blodget, his grandfather, who died in 1807, Thomas Stickney, the father of our subject, moved to Manchester and settled with his young family in the old Blodget homestead. His mother, Mary Ward, of West Brookfield, Mass., married Thomas Stickney in 1778, and though that town was the native place of Joseph H. Stickney, the home of the family was for many years in Manchester, and here the canals and farming interests of Judge Blodget occupied Thomas Stickney for a time.

To be numbered among the millionaires of the country at the age of eighty, with no help from inherited wealth, is proof of great business capacity and persistency of purpose. Fifty years of mercantile life did not spoil the fresh, youthful attachments of his younger days, or his ability for enjoying social life. His iastes and habits of expenditure were kept reasonable and simple, that he might form a Christian standpoint, and uplift and cheer humanity wherever his influence could be felt. The legacies left in his will — seventy six in number — do not comprise all his liberal gifts; these extended through all his life, in the building of churches and helps to deserving and needy educational institutions. Many of these benefactions are so well known by the public that it is needless to enumerate them here. He had great love for historical and genealogical research. Monuments have been reared and historical collections accumulated by his liberality. Of such men the world has too small a number; but, verily, when they are taken from us, " they do rest from their labors, and their works do follow them."

# Bibliography on Stark. Addenda to p. 211.

FISKE, JOHN. The American Revolution. Sketches, Reminiscences, Relics etc. Cambridge, 1896.

HEAD, NATT. Adjutant-General's Report of New Hampshire, Vol II, Military History of New Hampshire. Concord, 1866.

HOUGHTON, GEORGE FREDERICK (with James D. Butler). Addresses on the battle of Bennington, and memoirs on Colonel Seth Warner, before Legislature of Vermont, Montpelier, October 20, 1848. 8vo. pp. 99. Burlington, Vt., 1849.

IMPARTIAL HISTORY OF THE WAR IN AMERICA. Chapter on the part of New Hampshire and her Generals. London, 1787.

IRVING, WASHINGTON. Chapter on John Stark in his " Life of Washington." Vol. I, p. 471. New York, 1856.

JOHN STARK. British Gun captured by John Stark, probably at Bennington. The gun to be placed in Stark Memorial Park. In *Daily Mirror*, November 9, 1897. Manchester, N. H.

JOHN STARK. A biographical sketch in *The Metropolitan*, Manchester Semi Centennial Number. Full page portrait. Published by the Metropolitan Life Insurance Company, New York, 1896.

JOHN Stark. The Hero of Bunker Hill and Bennington. Portrait and Illustrations. In *Daily Union*, March 4, 1893. Manchester, 1893.

KENT, HENRY O. Tribute to General Stark. Address before the New Hampshire Society of Sons of American Revolution. In *Daily Mirror*, April 25, 1896. Manchester, 1896.

KIDDER, FREDERIC. History of First New Hampshire Regiment. Chapter on John Stark. Pp. VIII+184. Albany, 1868.

LOSSING, BENJAMIN J. Field-Book of the Revolution. Battle of Bennington. 1857.

MORRISON, WILLIAM H. New Hampshire Men at Louisburg and Bunker Hill. Address before Manchester Historic Association, June 17, 1896. In Man. Hist. Association " Collections," Part I of Vol. I, p. 25. Printed in *Notes and Queries*, Vol. XV, May, 1897.

POTTER, CHANDLER E. Military History of New Hampshire, 1623 to 1861. Concord, 1866.

STARK, GEN. JOHN. Sketch of Reprinted from " New Hampshire Patriot," on four folio 2-column sheets.  (87 titles.)

# Stark's First Fight with the British.

### CONTRIBUTED BY FRED W. LAMB.

After Stark had been stationed at Medford there were several expeditions set on foot by the patriots to seize the supplies of live stock and hay which had been gathered on the islands in Boston harbor. One of these, and the most memorable, occurred on the 27th of May, 1775, at which time considerable of an engagement took place. Col. Stark was sent with a detachment of three hundred men to drive the cattle and sheep from Hogg and Noddle's Island, (now East Boston), across Chelsea Creek, which could be forded at low water. While engaged in this task they were discovered by the British guard of marines. The British admiral hoisted a British flag at the main mast head and an armed schooner and sloop were sent up Chelsea Creek to cut off the return of the patriots. A force of grenadiers was sent to aid the marine guard on Noddle's Island and Stark was obliged to withdraw to Hogg Island, (now Breed's), and then to the mainland. He succeeded in carrying off a large part of the live stock. The schooner continued to fire at the Americans after they had reached Chelsea Neck, but Gen. Putnam, who fortunately came up with reinforcements, opened a brisk fire in return. The British were unable to get the schooner out of range, and the crew being forced to abandon her, she fell into the possession of the Americans with all her stores and equipments, four six pounders, twelve swivels, and a few small arms. The Americans had three or four wounded. The British loss was greatly exaggerated at the time. Gage stated in his official report that "two men were killed and a few wounded." The New Hampshire *Gazette*, of June 2, 1775, said that "'Tis said between 2 and 300 marines and regulars were killed and wounded, and that a place was dug in Boston twenty-five feet square to bury their dead." One man stated that he saw sixty-four dead men landed at Long wharf from one boat. This occurred before the Battle of Bunker Hill and should, I think, be accorded a place as the second fight of the Revolution, Lexington and Concord being the first actual clash of arms between the English and American troops.

# Anecdotes of General and Molly Stark.

CONTRIBUTED BY FRED W. LAMB.

When John Stark received the news of the Battle of Lexington he was working in his sawmill. He did not stop to go home, but jumped upon his horse in his shirt sleeves and rode furiously down the valley of the Merrimack, calling upon his old friends and neighbors to follow him. He sent to his wife for his uniform. She at once packed up his clothes, mounted a horse and followed him, but did not overtake him until she reached Medford, Mass. Here she gave him the clothes, stopped over night and then returned over the lonely way through the unbroken forest to her home and family at Amoskeag Falls.

One morning while dressing, Molly Stark heard the dogs owned by the family making an unusual noise in the woods not far away. She hurried down stairs, secured a gun and ascended a hill where she found that the dogs had treed an immense bear which lay upon the limb of a tree. She shot and killed the bear, returned home and sent the boys with a horse and they hauled him home. The family had bear steak for dinner that day.

Once when John Stark was encamped near Ticonderoga the weather being cold, the soldiers badly clad and poorly fed Stark grew disheartened. To make matters worse smallpox broke out among them. Mrs. Stark immediately sent word to him to send the sick home to her. She made a hospital of her house and performed the varied duties of nurse and physician and did not lose one of the twenty odd patients.

At the Battle of Bunker Hill, when his volunteers were facing the best soldiers in the English army, some one ran up and told General Stark that his young son, who was in the battle, had been shot and killed. General Stark's answer was, " This is no time to talk of private affairs, get back to your post." Fortunately the report was erroneous.

At one battle during the Revolution an officer who had never been under fire ran up to General Stark and said, "General, the enemy are upon us, what shall we do?" The General answered him quietly as follows, " Take a pinch of snuff and go back to your duty."

Just before the Battle of Trenton, General Stark, not liking Washington's methods, told him that " your men have long been accustomed to place dependence upon spades and pickaxes for safety. If you ever mean to secure the independence of the United States you must teach them to rely upon their firearms and their courage. Washington's reply was, " This is what we have agreed upon ; we are to march tomorrow upon Trenton. You are to command the right wing of the advance guard and General Greene the left." Stark said in reply, " I could not have been assigned to a more acceptable position." History tells the result.

Stark was prevented from making an immediate attack on Baum at the battle of Bennington by a furious rainstorm, during which Stark was joined by the militia from Berkshire, Mass. They were anxious to engage the enemy at once and their leader, Rev. Mr. Allen, approaching Stark, said, " General, the people of Berkshire have often been called out to no purpose ; if you don't give them a chance to fight now they will never turn out again." Stark answered smilingly, " You would not turn out now, while it is dark and raining, would you ? " " Not just now," was the answer. " Well," said Stark, "if the Lord should once more give us sunshine, and I don't give you fighting enough, I'll never ask you to turn out again."

# SKETCHES OF DECEASED MEMBERS.

CONTRIBUTED BY FRANCIS B. EATON.

These brief sketches are compiled with the view to preserve in accessible form such facts as are now to be obtained in the lives of our deceased and much lamented associates. Time fades or destroys the memory even of the most widely known and influential among men and it is only with the hope that in after years these records may prove to be of interest to the citizen whose historic studies should begin at home, that they are recorded in this volume.

For any who may desire to know more of the local sentiment or to read eulogies or editorial comments we have preserved extracts from the daily press which may be seen at the library of the Manchester Historic association, and are accessible to all members.

## JOHN C. FRENCH.

John Cate French, son of Enoch and Eliza (Cate) French, was born in Pittsfield March 1, 1832. His father was a carpenter and farmer and the son, the second of five children, spent his boyhood on the farm where his advantages for education were very limited. His life, was one more proof of the truth of the saying "where there's a will there's a way." He made such good use of the free public schools of the town, that he was soon able to teach winters. With the money earned in this way and what little he received for farm labor from his neighbors he managed to pay his expenses at the academies in Pittsfield, Gilmanton and Pembroke. At the age of 21 he was engaged by the well-known firm of J. C. Colton & Co. to solicit orders for their mounted maps. In this business requiring so much tact and perseverance his success was so great that his employers gave him the Boston agency for "Colton's Atlas of the World." In 1855 he was appointed New England agent for the sale of Colton's school publications and was afterwards in the employ of Brown, Taggart & Chase and of Charles Scribner & Co. in bringing out their publications. During this time he frequently visited his parents on the old homestead in Pittsfield. In 1866 Mr. French established his residence in Manchester, having been appointed state agent of the Connecticut Mutual Life Insurance company. Three years later, having satisfied himself of what might be done along insurance lines, he organized and set in operation that now famous institution, the New Hampshire Fire Insurance company. Some of the best known and most reliable business men of the city and state were attracted to this enterprise by the reputation Mr. French had already acquired. He was appointed general agent. The assets of the first year's business amounted to $134,568, with surplus or net profit of $8029. At the close of the year 1899 the gross assets of the company amounted to $3,163,880.05 and the net surplus was $946,783.34. The business which was done by the aid of one clerk in a modest office in Merchants' Exchange now occupies a fine building of its own erection on land held by a long lease and requires the services of twenty-three clerks and reaches the sum of one and one-half millions annually. In 1895 Mr. French was made president, succeeding ex-Govs. E. A. Straw and James A. Weston. Mr. French was a great reader and had marked literary tastes. He was a member of the New Hampshire Historical society, one of the founders and president of the Manchester Historic association and a trustee of the public library. He was thoroughly versed in the early history of the state and presided over the discussions which arose in our local society, with a grace and easy dignity which added greatly to the interest and value of the occasion. Although his extreme modesty made him very reticent about public speaking he always had some interesting remark or suggestion to make at the sessions of the association, and he has contributed one paper of peculiar interest to this volume (p. 73.) Mr. French was ever loyal to his native town and ready to help on any enterprise which promised to promote its welfare. Thus he heartily advocated the building of the Suncook Valley railroad, and assisted in raising the money necessary for its completion. To this end he established the *Suncook Valley Times* a weekly paper, and for two years contributed to its columns historical and biographical articles which attracted wide notice and were often copied into other papers. While his great and growing life work of necessity demanded most of his thought and time he would not be debarred from his favorite studies. On the publication of a certain town history a few years since, he remarked to the compiler of this sketch that he had set up all night to read it through. His interests and thoughts, however, were by no means confined to one channel. All public affairs of city and state received his intelligent attention. He was a constant attendant at the Franklin Street church and was president of the society. He was a member of Trinity Commandery, Knights Templars, a 32nd degree Mason and a director of the Merchants' National bank. On May 7, 1899, Mr. French and his wife were out driving in the town of Peterborough. The horse proved unmanagable, the carriage was overturned and both Mr. and Mrs. French were severely injured. This accident is thought to have brought on, or at least hastened, the development of Bright's disease of the kidneys, of which disease Mr. French died on Monday, Jan. 8, 1900, at his residence, corner of Bay and Webster streets, at the age of 67 years, 10 months and 7 days. On the following Thursday services were held at the home by the Rev. Dr. Lockhart, pastor of the deceased, at 11 a. m. From noon until 1 o'clock the body lay in state at the Franklin Street church, during which time a guard of honor from Trinity commandery, Knights Templars, was in attendance. A large audience assembled to hear the eulogy pronounced by Dr. Lockhart. There was singing by the Herbert

Johnson quartet of Boston. A wealth of floral tokens attested the regards of family and friends and the impressive funeral rites of the Uniformed Rank of the Knights Templars concluded the services..

Mr. French married in 1858 Annie M., daughter of Levi B. and Miribah Tilton (Seavey) Philbrick of Deerfield. He is survived by his widow, two daughters, Lizzie A., wife of Frank W. Sargeant of Manchester, Susie P., wife of Benjamin S. Brown now of Nebraska, and one son, George Abram French, of Manchester.

## HERBERT W. EASTMAN.

Herbert Walter Eastman, son of Ezekiel Webster Eastman of Moultonborough and Livonia Choate (Bean) Eastman of Boscawen, was born in Lowell, Mass., Nov. 3, 1857. He attended the public schools of that city until 1870, when he found employment in a large mercantile establishment in Boston. In 1873 he removed to Manchester and graduated at the Lincoln grammar school in the class of 1874, taking the highest honors in penmanship and drawing. Soon after he began work in the *Mirror* office, meantime studying wood engraving and making illustrations. In 1875 he entered the employ of Campbell & Hanscom of the *Union* where he continued for six years, when ill health compelled him to relinquish his position. He had arisen from the press room through every department of a daily paper — reporter, proofreader and city editor. With numerous and prolonged interruptions from sickness he did some business at job printing in connection with Mr. Frank H. Challis and later with Mr. Challis purchased the *Weekly Budget*, for which he had acted a while as city editor and to which he had contributed numerous articles on historical and industrial subjects. March 5, 1888, Messrs. Challis and Eastman started the publication of the *Daily Press* of which Mr. Eastman was the city editor. In 1891 he disposed of his interest to his part-

## SKETCHES OF DECEASED MEMBERS. 303

ner and was made secretary of the Board of Trade. His administration of this office, to which he was annually re-elected until 1898, was eminently successful. Expenses were diminished and membership increased. He started the publication of the *Board of Trade Journal* devoted to busisness interest which is now issued once a week with numerous illustrations of local public buildings and portraits of prominent citizens. He also wrote and published a history of the semi-centennial celebration, for which his position as secretary and treasurer of the general committee gave him peculiar fitness. Mr. Eastman was a past grand of Wildey lodge and a member of Mt. Washington encampment, I. O. O. F. ; Arbutus lodge, D. of R. ; Hillsborough council, Order of United Friends : Amoskeag Grange, P. of H ; an 'ex-president of the Manchester Press club ; secretary of the Manchester Historic association and president of the Manchester Cadet Veteran association. He was a Republican in politics, active in the exercise of his political duties and eager to assume all the responsibilities of a good citizen. His wide acquaintance among professional and business men made him universally respected for the evident sincerity and honesty of his intentions and loved for the unassuming goodness which characterized his nature. He cherished worthy and noble ambitions. He did his best against the great odds which fettered his progress, and he leaves an honored name. He was an attendant at the Unitarian church. Jan. 9, 1890, he was married to Nellie Clough (Eaton) daughter of George E. and Lucinda (French) Eaton of Candia. Mr. Eastman is survived by his widow residing in this city, by a sister, Mrs. D. L. Hill of Boston, and a brother, George W. Eastman of Malden, Mass.

Almost from boyhood Mr. Eastman had been subject to attacks of rheumatism, often severe and prolonged. On Wednesday, Dec. 22, 1897, he was obliged to take to his bed with the last and fatal onset of his old foe and notwithstanding affectionate care and medical skill died on the 10th of the following January, aged 40 years, 2 months and 7 days.

## MOODY CURRIER.

Moody Currier, the 43d governor of New Hampshire, was born in Boscawen April 22, 1806, of lowly parentage, but nature was prodigal to him in other ways. He was gifted with good health, a retentive memory, a worthy ambition, and he was heir to the rugged training New Hampshire gives the sons of whom she designs to make strong men. At 7 years of age he was put out to work on a farm and from that time onward earned his own living. From the district school he entered Hopkinton academy where he was fitted for Dartmouth college from which he graduated in 1834, delivering the Greek oration. After graduating he taught school one term in Concord, during which time he edited the *Literary Gazette* in company with D. D. Fish and Asa Fowler. He then became principal of the Lowell, Mass., high school until 1841 when he removed to Manchester, and having pursued the study of law in connection with his school work was admitted to the bar. After a partnership of two years with George W. Morrison he continued in his profession until 1848, when upon the organization of the Amoskeag bank he was made its cashier, which position he held until 1864 when the Amoskeag National bank was incorporated and Mr. Currier was made president, which office he resigned on account of failing health in March, 1892. Mr. Currier's reputation as a wise and successful financier was such that he was chosen to many places of trust. He was treasurer and president of the Amoskeag Savings bank, a director of the People's Savings bank and of the Manchester mills. He was treasurer of the Concord railroad in 1871-1872, was treasurer and director of the Concord and Portsmouth for many years, president of the Eastern railroad in New Hampshire since 1877, director of the Manchester Gas Light company, of the Blodget Edge Tool company, director and treasurer of the Amoskeag Axe company and treasurer of the New England Loan company. In politics Mr. Currier was a Democrat until 1852, and for a time editor of the Manchester Democrat. He was clerk of the state senate in 1843 1844. The anti-slavery movement found him in the ranks of the Free Soilers and he continued an active and influential member of the Republican party from its inception. He was a member of the state senate in 1856 and 1857 and its president the latter year. In 1860-1861 he was a member of the governor's council and chairman of the committee for raising the troops required to fill the state quota in the War of the Rebellion. In 1876 was one of the presidential electors who cast the vote of New Hampshire for Hayes and Wheeler. In 1884 and 1885 he was governor of New Hampshire. In all these places Mr. Currier had discharged his duties with absolute fidelity and to the great acceptance of all concerned. He was a great lover of nature, a diligent student of the natural sciences, and his neighbors around Tremont square will remember his beautiful flower gardens and his solicitous care for the trees on the common. Beginning with his Greek oration at college, in his later years he was familiar with the French, German, Italian and Spanish languages. In 1880 he published a volume of poems. It is understood that there is in press a volume containing his official speeches, messages and poems. For several years Mr. Currier was president of the Manchester Art association. He was a charter member of the Historic association and although his failing health prevented his presence at our meetings he was the first to affix his signature to the articles of incorporation. Up to and beyond what is considered to be the alloted age of man Mr. Currier's health continued good, his mental powers unimpaired, his interest in affairs of state and nation unabated and his attention to business exacting. The inevitable time came, however, when he had withdrawn from the activities of the street and the banking house, to pursue his favorite classical studies at his home, where he died from diseases incident to old age Aug. 23, 1898, having lived ninety-two years, four months and one day. His funeral took place from the Unitarian church and eulogies were pronounced by the Rev. Charles J. Staples and Rev. B. W· Lockhart of the Franklin street church. Mr. Currier was three times married and is survived by a widow but by no living children. Moody Currier received the degree L L. D. from his Alma Mater and from Bates college.

## DAVID L. PERKINS.

David Lane Perkins, son of David P. and Lydia C. (Lane) Perkins, was born at Pittsfield March 2, 1838. His mother died in the following October and soon after the family removed to Manchester where the father was teacher of the first high school and where David received his education, supplemented by a course at the New Hampshire Institute. He studied law with the firm of Morrison, Stanley & Clark and was admitted to the bar March 22, 1862. Meanwhile his father having a position in the pension bureau at Washington, D. C., he was often in that city in government employ and in 1858-1859 was private secretary to Stephen A. Douglass. From 1865 to 1869 he resided at Henniker and returning to Manchester was city solicitor in 1875. On the election of Mr. Cleveland he received a position in the treasury department which he held for four years. At the expiration of this term he again returned to Manchester and resumed practice of the law in the office with his father, who after a varied experience in teaching, book selling, office holding, acting as government detective in cases of pension frauds, etc., had found time to study law in the office of Hon. Moses Norris and settled down to whatever practice his profession might bring him. In politics Mr. Perkins was a Democrat. In July, 1864, he served for a short time as a volunteer soldier during the threatened investment of Washington by the Confederates. He was the first agent in Manchester for the Associated Press and did considerable work of a literary nature. He expressed himself well in plain English. He had a fund of interesting reminiscences of Washington life and a taste for historic research. As a member of this association he was an interested attendant on its meetings and ready to do whatever lay in his power that might properly be done to promote its interests. He contributed two valuable and entertaining papers which were read before the association and are published in Part I of this volune. It was apparently his intention to furnish other papers. About the time of the semi-centennial of this city he published under his own signature a brochure entitled "Manchester to Date." Mr. Perkins was interesting in conversation, of courteous and friendly demeanor to all, and so unusually cheerful that nothing in his outward seeming suggested his sudden and tragic ending on the 60th anniversary of his birth, March 2, 1898, at the Clifton House, Massabesic, the fatal bullet being discharged by his own hand. A paper was found on his desk in his office with this title, "My Sermon When I Die." It disclosed thought and ability on the part of the writer, but bore unmistakable traces of mental aberration. Portions of it were read at his funeral, the services of which were observed at the People's Baptist Tabernacle.

"Luck has befriended me only in spots. I have been no child of fortune, but rather of misfortune."

"Why wait until I have become moribund, and like Job learn to curse my fate."

"With me the past is past, and looking forward I can only hope, but hope is better than despair."

These sentences from the paper referred to above may fitly close this brief notice of our departed associate.

## ANDREW BUNTON.

Andrew Bunton, son of Andrew and Lettice (McQuesten) Bunton, was born in Manchester August 6, 1842. He was educated in the public schools of the city, but before completing his course at the high school entered the employ of Cheney & Co.'s express at the age of 14 years. Here he was industrious, reliable and so thoroughly devoted to his work that he soon acquired a knowledge of its details and upon the death of Col.

James S. Cheney in February, 1873, he was made agent for Manchester, a position he held for sixteen years, when he was appointed superintendent of the New Hampshire division of the American Express Co. His close confinement to the duties of his office had somewhat impaired his health, but he continued to discharge the duties of superintendent to within a short time of his death, which occurred on Friday, June 18, 1897. He had discharged his manifold duties faithfully and with promptness, and had brought affairs in his division to such a prosperous state that the business had not only held its own but had made a net gain during the severe depression immediately preceding his decease. Mr. Bunton became early affiliated (1865) with the Masonic orders, and arose through their successive grades, was Worshipful Master of Washington Lodge, eminent commander of Trinity Commandery, Knights Templar, in 1877-78-79, grand master of the grand lodge of New Hampshire in 1880, grand commander of the grand commandery of New Hampshire in 1883, and grand scribe of the grand chapter in 1883. He was a member of all the Scottish Rite bodies in the Valley of Nashua from the fourth to the thirty-second degrees, and in September, 1885, was given the thirty-third degree in the supreme council northern jurisdiction. He was one of the two active members in New Hampshire of the supreme council, of which there are but fifty or sixty members in the country.

While Mr. Bunton never sought or held public office he was not neglectful of his civic duties, served on the grand jury of Hillsborough county and was one of the most efficient of committeemen at the semi-centennial anniversary of Manchester in 1896 At the time of his death he was a trustee of the Gale Home for Aged and Destitute Women, a trustee of the Masonic Orphans' Home, a director of the New Hampshire Fire Insurance company and a director of the Merchants' National bank. He was the first member of the Manchester Historic Association to be removed by death. He was a member of the Board of Trade and a director of the New Hampshire

Trust company. In his personal relations Mr. Bunton was a very agreeable and social companion, a favorite among his associates and of a distinctively cheerful and optimistic temperament. He married Mary Elizabeth, daughter of Jefferson and Abigail Batchelder Knowles of Manchester, who died some years since, by whom he had one son, Arthur Stanley. He is survived by a sister, Miss Nancy Bunton, for many years a teacher in the public schools of Manchester, and by the son. He was an attendant at the Unitarian church, where his impressive obsequies were held on Monday, June 21, 1897. Prominent Masons were present from this and neighboring states. Religious services were conducted by his minister, Rev. C. J. Staples, and the Knights Templar service was performed by officers of Trinity Commandery.

# INDEX.

## PAPERS READ AND CONTRIBUTED.

| | |
|---|---:|
| Articles of Association and Constitution, | 3–6 |
| Address of Welcome of Union Meeting of Historic Societies, | 201 |
| Anecdotes of General and Molly Stark, | 297 |
| Bibliography on Major-General John Stark, | 205, 295 |
| Boating on the Merrimack, | 35 |
| Captain John Moore's Company, | 32 |
| Castle William and Mary, | 51 |
| Colonel John Goffe, | 233 |
| Derryfield Men at Bunker Hill, | 32 |
| Derryfield Social Library, | 44 |
| Election Sermons in New Hampshire, | 117 |
| Grace Fletcher, | 73 |
| Home Life of Major-General John Stark, | 194 |
| Indians of New Hampshire. Etymology of their Language, | 177 |
| Joseph Henry Stickney, | 292 |
| Manchester Fire Department, | 217, 273 |
| New Hampshire Branch of the Society of Cincinnati, | 66 |
| New Hampshire Men at Louisburg and Bunker Hill, | 27 |
| Old Derryfield and Young Manchester, | 84 |
| Proclamation Money, | 212 |
| Reminiscences of Manchester, 1841 to 1896, | 9 |
| Samuel Blodget, the Pioneer of Progress in New England, | 121 |
| Semi-centennial of Manchester, | 112 |
| Sketches of Deceased Members, | 299 |
|     Hon. John C. French, | 299 |
|     Herbert W. Eastman, | 302 |
|     Hon. Moody Currier, | 304 |
|     David L. Perkins, | 306 |
|     Andrew Bunton, | 307 |
| Stark as Citizen and Soldier, | 201 |
| Stark's First Fight with the British, | 296 |
| The Manter Mills, | 189 |
| "The Sweet By and By," | 81 |

## AUTHORS, PAPERS, AND CONTRIBUTIONS.

BROWNE, GEORGE WALDO.
  Boating on the Merrimack, . . . . . 35
  Hon. Samuel Blodget. Pioneer of Progress in N. E. 121

CRAWFORD, HON. JOHN G.
  Castle William and Mary, . . . . . 51
  Indians of New Hampshire. Etymology of Language. 177
  Proclamation Money, . . . , . . 212

EATON, FRANCIS B.
  Sketches of Deceased Members, . . . . 299

FRENCH, HON. JOHN C.
  Address of Welcome at Meeting of Historic Societies, 201
  Grace Fletcher, . . . . . . . 73
  New Hampshire Branch of the Society of Cincinnati, 66

GILMORE, HON. GEORGE C.
  Derryfield Men at Bunker Hill, Capt. John Moore's Co. 32

GOULD, SYLVESTER C.
  Bibliography on Major-General John Stark, . 205, 295
  Election Sermons in New Hampshire, . . . 117
  "The Sweet By and By," . . . . . 81

PERKINS, DAVID L.
  Old Derryfield and Young Manchester, . . . 84
  Reminiscences of Manchester from 1841 to 1896,. 9

MORRISON, REV. WILLIAM H.
  New Hampshire Men at Louisburg and Bunker Hill, 27

HERRICK, HENRY W.
  Home Life of Major General John Stark, . . 194
  Joseph Henry Stickney, . . . . . 282
  Stark as Soldier and Citizen, . . . . 201

HUSE, WILLIAM H.
  Derryfield Social Library, . . . . . 44
  The Manter Mills, . . . . . . 189

LAMB, FRED W.
  Anecdotes of General and Molly Stark, . . 297
  Manchester Fire Department, . . . 217, 273
  Semi-centennial of Manchester. . . . . 112
  Stark's First Fight with the British, . . . 296

WOODBURY, GORDON.
  Colonel John Goffe, . . . . . . 233

## INDEX

----, Benj 138 John 47 Nehemiah
   255 Susan 122 Susanna 122
ABBOTT, E O 280 J J 279 Mayor
   13 Susan P 206
ABERCROMBIE, Gen 267
ADAMS, Capt 61 Charles Francis
   12 Col 159 David 48 John 67
   Phinehas 17 275 President 173
   Rev Mr 59 Robert 48 Samuel
   57 67 William 153
ADDINGTON, Jas 125
AGNEW, 218
AINSWORTH, O W 221
ALDRICH, 280
ALEXANDER, 199 James 153
ALLDS, John 33
ALLEN, Rev Mr 298 William 118
AMHERST, Gen 267 268
AMORY, 57 Mr 54
ANDERSON, Allen 190 Capt 113
ANDRE, Major 71
ANNIS, 192
APPLETON, Grace 77 Samuel 77
ARCHIBALD, Jno 190

ARNOLD, 33 34 109 Benedict 32
ATKINSON, Col 271 Theodore
   249 272
AUBURY, Father 182
AYER, R H 18 Richard H 160
   Robert 17
AYERS, Hannah 129 John 128
   Obadiah 128 Samuel 129
AYLING, Adj-gen 113
BABSON, Mary 198 Polly 198
BADGER, Gen 155
BAGLEY, O W 225 Orlando 221
BAKER, Benjamin 33 87 H M 211
   Jesse 48 Jonathan E 210
   Nathaniel 99 William 136
BALDWIN, 34 226 Col 167
   Loammi 159
BALEY, Phineas 48
BALLOU, Hosea 47
BARNARD, 150
BARNES, Dick 114 G A 228 J M
   228
BARRELL, Joseph 157
BARRETT, Henry B 99

BARSTOW, George 12 205
BARTLETT, Asa W 74 Charles H
    205 Col 60 E W 280 Ichabod
    75 84 Joseph 53 Josiah 60 Lt
    61 Samuel C 205
BARTON, 280
BATCHELDER, Abigail 309 H
    228
BATCHELDOR, J S 275
BATTEY, William 190
BAUM, 108 298
BEAN, Fred S 283-286 289 Livo-
    nia Choate 302 N S 274-277
    Nehemiah S 22
BEEDE, Thomas 117
BELKNAP, Jeremy 117
BELL, Gov 57 John J 109 115 Mr
    218 S D 22 Samuel D 17 223
BELLOWS, Col 270
BENNETT, Capt 58 Mr 57 Samuel
    F 82 Samuel Fillmore 82
BENOIR, George 287
BESSON, 217
BIXBY, Edward 33
BLACKBURN, David 153
BLACKMER, 280
BLAIR, Henry W 211
BLAKE, Ezekiel 222 223
BLANCHARD, Col 250 253 262
    263 J 253 Joseph 89 129 253
    255 260 283 Thomas 245
BLENUS, Walter 288
BLISS, Charles M 205 Ira 222
BLODGET, 41 Abigail 144 172
    Benjamin 157 173 Billy 148

BLODGET (continued)
    6 144 150 173 Capt 143 144
    Dorothy 172 Elizabeth 173
    Hannah 128 129 172 Home-
    stead Illus 161 Judge 96 98
    121-176 293 294 Mary 172
    Nathan 136 144 150 172 Polly
    144 Rebecca 173 S Jr 148
    Samuel Frontispiece 36 91
    121-176 294 Samuel Jr 136
    143 172 Sarah 172 173 Wil-
    liam 136 151 157 158 165 172
    173
BLODGETT, Nathan 127
BLOGGET, 121 Caleb 124
    Samuel 124 125 William 124
BLOGGETT, Caleb 122 123
    Daniel 122 Elizabeth 123
    Huldah 122 Martha 122 Mary
    122 Mrs Thomas 122 Rebecca
    122 Ruth 122 Samuel 121 123
    Samuel 2d 122 Samuel Jr 122
    Sarah 122 123 Seth S 122
    Susan 122 Susanna 122 123
    Thomas 122
BOLYSTON, Edward D 205
BOND, Mr 124 Nathan 157
BOUTON, Nathaniel 118
BOWDITCH, Galen M 288
BOWDOIN, James 147
BOWMAN, Jonas B 105
BOYD, Hugh 49 W 222
BOYNTON, John 67
BOYS, Hugh 48
BRADDOCK, Gen 262

BRADFORD, Ephraim P 118
    Hannah 244 John 244 Moses
    118
BRADSTREET, Mr 240 Nathan
    117
BRANCH, A 228 275 Alpheus 275
BREED, Dr 110
BREEDAN, Capt 237
BREYMANN, 108
BRIGHAM, A 221
BRIGHT, S E 83
BROOKS, Gertrude H 116
BROWN, 228 278 280 300
    Benjamin S 302 Charles S 226
    Eunice K 151 Eunice Kidder
    205 Hiram 17 218 J N 228
    Peter S 229 230 Susie P 302
    Thomas 17
BROWNE, George W 4 7 George
    Waldo 35 121 205
BRUCE, J N 113 230 J R 113 John
    N 113 280 John R 275
BRUGGER, John 277
BUCK, 279
BUCKMINSTER, Joseph 117
BUMFORD, 155 Jere 156
BUNTON, A 280 Andrew 307-309
    Arthur Stanley 309 David A
    218 Lettice 307 Mary Elizabeth 309 Nancy 309
BURBANK, Caleb 256 Jonathan
    256 Samuel 256
BURFORD, Jacob 154
BURGOYNE, 112 204 206 270
    271 Gen 108

BURNAP, Jacob 117
BURNHAM, John A 222 223
BURNS, John 255
BURR, Aaron 109
BURRIL, 237
BUSHELL, Ephrm 249
BUTLER, Benjamin F 84 James D
    295 James Davie 205
BUTTERFIELD, 14 104 James 33
    Joseph 41
BUTTON, 218
CALDWELL, Samuel 34
CALFE, Mary 129
CALLAHAN, John 33
CAMPBELL, 98 132 302 Hugh 33
    Z F 18
CAMPEAU, Olivine 284 Philomine 284 Prospire 284
CARGILL, David 242
CARLETON, Kimball 153
CARPENTER, 277 280 Josiah 4
    W H 114
CARR, James R 232
CARRIGIAN, Philip 46
CARSWELL, N H 83
CARTER, T J 220 221 Timothy J
    218
CARTWRIGHT, Dr 151
CASS, Jonathan 67 Lewis 84
CATE, Eliza 299
CEWORTH, John 287
CHACE, Stephen 154
CHALLIS, Frank H 302
CHAMBERLAIN, Uncle 76
CHAMBERLIN, Georgietta 286

CHAMPLAIN, 35
CHANDLER, 104 Elijah 277 280
  Hannah 244 Thomas 244
  William E 211 Zachariah 84
CHAPIN, Bela 208 Edwin H 205
CHARLES, I King Of England
  234 235 II King Of England
  235 236 King Of England 238
  XII King Of Sweden 199
CHASE, 127 143 156 300 Charles
  223 Francis 206 Jacob 48 Mr
  135 Salmon P 84
CHENEY, 307 James S 308 P C
  20 103 220 225 Samuel 67
CHILD, Lydia Maria 84
CHURCH, John H 118
CILLEY, 70 Bradbury 68 Bradbury P 110 232 Col 110 112
  Gen 201 J G 225 228 John H
  110 Jonathan 67 Joseph 67
  Major 61 63 Martha Poor 112
CLARK, 306 Capt 154 D 228 D J
  228 Daniel 224-226 George 41
  John 125 N S 280
CLARKE, John B 226 230 W C
  225
CLAY, John 34
CLEMENT, 140 142 C W 113
CLEVELAND, Mr 306
CLIFFORD, Nathan 84
CLOUGH, Capt 61 James M 280
COBURN, Frank W 206
COCHRAN, Capt 56
CODMAN, John Jr 147
COGSWELL, 70 Amos 67 68

COLBURN, Capt 253 254
COLBY, Fred Myron 206
COLLEY, 228 278 280
COLSON, Israel 41
COLTON, J C 300
CONCANNON, John 289
CONGDON, J B 222
CONNANT, Nathaniel 48
CONNELLY, John 280
CONNER, 288
CONVERSE, Hannah 122
CONWAY, Gen 196
COOK, Thomas 256
COOKE, Phineas 118
COPP, 22
CORCORAN, John 54
COUCH, Ann E 48
COUSINS, Charles E 193
CRAWFORD, John G 4 51 177
  212
CROMWELL, 236 Gen 235
CROSBY, Jaazania 118 R R 83
CROSS, Allen Eastman 206 David
  4 11 100 230 Nathan 245
CROWN, Col 236
CROWNINSHIELD, Hannah 207
  Harriet 192
CURRIER, Jacob 41 M 228
  Moody 4 17 222 223 304-306
CUSHING, 150 A B 283
CUSTALOW, John 280
CUSTER, 116
CUSTIN, 290
CUTTING, Jonas 33
CUTTS, Samuel 53 56

CYPHERS, John 34
D'ESTAING, Count 110
DALE, Charles 41
DALTON, 102
DANA, Charles A 84 Daniel 118
DAVENPORT, Mr 237 238
DAVIDS, James 240 Mr 239
DAVIS, 150 218 Daniel 45 46 48
  Gershom 127 Moody 47
  Moses 48 100 Samuel 48
DEAN, Benjamin C 285
DEARBORN, Henry 67 70 Josiah
  G 4
DECOVERLEY, Roger 50
DEVENS, Gen 32
DHU, Roderick 29
DICKEY, 95 David 48 John 48
DICKINSON, Pliny 118
DIESKAU, Baron 129 263
DIGNAM, J F 287
DIX, John A 75 84
DIXWELL, Col 239 240 James
  240
DOBBIN, John 33
DODGE, Levi W 206
DOUGLASS, John 189 190 Stephen A 306
DOW, 121 140 Israel 232 275-277
DOWST, John 4 107
DRAKE, 277 280 Samuel G 206
DRAPER, Richard 131
DUDLEY, George H 281 H O 109
DUNBAR, Charles 275 Herbert
  113 S W 286

DUNCAN, George 190 Major 153
  154 Mr 250
DUQUESNEL, 28
DURNFORD, Lt 206
DUSTIN, Frank J 285
DUTCHESS, Of Burgundy 204
DUXBURY, C 226
DUYCKINCK, E A 206 G L 206
DWIGHT, Joseph 127 Mrs 78
DWINELL, John 48
DWINNELL, 101
EAGAN, Luke 33
EARL, Of Manchester 240
EASTMAN, 261 262 Ezekiel
  Webster 302 George W 303 H
  W 107 Herbert W 4 302 303
  Herbert Walter 302 Joel 75
  Livonia Choate 302 Moses 144
  Nellie Clough 303
EATON, F B 17 107 Francis B 4 7
  299 George E 303 Lucinda 303
  Nellie Clough 303
EDGAR, Ladderman 288
EISMANN, Margerita 287
ELKINS, Capt 61
ELLIOT, George 219 William H
  228
ELLIOTT, Robert 212
ELLIS, Ferdinand 118
ELLSWORTH, F H 228
EMERSON, Amos 67 Charles 33
  George 33 109 J C 222 Jonathan 109 Peter 48 W P 285
ENDICOTT, Mr 236 240

ENGLISH, Thomas D 206
ERICSSON, John 273
EVANS, Israel 117 W T 280
EVERETT, Edward 7 194 206
   Gov 199 Henry 142 Mr 136
FAHEY, Margaret 285
FAIRFIELD, 280
FARLEY, Mark 84
FARMER, David 34 I W 231
   Joseph 48 W P 221 William 48
   William P 218
FARWELL, 245
FASSETT, J H 207
FERREN, 287
FESSENDEN, 192 Wm Pitt 75 84
FIREMAN'S, Muster On Merrimack Common 282 Illus
FISH, D D 304 Hamilton 69
FISHER, Charles S 280
FISK, Sarah 289 William H 208
FISKE, John 295
FLAGG, Ebenezer 126
FLANDERS, B S 275 I C 224
   Isaac C 221 223 225 232 S L
   112 Walker 221
FLEGG, Ebenezer 126
FLETCHER, Bridget 74 Elijah 73
   Grace 73-80 Mrs Elijah 73
   Rebecca 75 Robert 157
FLING, D W 275-277 Daniel W
   275 276 Patrick 33
FLINT, David 48
FOGG, Daniel 79 Jonathan 67
FOLLINSBY, Moses 34

FOLSOM, Col 53 59 Dorothy 172
   Gen 60 63 Mr 64 Nathaniel
   172 Samuel 66
FORD, Isaac N 218
FORSAITH, Hiram 112
FOSS, C H G 275 Charles H G
   276
FOSTER, E C 222 Herman 17
FOULSOM, Abm 155 156
FOWLE, James 126 138 139
FOWLER, Asa 304
FRADD, Horatio 283 284
FRANKLIN, Benjamin 259
FRAZER, 132
FRAZIER, Q M G 143
FRENCH, Abram 74 Andrew 100
   Annie M 302 Eben 230 275
   Eliza 299 Enoch 299 George
   Abram 302 Hannah 74 128
   John C 4 66 73 80 107 201
   299-302 John Cate 299 Jonathan 118 Lizzie A 302 Lucinda
   303 Mrs John C 301 Mrs
   Theodore 280 Susie P 302
   Walter 17 221 223 225
FRISSELLE, Frank M 230 232
   289 291
FROTHINGHAM, 211 Richard Jr
   207
FRYE, Francis 67 I C 223 John 48
   49
FURNALD, David O 278
GAGE, 30 296 Gen 29 31 55 56 62
   Joshua 34

GALLINGER, J H 211
GALVIN, Mrs 289
GAMBEL, John 48
GAMBELL, John 49
GAMBLE, 95 John 99 William 91
GARCEAU, Emma 289
GATES, 109 Gen 199 270
GEDDING, John 53
GEORGE, Benjamin 33 I King Of England 245 Ii King Of England 243 King Of ?? 142 The First Of Scotland 204
GERRISH, Steven 261
GIBSON, James 34
GILL, Moses 157
GILLIS, David 225 Jotham 98
GILMAN, 70 Betsey 149 Capt 61 Edward 128 Elizabeth 128 J T 46 John 128 Lydia 128 M 149 Mary 172 Mr 150 151 Mrs 149 150 Nicholas 60 61 67 Peter 157 Polly 144 Samuel 172
GILMORE, Adam 41 George C 4 32 119 207 219 232 291
GLAZIER, William B 207
GLICK, Lt 209
GLIDDEN, James 34
GLINES, George E 283
GLOVER, Henry 34
GOFF, John 33
GOFFE, 95 220 Col 131 233-272 Dunkin 253 Ebenezer 244 Elizabeth 244 Esther 244 Gen 241 Hannah 234 243 244 Hunter John 247 Jemima 244

GOFFE (continued)
233-272 John 2d 243 John Jr 94 242 243 248 John Sr 243 Joseph 271 Margaret 244 Mary 244 Mrs 239 248 Mrs Gen 241 Mrs John 272 Rebecca 244 Sarah 244 Stephen 234 241 Theodore Atkinson 272 Thomas 249 William 234 241
GOLDSMITH, Francis 239 Walter 239
GOODWIN, Officer 283 Thos 235
GOOKIN, 70 Daniel 67 68 John W 67
GORDON, Horace 221 Nathaniel 61
GORMAN, James 94 Thomas E 289
GOULD, Mr 82 S C 81 117 204 205 207 Sylvester C 4 7
GOVE, M W 280
GRAFTON, Mrs 116
GRANT, 132
GRAY, Billy 165 166 Robert 117 William 165
GREELEY, Gilbert 101 Horace 25 84 S P 222
GREEN, Samuel A 131 134
GREENE, Charles G 75 Gen 110 298 John 135 Nathaniel 75
GREENWOOD, Chief 274
GREGG, James 242 John 34
GRIFFIN, Edward 221 James 48 98 Jim 41 Margaret 289
GRIGGS, Hannah 244

GRIMES, D W 222
HADLEY, Benjamin 93
HALE, John 100 John P 84 Nathan 143 270
HALL, 95 Aaron 117 Arthur N 275 Daniel 48 49 101 George 221 Hiland 207 James 101 John 48 87-90 94 100 269 270 Joseph B 99 Robert 48 Sam 101 Samuel 40 99 Willis 157
HALLECK, Fitz Greene 207
HAMPTON, 109
HANCOCK, 154 John 199
HANDCOCK, 154 156
HANSCOM, 302
HARDY, Old Mr 103 Reuben 103
HARMAN, Capt 125
HARPER, 194 206 Wm 157
HARRADON, James 112
HARRIMAN, Mrs Daniel 286
HARRINGTON, 278 E W 17 276 Ex-mayor 18 Mayor 231
HART, Arthur 33 Col 267
HARTSHORN, C E 276
HARVELL, James 104
HARVEY, 70 81 95 165 John 67 Lemuel 33
HARWOOD, 102 William P 41
HASELTINE, Philip 48
HAVEN, 272 Samuel 117
HAVERGAL, John 136
HAYES, 305
HAYWARD-PHILLEN, Judith 122
HEAD, Annie S 286 Natt 295

HEADLEY, 54 Joel T 208
HEATH, A 287 A C 275 276 A S 283 Albe C 275 276 Clara B 208 W S 287 Will H 115 William 114
HENRIETTA, Maria Queen Of Charles I 234
HENRY, VII 204
HERRICK, H W 107 110 112 113 Henry W 4 96 97 194 201 202 208 292
HESELTINE, Asa 48 Moses 48
HESELTON, Moses 49
HIDDALEY, Benjamin 93
HIGGINS, Freeman 276 277 281
HILL, Hiram 19 Mrs D L 303 W S 280
HILLS, Peter 48
HINKER, John 212
HOGG, Abner 114 George 33 James 34
HOITT, J B 228 Nathan 157
HOLBROOK, 228 280 George 277
HOLDEN, Jemima 244
HOLLAND, Denis Augustine 209
HOLMES, G S 280
HOLT, Peter 118
HOOPER, H N 276
HORR, 230
HOUGHTON, George Fred 205 George Frederick 295
HOUSTON, James 33
HOWARD, 218 Misses 280
HOWE, James B 118

HOYT, William G 18
HUDSON, Chas 127
HUNKINS, G W 280
HUNNEMAN, 218 290
HUNT, J T P 17 221 230 275 Peter 127
HUNTER, James 191 John 34
HUNTINGTON, Ezra 276 277
HUSE, 95 Isaac 48 101 Thomas 34 W H 115 William H 44 189
HUTCHINS, Nathaniel 34
HUTCHINSON, Alexander 119 Frank 283 Gov 235 241 John G 4 Solomon 34
IGGLEDEN, Ruth 122
INDIAN, Chief Joseph 116 Eliot 24 Paugus 247
IRELAND, Wilberforce 277 280 281
IRVING, Washington 295
JACK, Andrew 190
JACKSON, 280 Gen 105 Samuel 41 48 101
JAMES, 278 Jacob F 226 230 232 S 228 Stephen 280
JEFFERS, 218
JEFFERYS, T 131
JENNES, Mr 52
JENNIS, Richard 137
JEWELL, 280
JOHNSON, 278 Abraham 34 Calvin 33 Col 130 Edward 123 Esther 123 Gen 263 Herbert 301 302 Nathan 48 Susan 123

JOHNSON (continued) Susanna 123 W B 280 William 123 262 264
JONES, 228 237 Daniel 41 Dr 280 Elisha 256
JORDAN, John 34
KELLEY, 280 Israel W 75 J L 226 Rebecca 75
KELLOGG, Nate M 115
KELLOND, Thomas 237
KENDALL, B C 230 276 277 280 281 283
KENNARD, 290 Samuel C 4
KENT, Henry O 295
KERR, John 33
KIDDER, 95 123 Benjamin 91 244 246 247 266 Col 96 97 102 105 Frederic 295 John S 97 98 219 222 Joseph 4 98 N P 4 Nathan P 205 S B 108 115 162 S P 99-101 Saml Phillips 157 Samuel B 98 99 162 165 Samuel P 41 45 46 48 98 100 157
KILLICUT, Edward 41
KIMBALL, Frederick 97 G H 277 Orrin E 229 232 283 284 Reuben 41
KIRK, Thomas 237
KITREGE, Hezekiah 41
KNIGHT, Ellen 285
KNOWLES, Abigail 309 Jefferson 309 Mary Elizabeth 309
KNOWLTON, 31 280 Edgar J 4 7 J H 221

L'ISLE, John 235
LADD, Col 156 Sam'l 155
LAFAYETTE, 112 113 196 200 Gen 71
LAMB, F W 107 Fred W 107 108 217 273 296 297
LAMBERT, John 235
LAMSON, Gideon 57
LANE, Chief 284 286 287 Hannah 74 J G 113 Lydia C 306 Thomas W 232 281 283 291 W L 222 225 Warren L 17
LANGDON, Gov 211 John 54 55 84 Samuel 117
LANGLEY, S G 275 Saml G 275
LANMAN, 75
LARKEN, E 44
LATTA, A B 273
LAWLER, David 34
LEAVITT, Orrin H 81
LEE, Gen 110 143
LEEDS, Harry 226
LEETE, Mr 238
LEGAND, Louis 208
LESLIE, Benjamin 48
LEVERETT, 240
LINDSEY, James 190
LINGFIELD, Edward 244 246
LIVERMORE, Samuel 84
LOCKHART, B W 305 306 Rev Dr 301
LODGE, Henry Cabot 209
LONG, Gov 293
LORD, John P 192 Nathan 118

LOSSING, Benjamin J 295
LOUDON, Earl Of 264 Lord 131
LOUIS, XV King Of France 245
LOVEJOY, Mr 261
LOVEWELL, 125 247 271 Capt 122 Jon 246
LOWELL, A H 280 281 Sam C 281 283
LYMAN, Gen 262
MACCLINTOCK, William 89
MADISON, James 209 Jim 198
MANNING, Orrin A 284 Ruel G 283 284 286
MANTER, Col 192 Francis 191 George 191 George W 192 Harriet 192 Harriet M 192 Mary F 192 Samuel 191
MARA, William H 287
MARCH, Clement 53
MARION, Isaac 134
MARSHALL, Dustin 221
MARSTON, Alfred 79 Gilman 84
MARTIN, Benjamin F 275 Mary 244 Nathaniel 33 244 Samuel 34 Timothy 33 William 231
MASON, John Tufton 249
MATHER, Cotton 24 Increase 234 241
MATTHEWS, Hugh 33 Joseph 33
MAYNARD, John H 218 226 229
MCALESTER, George 48
MCALLESTER, Samuel 48
MCCLARY, Andrew 70 Jas H 67 Michael 67 68 Thomas 33

MCCLINTOCK, 54 Michael 91
　Nathaniel 63 Samuel 117
　William 270
MCCLINTOS, William 88
MCCLURE, Thomas 34
MCCRILLIS, 23 228
MCCURDY, Matthew 40
MCCUTCHENS, John 40
MCDOUELL, Mr 88
MCDOUL, Mr 88
MCDUFFEE, Daniel 193 John 190 193
MCFARLAND, Asa 117
MCGAFFEY, Neal 67
MCGILVARY, William 119
MCGREGOR, 104 Col 153 James 108
MCGREGORE, Mr 242
MCHUGH, Richard J 209
MCKEAN, R E 287
MCKEEN, Mr 242
MCKENZIE, 132
MCKEON, John C 290
MCKINLEY, President 203
MCKNIGHT, David 33
MCLAUGHLIN, Thomas 33 34
MCMUPHEY, Alexander 88
MCMURPHY, John 34 85
MCNEIL, John 91 95 John C 33
MCPHERSON, James 34 John 34
MCQUADE, James 255
MCQUESTEN, John K 104 Lettice 307
MCQUESTION, John K 109
MCQUESTON, Edward 222

MCQUIG, David 34
MERRIAM, Isaac 134
MERRILL, 95 280 Clarence R 286 289 Daniel 118 Israel 40 Joseph E 281
MERROW, Joshua 67
MESERVE, Col 264
MILLS, Charlotte 68 John 34 Joseph 67 68
MILTIMORE, James 117
MITCHEL, Mr 240
MITCHELL, 286 287 J W 228 Joe 105 Joseph 280
MONROE, Col 264 James 204 Jim 198
MONTCALM, 132 264 265 Gen 108 Marquis De 131 132 266
MONTPLAISIR, John 289
MOOERS, R D 226
MOOR, Capt 271 John G 48 Joseph 48 Nathaniel 48 Samuel 271 Widow 48
MOORE, 263 280 Arthur C 114 David 33 Frederick A 208 Goffe 33 Humphrey 118 Jacob Bailey 210 James 119 John 32-34 91 129 207 244 262 266 270 Margaret 244 Nathaniel 244 Rebecca 244 Samuel 34 48 244 W E 280 William E 4
MORETON, Mr 60
MORGAN, Charles 219 John T 219
MORRILL, A B 222 Amos 69
MORRIS, Gov 174

MORRISON, 306 E 156 Ebr 154
George W 17 19 105 230 304
John 291 William 117 William
H 4 7 27 295
MORSE, Samuel F B 211
MORTON, Perez 157
MOULTON, Capt 125 John 275
Mace 17 218-221
MUNRO, Col 131 132 Josiah 67
MUNROE, Col 265 James 196
MUNZO, Gen 147
MURPHY, Patrick 33
MURRAY, Gen 268
NATHANIEL, Boyd 33
NEAL, 228 280 Capt 110
NEGRO, Caesar 81
NESMITH, George W 209
NEWMAN, William 33
NEWSHAM, Richard 217
NICHOLS, Col 134 Isaac 41
Nicholas 61
NOBLE, Oliver 117
NORRIS, Capt 61 Moses 306
NOYES, N E 292
NUTT, Eliza A 48 James 48 Myles
123 Rodnia 95 Sarah 123
O'BRIEN, Mary Ann 284
O'NEIL, John 33
OFFUT, E P 230
OGDEN, John C 117
OLD, Harry 25
OLIVER, 235 239
ORLEANS, Regent Of France 245
ORR, James 33

PAGE, Charlotte 68 Christopher
73 74 James W 74 Mrs Christopher 73 Rebecca 74
PAIGE, Christopher 73 74 Reed
117
PALMER, Clarence D 285 286
Dan 225 Jonathan 219 William
41
PARENT, Elize 284 Justine 284
Leonard 284
PARKER, Francis J 209 Henry E
118 James 48 Joel 84 John 105
219 Jonas L 19 Nathan 17 118
Pigeon 104 William 67 104
PARKINSON, Henry 195
PARKMAN, 262 Samuel 153
PARRISH, Hannah 234 243 Mrs
Robert 243 Robert 243
PARSON, 280
PARSONS, Samuel 275
PARTON, James 175 209
PARTRIDGE, Edward I 114
PATTEN, Hoseman 288 Saml 33
PATTERSON, James W 207 John
281 Mr 165 Robert 190 S G
221 William 34
PATTY, Asa 140
PAYSON, Seth 117
PEABODY, Stephen 117
PEARSONS, M O 276 Moses O
276
PENHALLOW, 246 Samuel 212
PENNOCK, 218
PEPPERELL, 28

PERHAM, John 48 94 Robert 48 William 48
PERKINS, 283 David 4 107 David L 4 9 84 306 307 David Lane 306 David P 306 Jonathan 67 Lydia C 306 Samuel B 231 Sarah 172 Stephen 172
PERRY, George 221 J A 228 S H 114
PETERES, James 94
PETTINGILL, Phineas 48
PHERSON, James F 281 283 284
PHILBRICK, Annie M 302 Hannah 128 Levi B 302 Miribah Tilton 302 Samuel 61 Thomas 128
PHILIP, King Of ?? 121
PHILLIPS, John 134
PICKERING, John 53
PIERCE, Benjamin 69 Benjamin K 69 Capt 235 Franklin 69 84 Gilbert 191 Henry D 69 Kirk Dearborn 69 Thomas P 18 232
PINGRY, Stephen 48
PINKERSON, Deacon 191
PINKERTON, John 190
PIPER, 280
PITT, William 266
PLAISTED, John 212
PLATTS, Clarence M 193 George W 192 Harriet M 192 James M 192 Mary F 192
PLUMER, William 110
POLLARD, 165
POND, Mayo 219

POOR, 199 Col 61 Enoch 30 71 112 143 Light Infantry 71 201 Martha 112 Mr 60
PORTER, Fitz John 84 George 101 221 John 105 Nathaniel 117
POST, Louis Bell 114
POTTER, 87 95-97 135 143 166 218 222 232 240 Chandler E 209 295 Judge 127 133 136 146 Mr 44 47
POWERS, Grant 210
PRENTICE, John 46
PRESCOTT, 31 32 Henry 53 William 209
PRESSEY, 228
PRESTON, Ebenezer G 41
PRIDEAUX, Gen 268
PROCTOR, Edna Dean 84 John 48 Luther S 110 Mrs Luther S 110
PRYOR, Roger A 109
PUTNAM, Gen 30 296
PUTNEY, C A 228 C M 228 P B 280 William A 228
QUIMBY, 101 Moody 219
RAN, William 252
RAND, Elizabeth 249 252 Elizath E 252 John 244 Mrs 254 Robert 249-251 253 Sarah 244 William 250 252
RANDOLPH, Edward 240 Peyton 57
RANN, William 252
RANSOM, Col 18
RASLE, Pere 125
RAY, James 41 99 John 40 48 97

RAYMOND, L 228 Lyman 228
RAYNOR, William 283
REED, 31 209 Agent 14 James 190
REID, 70 211 James 67
REVERE, Paul 29 54-57 234
RICHARD, 140
RICHARDS, Jeremiah 67
RICHARDSON, E P 107 112 113 115 277 Edwin P 4 Jacob 41 Mrs E P 112 S C 280
RICKER, 280 David 221 J C 275
RIDDLE, 104 George W 220 Gilman 222 Isaac 36 219 Isaac Jr 219 William P 105
RIDILL, John 88
RITNER, H W 275
RIVINGTON, Mr 55
ROBBIE, John 287
ROBERTS, 218
ROBISON, John 50
RODMAN, Thomas P 210
ROGERS, 130-132 209 264 272 Major 110 Richard 265 Robert 129 204 210 262 264 265 267
ROOSEVELT, Theodore 209
ROW, John 235
ROWE, Capt 61
ROWELL, Daniel 100 Ephraim K 20 Job 48 100 140 Joseph 41 Joseph M 39 40 42 220 221 Z 67
ROWLAND, William F 117
RUGG, David 255
RUMFORD, Count 122

RUSS, Thomas 93
RUSSELL, Mr 35 238 Thos 157
RYDER, James H 192
SALTONSTALL, Richard 239
SANBORN, Edwin D 210 Jeremiah 154
SANDBORNS, J 156
SANDERS, Martin 80
SARGEANT, Amanda 289 Frank W 302 J Miner 289 Lizzie A 302 Nancy 287
SARGENT, J Q A 280 Q A 226
SAUNDERS, Abiel 41 Jesse 101 102 Ziba 41
SAVORY, Charles A 286 Mrs Charles A 286
SAWYER, Joseph 109 Joseph B 114 Reuben 48
SCAMMEL, Yorktown 201
SCAMMELL, Alexander 71 Yorktown 71
SCAMMONS, Brig Maj 143
SCHOFIELD, Isaac 153
SCOTT, 280 A M 114 Thomas 274 Walter 29 72
SCOVELL, A D 108
SCRIBNER, Charles 300
SEAVEY, Aaron 48 49 Miribah Tilton 302
SECOMB, Elizabeth 252
SELLERS, 217
SEVERNS, Ephraim 134
SEWALL, 123
SHATTUCK, Misses 280 Philip 124

SHAWK, Abel 273
SHEPARD, 280 Amos 46 William 21
SHEPHERD, William 223 225
SHERBURN, John 140
SHIRLEY, Gen 262 264 Gov 255
SHURTLEFF, Roswell 117
SIMONDS, Hudah 122 James 122 Judith 122 Ruth 122 Susanna 122 William 122
SLATER, 151
SMART, 154-156
SMITH, Abiel 157 Alonzo 17 Capt 130 Col 261 Isaac W 210 John 117 190 Jonathan 34 Mrs Isaac W 210 R G 222 225 Rebecca 173 Thomas 280 William 173
SMYTH, Ex-gov 201 Frederick 112 115 Gov 11
SPARK, 206
SPAULDING, W A 114 W L 112
SPERRY, 237
STANLEY, 306
STAPLES, C J 309 Charles J 210 305
STARK, 31 91 114 165 219 277 Abby 92 98 Archibald 33 88 91 93 95 96 Benj F 48 Caleb 33 36 194 203 208-210 Caleb Jr 203 Col 296 Eliza 48 Elizabeth 48 198 F G 98 Frank 98 Frederick G 41 92 98 106 Gen 11 95 97 194-211 271 298 George 203 210 Jerome B 206 John 14 29-32 48 62 84 91 94

STARK (continued) 95 108 129 173 194-211 272 294 295 297 John Jr 92 98 102 Judge 98 99 Lizzie B 102 Mary 294 Molly 198 207 211 297 Mr 11 Samuel 94 Sarah 173
STEARNS, Ezra S 4 J A 226 Nathan 41
STEPHENS, P H P 148
STEUBEN, Maj Gen Baron 66
STEVENS, Alpheus 41 Ann Melissa 230 Benjamin 88 99 Capt 101 127 David 100 Ephraim 48 91 100 Ephraim Jr 48 Ezekiel 95 Joseph L 101 Mr 256 Philip 101 103 Phinehas 210 Robert 101 Robert I 101
STICKNEY, 149 Abigail 144 172 B F 294 Elizabeth 293 Joseph Henry 172 292-294 Mary 294 Thomas 48 172-174 294 William 292 293
STODDARD, Richard A 211
STOUGHTON, John 147
STRAW, 228 E A 17 223 300 Gov 14 100 Hannah F 287
STURTEVANT, Chas B 4
SULLIVAN, 199 Ebenezer 67 Gen 51 61 110 143 James 35 152 157 John 54 55 57 58 62 63 66-68 70 84 109 201 Major 59 Patrick 281 R G 287 Thos 280
SUMTER, Gen 200
SUTCLIFFE, Frank S 208

SUTHERLAND, David 118
SWETT, S 211
TAGGART, 300 E M 280
TEWKSBURY, 228
THATCHER, James 211
THAXTER, Celia 84
THAYER, 218 223
THOMAS, 131 228
THOMPSON, Benjamin 122
    Ebenezer 122 Frances 122
    Hannah 122 James 122 James
    Sr 122 Jonathan 122 Jonathan
    Jr 122 Mrs James 122 Ruth
    122 Samuel 134 Susanna 122
THORNTON, Matthew 89
THORPE, Thomas L 192
THYNG, J Warren 211
TICKINGS, A C A 20
TICKNOR, Mr 78 Mrs 78
TIDD, Rebecca 122
TILDEN, George W 218
TILTON, Capt 61 63
TITCOMB, Capt 61
TODD, 272
TOMPKINS, 238
TOWLE, Marlene A 13
TOWNE, Foster 221
TREWORTHY, Ellizabeth 128
TRUESDALE, 287
TRUMBULL, Gen 143 Henry 211
TUDOR, William 157
TUFTON, John 252
TURNER, Hiram 100 John 34
TYLER, Bennet 118
TYNG, William 124 125

UMPHREY, James 89
UNCLE, Ebenezer 47
UNDERWOOD, James 269
VANDERHEIDE, 217
VARICK, John B 69 286 Richard
    69
VARNEY, 226 David B 275
VARNUM, James M 24
VAUGHAN, William 28
WAITE, 280
WALDO, Samuel 127
WALDRON, Capt 53
WALKER, 95 228 Charles K 219
    Esther 244 F G 114 James 244
    250 252 Mr 220 Nathaniel Jr
    135 Robert 250 William 48
WALLACE, A C 17 104 105 278
    280 281 283 Andrew C 277 C
    W 17 Col 279 James 218 220
    221 Jno 190
WARD, Gen 30 Mary 294
WARNER, Cy 162 Seth 205 206
    295
WARREN, 28 Amory 218
WASHINGTON, 54 62 110 112
    208 298 Gen 61 64 68 71
WAYNE, 109 Gen 111
WEBB, Gen 131 132 264 265
WEBSTER, 95 283 Black Dan 75
    Charles 77 Daniel 10 15 73-79
    84 211 David 48 Edwin 77
    Ezekiel 75 Fletcher 76 Geo W
    114 Grace 73 75-79 Israel 48
    John 94 Joseph P 81 82 Julia
    76 Mr 83 Viranus 41 W B 226

WELLES, Moses 93
WENTWORTH, Benning 25 84 139 Capt 61 Gov 52 56 138 139 142 255 271 272 J 141 John 53 137
WESSON, Ephraim 134
WESTON, 95 Amos 48 James A 300
WHALEN, N J 100
WHALLEY, 237 238 239 Col 235 Gen 241 Lt-gen 236 Miss 239
WHEELER, 305
WHIDDEN, Parker 41
WHITE, Bridget 74 Ephraim 48 Hannah 128 129 172 John 128 John Jr 128 Josiah 74 79 Lydia 128 Mary 128 129 Mrs 79 Nicholas 128 129 Ruben 48 William 128 235
WHITNEY, Eugene S 284 286 289 Henry S 218
WHITON, John M 211
WHITTAKER, 165
WHITTEMORE, Frances 122
WHITTIER, 201
WIER, John 34
WILDER, Marshall P 84
WILKINS, James Mck 105
WILKINSON, Gen 109
WILLES, Moses 88
WILLEY, George F 4 107 208

WILLIAMS, Col 130 263 Nath'l 118 Roger 178
WILSON, Geo W 112 Henry 84 Hugh 189 James 190 Robert 101 189
WINN, Joseph 122 Mrtha 122
WINSLOW, John Ancrum 203
WISWALL, Esther 123 Thomas 123
WITHERELL, J 211
WOLFE, 268 Gen 108
WOOD, Amos 117 M Seth 235
WOODBURY, Gordon 233 Levi 84
WOODMAN, Joseph 117
WOODWELL, David 256 Mrs David 256
WOOLDON, Constance Fennimore 84
WORCESTER, Noah 117 Samuel T 211
WORTHLEY, Stephen 48
WRIGHT, Mrs 228
WYMAN, Elizabeth 123 Esther 123 Francis 123 John 123 Jonas 127 Sarah 122 123 Seth 122 123 Thomas 123
YOUNG, Daniel H 281 David 41 Harrie M 108 109 Hezekiah 99 J C 275 Jonathan 48 Jonathan Jr 41

www.ingramcontent.com/pod-product-compliance
Lightning Source LLC
Chambersburg PA
CBHW070720160426
43192CB00009B/1253